Adolf Berle

Modern interpretations of the gospel life

Adolf Berle

Modern interpretations of the gospel life

ISBN/EAN: 9783337283322

Printed in Europe, USA, Canada, Australia, Japan

Cover: Foto ©Thomas Meinert / pixelio.de

More available books at **www.hansebooks.com**

THE GOSPEL LIFE

BY

ADOLF AUGUSTUS BERLE

MINISTER OF THE BRIGHTON CONGREGATIONAL CHURCH, BOSTON

BOSTON

The Pilgrim Press

CHICAGO

To the Memory of

MY FATHER

WHOSE INTELLECTUAL COURAGE AND ABUNDANT HUMAN SYMPATHIES

HELD UNDER THE SWAY OF A STEADY PURPOSE OF WILL

AND A RESOLUTE LOVE OF LIBERTY AND TRUTH

HAVE BEEN

The Inspiration and Ambition of my Life

PREFACE

THE New Testament is essentially a modern book. Engrafted into the life and permeating the thought of the
centuries as is the power of its Central Figure, the one thing
that impresses the student more than all else, as he endeavors
to catch the spirit of New Testament teaching, is its thoroughly modern tone. The setting is local and Oriental, but
the principles and their application are universal and human.
The discourses here gathered together are an attempt to
select from a ministry extending over a period of ten years,
most of it in a single pulpit, the ruling ideas and efforts of
that ministry to present a spherical view of the application
of the Christian gospel to the whole of modern life, as we
live it in America. Carrying out this purpose, I have made
several excursions into the region of apostolic psychology;
then again, I have tried to apply the teachings of Christ to
the social and political life of our time, an experiment always
fruitful of danger and misunderstanding, but none the less
necessary for that. I have further outlined the relations of
Christianity to our educational ideas and method, especially
the place of the Bible in university instruction, following this
with a literary criticism or two, in which I have made some
observations on the literary and dramatic portraiture of
gospel ideas. Then, too, I have added a number of discourses on the spiritual life itself, as distinguished from the
various modes of it which I have been describing.

These discourses are called modern because I have approached their themes in the spirit of the New Testament,
which I conceive to be the modern spirit at its best. I have

called them interpretations because that is what they are
rather than final declarations of opinion or dogma. As they
were all, with one exception, delivered extemporaneously,
I have preferred to retain the spoken form of address, as
most suitably preserving both the ideas and the temper in
which they were brought forth. There have not been wanting evidences that in their temporary form these messages
have been helpful and useful, and I send them forth in this
more lasting shape, in the hope that they may bring to
thoughtful men and women a somewhat larger vision of that
service of Christ, in whose ministry I have had so much
of happiness and blessedness.

Two acknowledgments are appropriate in this place.
One is to the men of the Brighton church, who have always
insisted that their minister should have the largest liberty
to think and speak as he believed, in accordance with the
teaching of the New Testament. This has utterly eliminated
anxiety for the temporal consequences of any utterance I
might make. The gospel, to them, has not been the proclamation of the ideas of a creed or a clique, but the announcement of Christ's purpose in the life of the world. I am
their grateful debtor. The other is to the Rev. Charles
F. Thwing, D.D., president of Western Reserve University,
who preached the sermon at my ordination, and to whom
since that time I have always turned for intellectual companionship and stimulus with never a disappointment or
failure to find light and encouragement. With these feelings
of love to the brethren, and that higher gratitude which I
feel toward the heavenly Father for the multitude of his
kindnesses to me and mine, I send forth these endeavors for
his greater glory.

EASTER, 1899.

CONTENTS

CONTENTS

NEW TESTAMENT BIOGRAPHY

ST. PAUL THE GOSPEL DEMOCRAT

ROMANS xiv. 7.

IN a call for independence addressed to the American people in 1776, Thomas Paine makes use of the following language as descriptive of the then existing situation: "The present state of America is truly alarming to every man who is capable of reflection. Without law, without government, without any other mode of power than what is founded on and granted by courtesy. Held together by an unexampled concurrence of sentiment, which is nevertheless subject to change, and which every secret enemy is endeavoring to dissolve. Our present condition is, legislation without law; wisdom without plan; a constitution without a name; and, what is strangely astonishing, perfect independence contending for dependence. The instance is without precedent; the case never existed before; and who can tell what may be the event?" If the requisite changes be made which allow for the difference of theme, point of approach, and the contrast between the mood of government and the mood of religion, this is a very fair description of the state of the apostolic Church till St. Paul made his appearance as a delegate of Jesus Christ. There had been attempts enough at the formulation of a church discipline and the definition of a church life. There had even crystallized sentiments which had the authority and force of law in the carrying out of certain apostolic desires. There were various rude attempts in the direction of a theocracy and some hints in the direction of a communal *régime*. But, scrutinized closely, the apostolic Church, till St. Paul appeared on its horizon, had very much the fluid character ascribed above by the eloquent and discerning Paine to the American government

in 1776.   It could not be said to be without law; but its
laws were not those of a real government.   It was precisely
so with the apostles.   There were agreements in the early
Church and certain votes embodying the majority decrees of
the earliest company of believers, but they never had the
force of potential government in the ordering of church
affairs.   There was an unparalleled fund of wisdom in that
company, yet it was very largely without plan.   And what
is truly enough "strangely astonishing" is that it was as true
of the apostolic Church as of the American Republic that
it had "perfect independence contending for dependence."

It was an amazing congeries of intellectual types which
gathered in that first meeting of the apostles at Jerusalem.
Probably there never was such a religious body assembled
in this world.   It was as truly an ecumenical body intellectually and spiritually as this world has ever seen.   It met under
as peculiar conditions and faced as original questions as ever
demanded the thought and insight of any congress that was
ever called to decide upon issues which were fraught with
life and death.   It is worth while to look at the personnel
of that remarkable body, for in that companionship we shall
find the explanation of many things which their subsequent
history would leave dark or inexplicable.   Each of that company must be seen in association with the others.   In this
way we shall discover the exceptional character of the whole
body, the essential differentiation of the various types present, and more especially shall we see the significance of the
great absent figure that was to unify and solidify the whole.
It was not a united body nor one that apart from its common
interest in Jesus Christ could be said to be even homogeneous.   Too great an effort has been made to show that
there was a single spirit present in the early days of the
apostolic Church.   Those passages in the text which show
this, or seem to show it, are rather the afterglow of the consciousness that unity as finally attained was not there present
and seen to be needful to the organization and success of the
infant Church in its career of winning the world to Christ.
The descent of the Holy Spirit on the day of Pentecost was,

as we shall see, less a unifying act of God in his Church than it was an edict from the highest authority that the Church was to be greater than any race, creed, color, or condition in life. The gift of the Spirit at Pentecost was rather the Church's emancipation proclamation, and with about the same result that was secured by our own great national document of that name. Few there realized, and, it may be said, even now recognize the essential thing that was sought to be conveyed in that marvelous expression of the divine authority and will.

In the first chapter of Acts we have this record as to the people who gathered in the "upper room" which appeared to be the meeting place of the nascent church : "both Peter and John and James and Andrew, Philip and Thomas, Bartholomew and Matthew, James the son of Alphæus, and Simon the Zealot, and Judas the son of James. These all with one accord continued steadfastly in prayer, with certain women and Mary the mother of Jesus, and with his brethren." A most remarkable assembly, as the mere recital of the names reveals. Just think for a moment of the after history of each of these individuals as the work of the Church expanded, and as the cause of Christ was seen to be something larger than the mere development of a national hope and the gratification of a national ambition. Reflect how gradually one after another of these men lost the personal element in the gospel and found the Christlike world-love which was both above and without themselves. And see in what a crude state the body which had in its keeping the future of the gospel of eternal life actually was. Never did a great movement begin under more perplexing conditions. Truly it had wisdom enough, but without any plan. It had great men, but there was little unity of purpose, hardly any real unity of perception, and it may be held doubtful if the true gospel of Christ, except as it is the message of the personal assurance of forgiveness and acceptance with God, had any currency among them. In this respect there may have been one single exception. Kept by the nature of the case apart from many of the practical aspects of Jesus' ministry and teaching, Mary had better opportunities for thought and observation than the active, zealous men who were by the Master's side. Pondering these things through the years and seeing with the maternal vision and feeling with the maternal heart, she may have known what the rest of the company did not even suspect. But that the rest had any proper idea of the extent and cosmopolitan purpose of the gospel is not only incredible in itself, but is evidenced by what subsequently occurred.

The most striking incident in the early administrative history of this congress of primitive Christians is that which records the choice of a successor to Judas the traitor. It is immaterial who was chosen, as he does not figure again in apostolic history. The interesting fact is that he was there, as probably many others were who were co-witnesses with the apostles according to the standard of apostleship adopted. What the influence was that probably led to this election we shall see later. It was here that a long series of contrasts and antagonisms began which has not ended yet and which marks one of the permanent differentiations of Christian thought to this very hour. Even at that early moment the practical aspects of the case called for an authoritative and unmistakable announcement of the true character of the Church of Jesus Christ. Notice how remarkably it came. While the whole of the Church, undoubtedly under the influence of St. Peter, was considering the office of apostle and the arrangement of affairs of external authority, the one fact which was of absolutely most importance was being lost sight of and was in a fair way to be strangled before it was fairly born. This was the priesthood and kingship of all believers. "His office let another take" was the ruling thought of the Church. But the Holy Spirit was not thinking of offices. He was thinking of believers and the fellowship of forgiveness and love. And the first great mandate of the Holy Spirit was what? the issue of an encyclical about the qualifications of bishops and the appointment of officers? By no means. The first great demonstration of God in the history of the Church and in the teeth of the expressed plan of the existing body of Christ was the announcement of the democracy of the gospel in the pouring out of the Holy Spirit upon the most cosmopolite and mixed assembly that was ever moved by a common impulse. Even the unwilling Church must be given new tongues that each man may hear in his *own* tongue the wonderful works of God. No Jewish gospel then nor national ambitions! No special pleas for apostolic bishoprics and peculiar qualifications, but simple Christian democracy. In every nation he that feareth God and worketh righteousness is to be accepted. And there they were, Parthians and Medes and Elamites and all the rest, dwellers of Judæa and Cappadocia and Pontus and Asia, Romans, Libyans, Cretans and Arabians, Jews and proselytes, moved by the great inclusive democratic message of the Holy Spirit to them all alike.

Now this crowd, as the record shows, had just one common quality. It was composed of religious, that is, devout men. Nothing else in common but a spirit of devotion which made them the proper subjects of the Holy Spirit's appeal. They were racially, socially, intellectually and culturally as diversified as it is possible to conceive such a body. They had varying ideas of life, government and law. They had probably no common ideas on the great social themes of the time. But they were the democratic assembly of devout men, and to them the Holy Spirit sent his most direct appeal. There is a touch of gentle irony in the fact that St. Peter was the chosen preacher on this occasion. But it is very clear that he did not perceive it. Imperialist as he unquestionably was, and full of authorities and rites and insistent upon decrees and ceremonies, he did not perceive how on this occasion he was standing utterly apart from all his cherished notions of the gospel and its administration. But we shall see this developed later on. The essential fact to be observed now is, that the first great act of the Holy Spirit was a proclamation of the democracy of believers, and that it might be without a single element of misgiving, the mixed and utterly heterogeneous crowd in Jerusalem on the day of Pentecost was chosen to illustrate the doctrine. How great the impression made was, may be seen in the first result which appears in the administrative life of the Church. They were not yet far enough advanced to see that it meant spiritual democracy, but, humanlike, they began at the lower stages. They at once introduced an experiment in material communism. Communism in spirit, spiritual democratic acceptance of the priesthood of every believer, was as yet a thing quite unthinkable to them. But community of goods, the democracy of things, they could grasp, and this was really quite an advance. It showed that though the Church did not learn the greatest lesson of the Pentecostal outpouring, it did learn something of that great message. And it made haste to apply what it had learned.

It has been necessary to dwell upon this aspect of the Pentecostal blessing at such length because this is really the key to St. Paul's life-story as the interpreter of democracy in the Christian Church. Paul had, if I may so speak, the rare good fortune not to be among the company which met in the upper room. That was a blessed place and had its great experiences. But the providence of God was larger than the spiritual trysting-place of the early disciples before the real Church was born. They were a company of persons of varied tastes and characters and experiences, each hardly understanding himself and not at all understanding each other. Their only recorded administrative act was a blunder, and whatever else they did was apparently not of sufficient consequence to be worth recording. Paul happily was not there. That fact of itself shows that certain types of mind and character had not yet been touched by the gospel preachers of the Church. When the Church secured a Stephen, it soon converted a Paul. But suppose Paul had been present. From what we know of the subsequent clashings of Peter with Paul, who can doubt that the issue of those early meetings would have been dreadful confusion? Their fundamental views of life and the world were so radically different. There was, even to the last, little in common between these two great expounders of gospel ideas. Brought together in the earlier stages, there would have been confusion, surely, if nothing worse. Paul was fortunate not to be there. The

apostles were equally fortunate. When the proper time came
they were brought together, though it is worth while noticing
that Paul had made for himself quite a Christian experience
before he came into actual touch with the other apostles.
He had his commission, as he himself proudly says, from
Jesus Christ himself, and there again spake the Christian
democrat who at once overleaps all churchly distinctions and
authorities and derives his power with democratic simplicity
from Christ himself.

Looking backward, then, in the spiritual history of St.
Paul's life, we now see that the great, shadowy figure behind
the Pentecostal outpouring was the figure of the real successor of Judas the betrayer ; that the democratic announcement of the Holy Spirit on the day of Pentecost was the
logical beginning of Paul's career ; that it was the preparatory stage of his life, and that it was the absolute prerequisite
to the appearance of Paul in successful and strong relations
to the remaining members of the apostolic Church. It is one
of those singular facts about the gospel which no amount of
conjecture can reasonably explain, that the greatest fact of
the apostolic Church should attain its largest significance in
the life of one then as yet spiritually unborn ; that the man who
was to teach the essential lesson of that great message to the
Church and the world and give it power and demonstration
was not only not a part of it, but as yet in no organic relations
to it. Paul developed the doctrine of the Holy Spirit in the
Church as no other apostle tried to attempt it. He preached
a democracy founded on the equal gift of the Spirit to all
Christians, which has been the refuge and strength of believers from his day to this. It was his democratic conception of the equal and free brotherhood of believers, based
again on this equal access to the gift of the Spirit, which prevented the apostolic Church from drifting into imperialism
almost from its inception. The first great protest was made
by God himself in the form in which the Spirit brought the
word of God to the multitudes. Its continuance and development was the distinctive contribution of St. Paul to the
spiritual life and history of the Christian Church.

The democratic idea is an idea of protest in its very nature. The whole tendency of human nature is to emphasize personality and to make the common welfare and interest subordinate to it. At the close of the nineteenth century the strength and persistence of the personal element in law, government, reform and administration is almost as clearly marked as at any period of the world's history, though the form of its expression has been slightly altered to the amelioration of the condition of those affected by it. With all the progress of democracy, the world figure, the national figure, or the community idol still survives. Our heroes are still turbulent spirits from the battlefield or the tireless manipulators of the cabinet. Democracy is the continual protest against the undue exaltation of the individual at the expense of the whole body. It is this for which St. Paul, in the work and extension of the gospel, peculiarly stands, and there is no finer embodiment of the rule and purpose of his own life than that which he himself penned to the Romans, " For none of us liveth to himself." That was democracy reduced to its absolute and lowest terms. That was at the same time the highest altitude of religious attainment. It was at once the statement of the dignity and the humility of the gospel life, and it is the only true epitome of St. Paul's career. It was this that made him take up the cause of Gentile Christianity and by the might of his idea literally break out the walls of Judaic Christianity so that the whole world could come in. It was this that made him see the strategic force of the conversion of the Roman army. It was this that made him the evangelist to the great cities of his time. It was this that made him see that schism for the sake of freedom was better than harmony with bondage. It was this that colored and modified every practical project, every spiritual purpose of which we have record in the great apostle's life.

Analyzing now this distinctive contribution of St. Paul as the type of democracy in the apostolic Church, observe first of all that he makes the individual life and authority absolutely subordinate to the Holy Spirit's purpose with respect to the whole Christian body. This is exceptionally revealed in a doctrine which is commonly understood to teach some-thing far different. When Paul uses the expression, the elect, Paul is never thinking, when the whole range of his use of that term is examined, of a selected body of individuals, but of the whole of the Spirit's purpose for the whole Christian body. When Paul announces his willingness to be the offscouring of the world for the elect's sake, Paul has no thought at all of offering himself for individuals, but for the totality of the Holy Spirit's purpose for the entire Church. To imagine St. Paul holding a doctrine of election which is an arbitrary selection is to pervert the whole message of Paul's life. It is to lose sight of the very thing for which he contended most and most earnestly. To St. Paul individuals were nothing. His own personality, he is often proud of boasting, has been utterly lost in his devotion to Christ. He loves to tell the churches that he himself is nothing, and speaks only by the authority of the Holy Spirit and the com-mission of Jesus Christ. His appeal for obedience, when he makes it, is on this ground, not the ground of an apostleship which has been sanctified or indorsed by ecclesiastical usage and habit. Indeed, there are not wanting evidences that he was somewhat contemptuous of constituted authorities, except as these registered the common will. Nor is it to be sup-posed that Paul made the blunder of meaning by the total purpose of the Holy Spirit merely the will of the majority. This is not democracy. Majorities sometimes become, under right influences, minorities. Righteousness and majorities do not necessarily go hand in hand. Paul saw this clearly enough and stubbornly refused to let the majority stand in the place of God. But he recognized the practical force of majorities, and yielded in the measure that a democratic soci-ety demands to the expressed will of the main strength of the body of Christ.

But Paul's democracy meant the whole purpose of the Holy Spirit for the whole body of Christ. These two ideas were to him the true gospel, and Christ was the expression of them both. In Christ the Holy Spirit had revealed his whole purpose. In Christ the whole body of Christ must meet on terms of perfect fellowship, which meant, to him, terms of perfect equality. There must be no respect of persons. There could be diversity of gifts. There could be a variety of administrations, but there must be the same Spirit and the spirit in all must be unified in the life and service of Jesus Christ. And this led naturally to the idea that in the second place such a democracy was the living demonstration of the principle of Christian coöperation and mutual helpfulness. Unity meant life, and division meant death. St. Paul's statement that none of us liveth to himself was much more literal in meaning than is often supposed. Life, to a man moved with the genuine democratic impulses of Christianity, means relation, organic and personal, with the rest of the body of Christ. Such a relationship to be a life relationship is one of helpfulness and coöperation, respecting and being respected. First of all it is self-respecting and finds its own usefulness and value to the social whole in that it has a genius and capacity for coöperation with all others like minded in expressing the total idea of the Holy Spirit in the revelation of Jesus Christ. Paul insists that the desire and will of God can be discovered only in the whole body of believers. That makes them democratic from the very necessity that by this means alone can they be personally acceptable to God. And following up this statement he insists that the only living relationship of those thus revealing the whole will of God is for all to be in coöperative activity, expressing each in his way and to the degree of his power, in helpful fellowship, the ruling purpose of all. God is not only in them all, but he works through them all. The coöperation in service is the immediate result of the unity in life.

Nor was Paul conscious, or if conscious willing to acknowledge, that there was any possible barrier to the realization of this ideal of Christian fellowship and service. To Paul there was no race nor tribe nor kindred other than that of Christ. His doctrine of the subordination of the personality to the purpose of the Holy Ghost in the whole body of Christ was so inclusive and absolute that he could not fancy any difficulty strong enough to stand in the way of its full realization.

To have imagined such an objection possible would have been
to him an impeachment of the authority of God or a division
of the Holy Ghost. Of both these ideas he was spiritually
incapable. But we are not to infer from this fact that Paul
had no conception of a possible separation of the individual
from the gracious circle of the Spirit's power and influence.
Indeed, on various occasions he fancied himself outside the
circle, and such moments were not always moments of depres-
sion either. They were sometimes the result of Paul's inabil-
ity to coördinate the various types of human life and thought
in such a way that the great main idea of his own life could
be seen through them. Christians have the same difficulties
to-day. It is hard enough to imagine in our enlightened time
such a reign of democratic feeling as Paul idealized for himself constantly. We know that it has not been attained in
civilization, in government, in the arts, nor in science. We
know that after twenty centuries of incessant striving, men
in the mass are very far from the idea of democracy as Paul
saw it to be the inevitable outcome of the Holy Spirit's gift
to each believer, and the announcement by this means of the
priesthood and kingship of all believers. Few believe the
doctrine, though there are many who affirm belief in it. But
because the world and the Church have not risen to the idea,
shall we abandon it? Shall we lose the grandest conception
of religion, to say nothing of the noblest thought of liberty,
because the world is still in the grasp of small and mean
principles for the regulation of its concerns, and especially
its religious life? Or shall we rather take up the same cause,
and with the heroic expositors of the idea in all ages press
on toward this mark for the prize of the high calling of God,
in freedom and brotherhood as Paul loved and strove for
them?

The world will continue for many years yet, in all probability, to exalt Paul or Cephas or Apollos, but Paul's analysis
of the relation of all these to the work and will of God remains the true one. Men are nothing, God is everything.
Left to themselves, they will be yet electing bishops without
power and officers without authority. They will be still

making distinctions which may be valid on earth but are invalid in heaven. They will be still making the life of a few or the abilities of a few the channels of the whole purpose of the Holy Spirit, which is nevertheless found only in the whole body of Christ. They will be still relying upon unexceptional gifts, and the hands will yet be arrogantly saying to the feet, We have no need of you. But it will still be true that none of us liveth to himself, and he that lives most among us lives least to himself. It will still be true that living friendship and organic touch with the whole body of Christian people on the earth are the only sure means of knowing the will of God in the common gift of the Holy Spirit. And through the coöperation of service and the loss of self to the glory of the whole, we shall find ourselves in the fulness of our partnership in the gifts and graces of the whole Church of God.

ST. PETER THE APOSTOLIC ECCLESIASTIC

MATTHEW xvi. 18.

IF mere language could confer an apostolic primacy, these words unquestionably confer such a primacy upon St. Peter. All the conditions which make such a feeling about the words of Jesus and the interpretation which gives to the apostle exceptional prominence among the disciples natural and satisfactory, are here present. It comes after an extraordinary exhibition of primacy in action and confession on the part of the favored disciple. The Master has been asking his disciples during a brief period of retirement in the region of Cæsarea Philippi what men are saying about him, and to whom they most liken him in their thought. Various answers are returned, as the disciples had discovered the sayings of the multitudes. Curious and possibly somewhat anxious, Jesus asks his disciples their own view of his person and work. Then the primate at once responds with energy and with spiritual exaltation, " Thou art the Christ, the Son of the living God." It was a noble answer. It was worthy of an apostolic primate. It has never been improved upon. It indicated a devotion, a discernment, a consecration and a spiritual fellowship which have not been excelled in the history of the Church. It was of the nature of a finality as regards the Person of Christ. It was clear, definite, decisive and true. If selective clearness and spiritual discernment were to be made the conditions for the bestowal of peculiar honors, here was the occasion for such a gift. And Christ unquestionably did regard the answer as at once noteworthy and praiseworthy, for it is apparently for this reason that he utters the words which give the added significance to St.

15

Peter's name, "Thou art Peter (Greek, *rock*), and upon this rock I will build my church." From that moment St. Peter and the Church became inseparably connected in the thought and life of the whole world.

Two things need to be said with reference to the interpretation here and its effect upon the subsequent history of the Church. The first of these is that St. Peter's personality was a minor matter in the supposed primacy which was here conferred. If personality is taken into account, the statement of Jesus becomes dangerously near being absurd. For though the saying of Jesus is obviously a play upon the name of Peter, there is no one of the whole apostolic company to whom the designation "Rock" as indicative of personal qualities of firmness, stability and fidelity is less applicable than to St. Peter. No member of the company of Christ was more variable in manner, speech and general dealings with the Master and the remaining disciples. No one was more often rebuked by the Master for false conceptions of Christ's mission to the world. No one was apparently more upon the Saviour's mind as creating anxiety and fear for his future. After his resurrection, there is evidence that Jesus had St. Peter specially in mind when he sends a message to the fallen primate who had denied him thrice. So that to assume that the Rock had a personal application to St. Peter as constituting him in any sense the head of the Church, is utterly misleading, not to say absurd. It would be a curious primate whose distinguishing characteristics are those which make for disruption, confusion and misconception of the gospel. The other thing to be noted here is the real significance of the word "church." The entire New Testament use of the word church seems to indicate simply an assembly. The word is variously used for any assembly, civil as well as religious. And when Jesus says that upon this Rock his assembly is to be built, he simply utters the constitutive principle of the Christian Church which is on the distinctive and clear announcement of the doctrine of his Person, namely, "the Christ, the Son of the living God." There is no ecclesiasticism here. There is nothing at all resembling the creation of a vicar of Christ.   There is not a syllable that demeans or subordinates any other disciple of Christ either then existing or yet to be.   It is simply the announcement of the constitutive principle of the Christian assembly.

But though the words of Christ conveyed no such authority, it is pretty clear that the habit of rushing in where angels feared to tread and otherwise asserting with reckless energy his own thought or desire did not utterly leave St. Peter on this occasion.   On the contrary, the words of Christ fastened themselves deeply into his mind.   The other disciples, not much better informed than St. Peter, and possibly with no such desire for physical leadership as he, helped to give the ideas even greater strength in his mind.   The result is that we find Peter, probably on the basis of this saying of Jesus, assuming a leadership and giving himself all the external powers of a real primacy.   After the ascension we find him dominating and probably directing the policy of the Christian Church.   We find him emphasizing the details of apostolic organization and insisting with rigor and severity upon the ritual observances of the Jews.   By St. Peter's influence and direction there was carried over into the early Church a mass of detail, of rite and symbol, which properly had no place in a Christian church whatever, and the remains of some of which are with us to-day.   The Church itself received a definition which probably excluded some Christians then and excludes others now.   The terms of Christian confession were at once extended so that they were no longer on the simple basis of the very confession of St. Peter which won such hearty approval of Christ, but upon various ritual observances. In other words, under Peter's conception of his own primacy, the Church was made coequal with Christ, not as a spiritual expression of Christ's body and life, but as the visible symbol of Christ in the world.   Thus it came about that the body of Christ, under St. Peter's thought and influence, became, not the assembly of Christians, but the gathering of churchmen. And in almost every part of the surviving tokens of the work of the great apostle of form, we see churchmanship practically elevated to the place of Christianity.

Against this easy and natural transition, perversion as well
as transition, there was apparently little protest at first.   The
men who were associated with Christ were Jews.   They had
all the sympathies and most of the prejudices of Jews.   The
idea of a world-wide and all-including Christianity was too
astounding to find a place in their minds, nor did it in the
Church at all until Paul brought it.   So that churchmanship
and Christianity soon became interchangeable terms in the
life of the early Church, and have to many so remained.   It
would be a beautiful realization if churchmanship and Christianity could be made interchangeable terms with any security
or confidence that each implied the other.   But no man who
is familiar with the history even of the apostolic Church can
for a moment hold such a belief.   The Church undoubtedly
has in it the vast body of those in whom is the spirit of Christ,
but that it has them all is simply absurd.   That the Spirit of
God limits his operations to those alone who are banded together in more or less varying visible forms of society and
worship is equally absurd.   In fact, in the very pages of the
New Testament, we have evidence that the Church would have
excluded, if it had dared, and if he had not been so energetic
in his own defence and so active in the announcement of his
own apostleship, St. Paul himself.   In St. Peter's visit to
Cornelius it is perfectly evident that the individual who
gained the most light and for whom the visit was apparently
most needful for spiritual enlightenment and growth in grace
was, not the centurion, but the apostle.   And this experience
is repeated in St. Peter's case more than once.   But wrong
though the idea was, it nevertheless grew to be very strong
in the days of the apostolic Church, that a certain churchmanship alone was Christianity, and thus even in that early day
did the shadow of ecclesiasticism hover over the path of
Christianity, suggesting what has since developed in the history of ecclesiasticism in the Church of Jesus Christ.   And
the mind who organized it and gave it force and power
was the ecclesiastic of the apostolic Church, namely, St.
Peter.   By nature, by training, and by the natural development of his mental type, St. Peter was an ecclesiastic,

and he may properly be called the apostle of churchmanship.

One of the great religious problems of our time is this very problem of churchmanship. When is a man in the real Church of Jesus Christ? Is it when he has subscribed to a given creed? But creeds differ, and such a definition must necessarily be a very narrow one. Is it when he has submitted to certain rites? But rites are nothing without the true spirit which gives them vitality and force in life. A Church Christ undoubtedly instituted in the earth, but unless the signs are very much at fault that Church is very much larger than we have been in the habit of supposing. Surely the men and women who have and live in the spirit of Christ are not apart from Christ. Surely the alliance of all good and spiritual persons is a natural and immutable alliance. All good is one. All spiritual life radiates from the common source. Protestantism has always held that where the Spirit of God is, there is the Church. It has also held as equally true that all the ceremonies in the world, however ornate and . impressive, cannot constitute the Church of God, unless the Spirit of God be there. It is the Spirit that quickeneth, said Jesus. So that the Church of Christ is a spiritual body, constituted through the authority and sustained by the power of the Holy Spirit. But even this spiritual life must have a habitation, and the organized fellowship of believers is this habitat of the spiritual body of Christ. It has all the weaknesses and all the failings of any merely temporary habitation. In this respect it is like the body of a man. Springing from dust it shall return to the dust, but the spirit unto God who gave it. Devotion to the external visible habitation of the Spirit is, however, not a useless or ignoble passion. And to say that St. Peter was the ecclesiastic of the apostolic Church is not to give him a small nor unworthy part in the carrying out of the Master's plan for the salvation of the world. If, amid splendid and imposing ceremonies, God in the elder day accepted the offering of his people when they built him a temple at Jerusalem and loved to dwell with them there, shall he not equally honor those who build him the temple, not of costly metals and the skilled workmanship of cunning artificers, but of human hearts and hands united in the common work of proclaiming and extending the gospel of his Son?

Speaking of the literary development of the twentieth century, a very distinguished French *littérateur* and critic, M. Joseph Texte, has recently said : "The capital problem in the literature as well as in the policy of the twentieth century will be the reconciliation of the fatherland with humanity. This reconciliation is possible, it is necessary. Should we fear to see the fatherland absorbed by and confounded with humanity? This fear is a chimera ; those who question the future of the principle of humanity despair of humanity itself, but those who fear for the fatherland do not realize the power of the bonds which attach a man to the soil. . . . We cannot conceive of an art without local moorings, a painting without definite horizons, a literature without a cradle. *Qui dit science, dit humanité ; mais qui dit art, dit patric.*" Here we have the contrast and relation between humanity and patriotism set forth in almost the precise terms in which we should set forth the relation of the Church to Christianity. We need not have any fear for the vast unknown body of the true lovers and servants of Jesus Christ. But just as no man can conceive of a painting without definite horizons nor a literature without a cradle, so no man can conceive of a Christianity which is without a Church, which is without form and without the symbols of self-expression and self-recognition throughout the whole circle of human life and activity. St. Peter's peculiar and distinct part in the organization of the apostolic Church was just this, to emphasize those horizons which localized and made definite the consciousness of the Church of Christ. To him it was peculiarly given to keep, in the assembly of the whole, due and necessary attention fixed upon those qualifications for external organic union through which alone the propaganda of Christian effort throughout the earth could be maintained.

What M. Texte calls the capital problem of literature in the twentieth century has already become the capital problem in the reconciliation of the form and spirit of religion. Christianity must have forms and symbols. These forms and symbols must not violate the spirit of the gospel, nor must they be oppressive in the demands which they make upon belief and life. How to make forms which shall be elastic enough to be true to the world-wide operations of the Spirit of Christ, and yet exclusive enough to be true to the fundamental ideas and tenets of the gospel life, is a problem which is vexing the whole Christian Church. The gospel must be proclaimed and upheld at all hazards. The Church must be upheld at all hazards, because the loss of the organic continuous life of the Church would soon lead to the loss of the gospel itself. But to make the Church and the gospel live in continuous harmonious relations together is the capital question. To insist upon the absolute liberty of the believer, with no regard to the requirements of fellowship, is to open the floodgates of no-churchism. To impose forms which have lost their vitality on the one hand or which challenge unbelief on the other, or, what is worse than either, to suggest assent without belief, is morally destructive. The only possible course is to keep the distinctive worth of actual liberty and church federation and union clearly and coördinately together before the minds of Christians, that they may see that though the spirit is life, nevertheless all life expresses itself in a body, and as the human spirit gives forth the tokens of its life in a perishable body of flesh, so the Spirit of God in the world makes his message known through the visible union of believers in the Christian Church. It was this truth, permanent, necessary and vital to the cause of Christ, which St. Peter grasped more than any other apostle. It was upon this phase of the gospel life that he laid the emphasis. If it is exaggerated sometimes, it is no more so than Paul's contemptuous rejection at times of all authorities and signs. If Paul can regard any day as holy and give the impression that any day may be God's holy day, as a token of Christian freedom, Peter can with no less propriety, and certainly with equal force of reasoning, point to the disciplinary value and the ministering function of a single and appointed holy day.

There is a most excellent case to be made out for the mere ecclesiastic, even when his ideas are neither the highest in type nor the clearest in thought. The history of civilization and religion alike is a history of organization. Universities are the organization of thought and knowledge. We do not think of the organizer and administrator of a great modern university as a man whose activity is pernicious to life and thought. On the contrary we delight to honor him whose insight and mastery of the needs of the world lead him to so apply the resources of his university that he can constantly increase its quick capital and enlarge the power with which it sends out its ideas into the minds of the youth and of the nation. The great factory is the organization of industry. It brings multitudes of incoherent powers and activities into living coöperative unity, lessens the cost of production, and soon makes what was the luxury of the few the common possession of the many. In a similar way the Church is the organization of religious life and activity, and, in a way, of religious thought. It provides for the maintenance of necessary and fundamental ideas. It provides channels for benevolence. It prescribes boundaries for special functions and secures an order and a discipline. And if organization is useful always, it was specially so in the early days of the Church. St. Peter had hardly creative skill enough to rapidly and accurately formulate a new church order, but to his mind it was infinitely wiser to stand by functions that had been sanctified by usage and which had not been clearly abrogated by the command of Christ, than it was to turn the whole band of new beginners in the gospel life over to their own caprices, letting each work out his own peculiar notions of service and worship. A dominating and organizing mind like St. Peter's shrank from such confusion, and well it might. To this very day the branch of the Christian Church which most closely adheres to the Petrine type is the one which has the closest organic union between its head and members. The fatal element in that union is that it is a union of helpless dependence, instead of one of mutual federated fellowship in Jesus Christ.

But when the ecclesiastic is one moved by an unselfish apostolic fervor, and vindicates himself by the earnestness

and self-sacrificing character of his efforts for the gospel,
there is a larger presumption even than that based on practical results that he has a real place in the development of the
life of Christ in his Church.   It has been a favorite habit with
the opponents of the Christian Church to point out that Christ
stood, most of his life, in relations of opposition to the religious organizations of his time.   This is both true and untrue.
As a statement of Christ's personal attitude toward the men
who stood in the places of leadership, thoroughly corrupt in
character, unsympathetic, selfish, and wholly lost to the spiritual obligations of their positions, it is true to say that he spent
most of his time in the opposition.   But as descriptive of
Jesus' attitude toward the temple and its services, the ordinances of the Jews and the religious life and practices of
the great body of his countrymen, it is misleading and false.
Even St. Paul, the most iconoclastic of the early teachers of
the gospel, held firm and true to the pride of his race and
training in the Jewish religion.   To the Jews there was to him
forever an advantage because to them had been committed
the oracles of God.   St. Peter went simply one step further
than Paul.   Paul conceded to the Jews precedence because of
their possession of the oracles of God; Peter simply placed the
ordinances of God on the same basis with the oracles.   This
was an error.   The Word remains, the ordinances perish with
the using.   The one is the breath and mind of God ; the other
must often be modified by the hardness of the hearts of those
whom God would make the custodians of his truth.   But St.
Peter's principle as a principle was as good as Paul's, and in
the opinion of many was as sound in the application.   Oracles
and ordinances are not so far apart as it might seem ; in fact,
one might argue with considerable show of success that ordinances were the oracles in practice.

St. Peter, therefore, by the natural movement of his mind
became an ecclesiastic.   His theology is the theology of an
ecclesiastic.   His appeals are the appeals of a mind moved
with a lofty sense of the necessity and supreme value of
the church discipline and order.   Whether the development
of the Petrine idea in its later, especially its mediæval,

form is to be ascribed to the apostle is a matter concerning
which there must always be differences of opinion, but there
can be no doubt that it was under St. Peter's strong and vigorous conception of a churchly life and a churchly authority
that the Church gathered itself into the compact mass which
so resolutely faced the persecutions of heathendom only a few
centuries later.   If Paul's teaching and message gave the individual disciple a sublime sense of his personal worth and
spiritual freedom, it was St. Peter's that gave him the sense
of Christian solidarity which made him everywhere look for a
united front against the assaults of godless men and persecut-
ing rulers.   And the idea of solidarity, of unity, is no less a
productive idea than the idea of freedom.   The enthusiasm
for humanity is not to make us forget our duties, nor our love
for the fatherland.   No rightly constituted man forgets the
soil out of which he sprang.   If in Paul's life there gleamed
always the splendor of a coming kingdom, wherein all were
kings and priests, in Peter's there was always the majestic
picture of the elders of Jewish history and tradition, the
mighty prophets and seers of old.   If the one was happiest
in the open forest where God himself had reared the stately
temples of oak and pine and fir, the other could not forget
the glistening temple front and the solemn march of the
priests, and the stately presentation of the nation to God for
forgiveness by its authoritative high priest.   Where the one
represented the centrifugal form of individualism and democracy, the other represented the centripetal force of concen-
trated authority and fixed tradition.   Both had their proper
note in the early Church, and both were men of God.

It is possible, under the sway of a science which is destroying many of our most cherished illusions, under the influence of a literature which has gained in beauty and exactness
of form what it has lost of impressional significance and
power under the disintegrations of thought which leave us
less theology than we ever had before, that perhaps we may
with wisdom make more than we have of our church order and
life.   Certain it is that order and form must ever be the
proper channels for the expression of the religious moods of

so complex a civilization as the world seems now to be enter-
ing upon. Of all calamities to which an emancipated intellect
and spirit are subject, the malady of rampant no-churchism is
the most pitiful and barren. Its natural fruits are sterility of
intellect, loss of spiritual responsiveness, and the extinction of
the higher sensibilities of heart which are the redeeming traits
of mankind. To base such a life upon a theory of gospel freedom is to crucify Christ anew and to pervert the sublimest of
sacrifices to the lowest of personal inclinations. The practical
aspects of the case fully bear out this analysis. Where there
is no church there is usually little or no religion. Where
there are no ordinances there is no conviction. Where there
is no Bible to preach there is no truth to maintain, and where
there is no Christ proclaimed there is no Christ to serve. It
is to the *ecclesia*, the church, the assembly of the men and
women of Christ, to whom in special and peculiar measure
these trusts are committed. And the figure of that small body
from whose loins all of our Christian types have emerged, who
at least once in his life uttered the final constitutive principle
of union in the announcement of the supreme and final word
of our Master, and the great Head of the Church, was the man
who said, " Thou art the Christ, the Son of the living God."
It was a truth which flesh and blood could not and did not
discover. It came from the Father in heaven. It was the
filial recognition of the fatherhood through the Son. It is
the uniting clause of all souls that have felt the divine fatherhood and have come into the relation of sonship and love. It
was not the utterance of a rebel against a spiritual order and
an organized fellowship of service and love, but the discerning
comment of a churchman in Christ uttering the basal truth of
the Christian life. Upon this faith the Church has been built.
Against this Church the gates of hell have not been able to
prevail. On its corner-stone shall ever be graven the name,
and in its heart ever be cherished the love, of the apostle of
churchmanship who first gave it utterance.

ST. THOMAS THE BELIEVING
RATIONALIST

JOHN XX. 29.

THERE are few terms in the vocabulary of modern Biblical learning and research which have had more terrors for Christian believers than the term "rationalist." To say that a scholar was a rationalist was for many merely a euphemistic way of saying that he was an unbeliever of some kind. The content which had been given and which still is given to faith was such that any inclination toward a rationalistic frame of mind was held to be evidence of spiritual degeneracy and the beginning of the decline of faith itself. And it must be confessed there was much to support this view. Those scholars and others who made the most use of the term, or who rejoiced most to be known as rationalists, were least prominent in the spiritual life and the practical activities of the Church. They appeared to be out of sympathy with the struggling masses of the Church for light and truth. Where these sought comfort and encouragement, they were usually received with a sneer or a rebuff. Humble and unquestioning faith in the final truth and authority of the gospel without a long career of antagonism, rebellion and interrogation was held by these rationalists to be evidence either of mental weakness or an unmanly spirit. And thus it came about that schools and seminaries controlled by humble and spiritually minded men warned their students against rationalism almost with the same vehemence and anxiety that they warned them against infidelity. They took pronounced steps against the encouragement of the habit of interrogation. They made strenuous efforts to confirm the feeble knees and lift up the hands that were hanging down by violent assertions concerning the nature of the Bible and the authority of its truths. In many cases they went so far that the recoil on the part of those whom it was designed thus to impress and strengthen in the faith was very much greater than it could possibly have been had they been freely acquainted with the writings of these rationalists themselves.

But this terror has almost entirely passed away. The term "rationalism" has grown along with other things. To say that a man is a rationalist in Christian thought in these days is no impeachment either of his character or his faith. It may still mean that he holds certain views which are not the common possession of all Christians; but it does not invalidate his claim to Christian fellowship or support. Indeed, we have all become rationalists in a sense. The desire of us all for evidence by which our belief can be confirmed, or otherwise made more tenable, is so strong that even the daily press has taken to printing elaborate accounts of any new discoveries which have any bearing on the problems of Christian belief. Our most conservative teachers have given us the example and inspiration of weighing and sifting evidence which has made us all in a measure rationalistic investigators of the gospel history. Our very methods of studying God's Word have taken on this general intellectual form and type. We believe, but we believe because we have made the reasons for our belief a part of it. We are steadily translating our religious life and beliefs into the terms of all our other knowledge. We have found that we cannot have one rule of evidence in the so-called secular portion of our lives, and another in the religious. We know now that belief and life are inseparably associated. It is no longer a question with us as to what we shall believe, but whether we are justified in believing what we do believe. We are more afraid than we used to be of taking sacred things into our hands and making sweeping assertions about matters of which at very best we can know but little. We are more hospitable to those who bring us light, from whatsoever source they derive it. We are learning to prove all things, and I hope are at the same time trying to hold fast to that which is good. This is a real spiritual and intellectual advance in the Church of Christ. It seems to be a step nearer to the ideal and practice of the New Testament.

It is a matter of surpassing interest, therefore, in view of all this experience, to find that one of the small band whom Jesus Christ selected to be the authoritative expounders of his life and teaching should have been a man to whom the term "rationalist" applies better than any other expression that could be selected. Thomas has been called the doubting apostle, but the expression is certainly misleading if it is not absolutely false. I do not contrast doubt with belief. Doubt is a phase of belief and a necessary part of its development and strength. A genuine doubt is not devil-born, as Tennyson suggests, but of divine birth. Almost the whole apostolic company asked questions of one kind or another before they became disciples of Christ. To that degree they were rationalists, every one of them. They would hardly have been worth having if they had not been men who asked questions. To be sure they were frequently answered by the simple invitation to "come and see," but nevertheless this was an answer as well as a recognition of the force and rectitude of the mental attitude which propounded the question at the outset. No, doubt is not devil-born. A genuine doubt may be God's open door toward a profound and satisfying knowledge of himself and of his Christ. And, besides, Thomas was not a doubting apostle. There is nothing in the New Testament that indicates in any sense that Thomas was not always clear, definite and positive in the views which he held. In what is called his supreme doubt, namely, that of the resurrection of Christ, his language is positive and clear: "Except I shall see in his hands the print of the nails, and put in my finger into the print of the nails, and put my hand into his side, I will not believe." There certainly is no note of dubiousness in that speech. It is as clear a statement of belief as can be found anywhere. It is more than a statement of belief. It is the announcement of a standard of evidence which is very explicit. How very absurd it is to call that the speech of a doubting man! Where is the hesitancy that belongs naturally to genuine uncertainty? Where is the feeling of insecurity which goes with what is uncertain and which is the unmistakable accompaniment of all irresolute or fearful men? Utterly wanting. Thomas was not in doubt at the moment he made this statement. In fact, he was in one of the most positive moods of his life.

This statement must be analyzed yet a little more to make it perfectly clear how absurd the designation of the doubting apostle is, as applied to Thomas. There is in this simple statement, observe, a clear and definite appreciation of the nature and consequences of certain causes. Thomas notes specifically the print of the nails in the Saviour's hands, and insists that he must put his finger into the print before he will accept Christ's resurrection as a fact. Notice that detail. The finger and the nail print. That is specific and definite. Again, he remembers that the Lord's side was pierced with a spear. Into that wound he must put his hand. Again a careful, minute detail. Now that shows how analytically Thomas had recognized the causes which produced Christ's death. He does not propose to be misled by any stories, nor barter his faith for vague hopes. Even apparitions do not win his intellectual assent to the fact of the resurrection. Not at all. A finger in the nail print and a hand into the wound in the Master's side are the conditions of his belief. Now this is the language of belief, not of doubt. His belief, here expressed in a negative way, is that a man whose side has been pierced with a spear and whose hands have been driven through with nails and who has been dead and buried does not come to life again. Notice that he asks no questions. The resurrection to him is intellectually out of the range of credible things. And there is a positiveness about this speech which makes it absolutely clear that Thomas had not the slightest expectation of seeing Christ or of making the test which he proposed. This is a statement of belief. This is not the expression of a man without opinions nor of one at all hampered by uncertainties. It is the statement of a man who has a definite notion of what evidence is, and has given due weight to the evidence which he has in hand

and has formed a conclusion. Thomas' reply to the disciple's statement that they had seen the Lord is probably the final word of a precise, cogent and for himself convincing, argument of his belief that the thing was absolutely incredible. And it sounds like the expression of a man who is making conditions which he knows are impossible of fulfilment.

Then again observe that word "will." There is a determination here which does not admit of the assumption of doubt. The precision of intellectual perception which specified conditions extends to the will, which shows that there is a determination behind them. Thomas was a man utterly devoid of sentiment. Whatever might be his desire to confirm or agree with his fellow disciples, he could not stultify himself, and, what is of more consequence, he would not. " I will not believe," is the revelation of a determination which was reached after mature and deliberate examination and reflection. And this is in thorough accord with all that we know of Thomas. His questions always have a directness and a form which show a man both of intellectual precision and strong will. When Jesus undertakes to go to Bethany after the death of Lazarus, it is this same Thomas who sees the perils with which that journey is fraught, and who knows that Jesus' life will be endangered by that nearness to the hotbed of conspiracy and hatred at Jerusalem. But he does not hesitate. We will go, he says, and die with him. Already he sees Jesus put to death by the conspiring and murderous priesthood. But he does not flinch. He is willing to go and die with him. And Thomas' speech on this occasion was not of that fluent, volatile character that so often distinguished St. Peter. On the contrary, his was the word of a man who meant every syllable that he uttered. To call such a man " the doubting apostle " is absurd in the extreme. There is no member of the apostolic college of whom we have so clear a mental picture as we have of this man. And everywhere the cartoon is in bold outlines and mentally clear and precise. And for this, too, there is a very interesting reason. All that we know of St. Thomas is found in the gospel of John. John, as I have remarked, was the philosopher of the apostolic band. It is he who notes these mental states and gives us the record of them. St. John probably appreciated Thomas' intellectual gifts and moods better than any other man present. It seems clear, too, that the others did not or could not understand him. Such a man could not have been obscure in the apostolic counsels. He could be misunderstood. No other gospel historian has aught to say of him but to record his name.

St. Thomas was a rationalist. To him faith was a product of mental life and mental effort. It was associated in his thought with the higher facts and forces of the intelligence. It is unfortunate that we have so little knowledge of his personality in other respects than the ones which St. John notes. He has been identified with Judas, the brother of our Lord, and by some it has been supposed was our Lord's twin brother. This would be interesting if we could confirm it. Eusebius, the historian, says that Thomas' real name was Judas, and in Matthew xiii. 55, there is mentioned a Judas, the brother of our Lord. But this is the extent of the evidence on the point. If Thomas was a brother of our Lord and a twin brother (Thomas means twin, Didymus being the Greek equivalent) at that, we have even greater insight into the explicit refusal of Thomas to accept the word of the disciples on the question of his resurrection. Another tradition is that he had a twin sister Lydia, and still another is that he was born at Antioch. Of these matters we may not speak in detail nor with any positiveness. The essential thing for our purpose is that here we have among those who formed the earliest nucleus of the Christian Church a man in whom the habit of rationalizing about the events of the gospel and the person of the Lord himself was highly developed. It is an interesting fact. It has in it an encouragement which has not always been appreciated at its full worth. When in the very company who walked and talked with Jesus there was a man who in those solemn hours of the Last Supper could say with uncompromising frankness and directness, "Lord, we know not whither thou goest; how know we the way?" surely we may bear with men of our own day,

who, amid perplexity and anxiety, are unwilling to make the
assumptions and walk in the brazen confidence which belongs
to less sensitive and less compelling intellects, when the great
facts of the gospel are brought into question.

Of St. Thomas' rationalism there are two characteristics
which it is very well worth our while to dwell upon, both for
the sake of understanding the apostle and for our own instruction and guidance in the mastery of this habit of mind.
It had the quality of uncompromising frankness. There is a
ring of openness about every utterance of this man that
endears him to us, little as we know of his personal traits.
There is no questioning the passionate, determined love
which he had for the Master. He was of the stuff that dies
for a cause in which he believes. And such men are notori-
ously slow to give their allegiance. But when they do give
themselves they give all that they have, and do not need to
go through the process twice. Once enlisted they go with
grim determination to the last stand of discipleship. There
is never any danger in a skepticism that finds a voice truthfully and frankly. Most of the difficulties about the gospel disappear when brought into the forum of practical life
and experience. Imagine the blunt man breaking in upon
Christ's tender mood at that last meeting by affirming that
he did not know the way. But it was frank, it was open, it
was saying what possibly the others thought but did not dare
to say. In fact from what happened it is perfectly clear that
Thomas was not the only one who did not understand what
Jesus was talking about on that occasion. But he spoke
right out, and they did not. There are such disciples of
Christ in the Church to-day who are often viewed with anxiety and suspicion. Where others maintain a discreet silence
and either pretend to know what they do not know or prefer
to let the specters of unbelief haunt them without giving
expression to their fears, this man speaks forth the question-
ings of his soul. It is a noble trait. It is wholly praiseworthy and deserving of commendation. The Church has
too often put a premium upon unbelieving silence instead of
upon vocal interrogation. It has too often made unquestioning assent take the place of inward confidence.

The other characteristic is the equally frank acceptance of new facts and evidence. Men of open, inquiring intellects are proverbially the readiest men in the world to give their faith and confidence when their just scruples have been satisfied. They do not make objections merely for the sake of argument. They are not talkative individuals who have no reason for talking. They are just in their intellectual demands, and when these have been fairly met they are equally just in surrendering their prejudices or mistaken opinions. Such a man was St. Thomas, and thus it comes about that we have from his lips the strongest affirmation of the divine character of our Lord that can be found in the New Testament. It is immaterial whether he actually did put his finger into the nail print or his hand into the spear thrust or not. The fact is that when he stood face to face with his Lord he surrendered his standard of evidence or verified it, and in either case he worshiped and said, " My Lord and my God." In this Thomas was exactly the man that we see him when he meets the disciples who had seen the Lord in his absence. There is here the note of positiveness and conviction. It is no more vacillating now than it was then. He has no more nor any less doubt now than he had then. It was in both cases the decisive utterance of a man who thinks he knows, and, whether he knows or not, is honestly expressing the judgments of his mind. And we have here the illustration of what I have been saying, that when a frank, open man has been in the wrong he is equally frank and open in abandoning his mistaken position. This is the true attitude of rationalism as the world has come to appreciate and understand that term applied to Christian things. A rationalist may be a devout believer in Jesus Christ and his salvation. Many rationalists are. The gospel is intellectually secure, but it is not intellectualism. It is mentally sound, but it is not on that account a mere mental phenomenon. It is all these, and more. It is being enlightened by the truth, as that truth is seen in Jesus Christ, and made the standard of personal behavior and conduct toward God and toward man.

There is a general impression that St. Thomas' intellect

was of a somber, gloomy cast, and that he was of a desponding turn of mind by natural disposition. But I find no evidence for this in the New Testament. Wherever I come
into contact with the character of Thomas I find it strong,
earnest and mentally alert. I feel certain qualities of hardihood and tenacity which are, perhaps, not consistent with the
best intellectual development, but I find nothing that indicates gloom. There is nothing in the incident about going
to Bethany to die with Christ that to me shows despondency.
I cannot find myself despondent under such conditions, and
the words, to me, are expressive of anything rather than
despondency. Incredulity, if that is a fair description of
Thomas' mind when the report of the resurrection reached
him, is not allied usually with gloom or despondency. This
is the error of the Middle Ages, still surviving in the light
and learning of the nineteenth century. When a man shows
any disposition to be clear and enlightened, and to give due
weight to the various moods of his reflection, the thoughtless
multitude is very likely to imagine that he is brooding and
gloomy. This has been the thinkers' heritage for many centuries. But it is a mistake. The evolution from the belief
that when a man shuts himself up with books and experi-
menting apparatus he was secretly conjuring up devils, to
the day when we are all anxious that the most recent discovery in any science or branch of human knowledge shall be
given to the world at the earliest possible moment, has been
gradual, but it has also been thorough. Still old superstitions linger. It is one of the interesting facts about heresies
in general that the heretics of one generation are the orthodox
of the next. The very word from which the name is derived
means, to think. Far better that we keep our thinkers in the
Church and try to think with them, and keep the channels
of intercommunication wide open, than to create the mental
and spiritual alienation which has in times past wrought
such enormous practical havoc in the life and usefulness of
the Church. It is one of the most pleasing things to notice
in connection with the apostolic Church, that the disposition
to brand as false the ideas of any disciple was notably lack-

ing during Christ's life and received no encouragement afterward. Orthodoxy throughout the New Testament is still simply Christlikeness and the disposition and determination to follow Christ. It has remained for later authorities to create conditions and demand obediences which Christ himself did not require.

St. Thomas was a believer. Let that fact never be forgotten. When he was announcing his rejection of the testimony of the disciples as to the resurrection of Christ, he was still a believer. There was nothing about him of the man who is a skeptic for the sake of skepticism. His was a believing mind, even in those moods where its rejection of certain facts appears in the strongest light. The difficulty at that time, and the difficulty as a general thing with all skepticism about the gospel and its Christ, arises from a false standard of judgment and false assumptions concerning the message of the gospel itself. Paul once asked a council, Why should it be thought a thing incredible among you that God should raise one from the dead? And we, in the light of the mysterious developments of our own day, when attempts are being made to give the doctrine of immortality a scientific basis, shall we stand skeptical, still holding theories of evidence and standards of belief which were unreasonable centuries ago? Has not science extended the limits of the admitted order of nature immeasurably in the last fifty years? St. Paul's question was a perfectly rational one, and one that never has been satisfactorily answered. The difficulty with Thomas was that he based his beliefs upon a standard which, if consistently carried through the world, would drive a man first to a monastery and then to a grave. The idea that a man must see to believe has been demonstrated again and again as too foolish for the practical needs of the world. And when to this is added St. Thomas' further condition, that of personally putting his finger and hand into the wounds of Christ, we have an already unreasonable standard made more so. The gospel of Christ has no quarrel with thoughtful and inquiring minds. The Son of God makes his appeal to the reason no less than to the heart and the feel-

ings and the will. But the appeal to reason must be a genuinely reasonable appeal.

Christ's forbearance and tenderness on this occasion are
also worthy of notice. Instead of meeting this unreasonable
man with a reproach and a rebuke, the Master, well knowing
the temperament and habit of thought of his rationalistic
disciple, accepts his own test and does it in his own way.
"Reach hither thy finger, and see my hands; and reach
hither thy hand, and put it into my side : and be not faithless,
but believing," — this was his kindly acceptance of the harsh
standard which Thomas had proposed. We do not know
whether he did what his Lord invited him to do. The prob-
abilities are rather, I should say, that he did it. The general
opinion has always been that he did not, but that, overcome
with his humiliation and shame, he at once gave forth his
wonderful and powerful testimony to Christ. My own thought
is different. Strong, resolute, determined man, I can see him
walking close to the Master, I can see him holding with the
wonderful tenderness of strength that nail-marked hand, I
can see him putting the great strong arms tenderly around
Christ as he feels the impress of the Roman spear. Then
out of the great revulsion of faith I can feel the welling up
of that powerful nature in its effort to give adequate expression to its profound emotions, and then I hear him say, "My
Lord and my God." But the lesson is not yet learned.
Christ has yet another word. "Because thou hast seen me,
thou hast believed : blessed are they that have not seen, and
yet have believed." Therein Christ taught the true rationalism ; to believe what is believable with a just appreciation
of the proper standards of judgment and with appropriate
scrutiny of all that requires our credence and acceptance.
But not with the flag of unbelief flying as the normal standard of human judgment, and skepticism as a rational habit of
mind. The heart and the mind of man were made for belief,
and when they are not elevated by the rational beliefs of
Christianity they have, as experience abundantly shows, been
degraded by the vulgar superstitions of pseudo-religionism.

But for the inquiry itself Christ had no word of reproach.

This outward skeptic, as skepticism is usually reckoned, had a heart of belief and love. Loyal to the end and faithful in that calling to which by the grace of Christ he was called, his name and his words have remained to us the type of that kind of life, and point of view, which dares to interrogate the sublimest facts of human life, and does not wear its faith upon its sleeve to be plucked at by every passing daw. And out of these lips we have that majestic, sonorous and moving declaration of personal faith, " My Lord and my God." Reason and emotion combined in that testimony, and it stands as converted Reason's testimony to Jesus Christ. And like all else that proceeds from the sanctified reason, it is the highest, the farthest reaching in significance and dignity, and rings with sonorous resonance through history as the witness of a strong mind's devotion to the Son of God.

ST. JOHN THE CHRISTIAN PHILOSOPHER

John i. 9.

THE favorite and Biblical designation of the apostle John is that of the "disciple whom Jesus loved." The origin of this title is not known, and there is little in the New Testament to indicate that there was anything peculiar in the relations of Jesus and John to warrant John's bold and apparently thoroughly artless application of this title to himself. There were disputes often enough among the disciples as to the prominent places in the company, and the mother of John had craved the right and the left hand of Christ in his kingdom. But there was nothing strange in this request, and it might, with equal appropriateness, have come from any other member of the company that followed Christ. Spiritual conceptions of Christ's kingdom were as yet almost, if not quite, nonexistent. Christ's power and authority were allied, in the minds of the men with whom he was associated, with earthly authority and earthly splendor. The true mission of Christ was not apprehended, or, if apprehended, in such vague and indefinite terms as to be hardly useful in directing the spiritual energies of the disciples, left to themselves, in such a way as would make for the true work of Christ in the earth. Jesus does seem to have made special associates of three of his apostles, Peter, James and John; and we have the word of John that he was himself "the disciple whom Jesus loved." It may be remarked that John's frank assumption of this title himself may show that it was habitually employed by the disciples in some such way as we frequently hear a favorite child spoken of as "the one whom mother loves." It is difficult

to believe that the apostle John would use such an expression if there were the slightest possibility of causing offense
thereby. On the other hand, the New Testament contains
nothing that warrants the special assumption of such a dignity by John. In this respect John's favorite title loses its
significance in precisely the same way as Peter's assumption
of the primacy of the apostolic college.

Jesus loved all his disciples. It is thoroughly inconsistent
with the character of Christ that he should take on a mode
of behavior toward any single disciple that would gain for
him such a precedence as is indicated by the words " whom
Jesus loved." If there had been, we may assume that it
would have appeared in some way in the history of the early
Church. But no such token appears. Nor is the thing reasonable in itself. Such a habit of regarding one disciple as
more lovable and better loved than the others would have
been the surest way of dampening the ardor and otherwise
restraining the enthusiasm of the remaining disciples of
Christ. This is hardly a fair thought about the Master,
whose own attention was never to individual men, anyway,
except as they marked the way to be followed in the salvation of mankind as a whole. Christ was not merely a leader
and Saviour of individual men, excellent as these might be.
He was the Saviour of the world, and individual men stood
to him merely as emblems of the world which it was his
mission to save. It is possible, however, that the relations
between Jesus and John were of a nature which marked a
greater fellowship of mental habit and life than was possible
with the other members of his chosen band. Jesus was undoubtedly impressed with the mental attitudes which John
habitually held toward himself and his words. He was,
without doubt, greatly interested in the view of his own
Person which John's mind should form and which he should
proclaim to the world. John represented a type of mental
life which was exceedingly rare among the Jews, and Jesus
probably knew this also and desired to take the largest advantage possible of it. The philosophic habit among the
Jews was exceedingly rare. Jewish ideas about religion

and God forbade the development of any great philosophic powers in the nation. This is seen in the fact that the speculative, philosophic habit is almost entirely absent from the Jewish literature, including the Old Testament. Whatever there is springs from non-Jewish sources. It was John who was destined to interpret the gospel to the non-Jewish mind on its speculative side. This of itself may have produced an unusual mental intimacy between John and his Master.

Hand in hand with the idea of a peculiar affection on the part of Jesus for John, and partly as a result from it, has come the idea that John was a quietist in religion, the representative of the moods of religion which are unconnected with the vigor and energy which we associate with others of the apostolic company. But such an idea is manifestly an error, as the mere reading of John's works proves. John had not the personal self-assertiveness of Peter, nor the demonstrative strength of Paul, but there was no bolder mind in the whole circle that Jesus gathered about him. It is John, be it remembered, who could on occasion rise even to the heights of personal aggressiveness, as when, in company with James, he wants to call down the fire from heaven on the offending Samaritans. But his boldness was not of the type that effects physical reforms directly. His courage was in the strong and unhesitating appropriation of the ideas of other nations and possibly other religions, certainly other philosophies, than those common or dominant among the Jews, and incorporating them into the faith and gospel of Jesus Christ. The true exhibitions of courage and energy are not always in the open field. There is a dash and movement of the cloister, and the cabinet as well. The true pioneers of human life are after all the pioneers of thought. The noblest heroism is the heroism of independent opinions. The reason why there was no clash on the subject of apostolic orthodoxy between St. Peter and St. John, as there was between St. Peter and St. Paul, is probably because Peter had absolutely no grasp whatever of the vastness of the spiritual reach and effect of St. John's opinions of Christ and the gospel. Philosophy Peter had absolutely none. To John the gospel was not

merely a life, but a philosophy of life also. And his problem
was the explaining of the philosophy of life which was expressed in the terms of the gospel life of Jesus Christ. This
conception of itself was a bold one in the mind of a Jew
trained in the habits of thought and in the precepts of Jewish
exclusiveness as John was. It marks John as a radical of the
most pronounced type. It was not personally self-assertive
nor ecclesiastically aggressive; but it was intellectually con-
tinental and human, as contrasted with the provincial and
insular modes of Jewish thought.

If the key-word of St. Paul's life-work is freedom, and that
of St. Peter's is authority, that of St. John's may be set down
as illumination. He is the apostle of light, that is, of the
light of the mind. John has more to say, directly and indi-
rectly, of the thoughts of Christ than all the other writers of
the New Testament together. He penetrates more deeply
into the springs of the Christian teaching. He is more
anxious about the reasons that lay at the roots of Christ's
own mind. He shows a deeper understanding of the self-
consciousness of Jesus than any of his contemporaries. He
tried to see the gospel from the standpoint of Christ's own
experience. He sought to bring the world-ideas of Jesus
naturally into harmony and relationship with the Jewish ex-
pectations of the Messiah. He endeavored to point out that
the Jews' Messiah was also the world-Christ. And, as is by
that fact at once seen, this was a question of a human and
world philosophy quite as much as it was the proclamation of
a faith. There was another reason for all this which lay in
the nature and rearing of St. John himself. St. John represents in many ways what may be called the urban view of
Christ and his work. It was the view of a man who had
relationships and interests at the center of the nation's life.
This was true of John even more than it was of St. Paul. St.
Paul feels impelled to boast that he is a citizen of no mean
city. St. John has the calm urban view of a native Jerusa-
lemite. There is no need of announcing that he is a city
man. There is no need of making it clear that he is taking
the view of a Jew whose interests and traditions are those of

an assured social and intellectual position. This appears in John's writings themselves. It is for this reason, too, that the Jerusalem ministry of Jesus has for him the deepest interest. It is for this reason, likewise, that he pays more attention to the discourses of Christ, and less to the events that induced the discourses. His doctrine of the *logos*, the Word, made the ideas of the gospel of infinitely more importance than the mere local clothing in which those ideas might appear.

It is at this point that an interesting contrast appears between the point of view of St. Paul and that of St. John. Paul's interests at the capital were those of a theologian, and hence we have a Pauline theology. It is hardly a right designation to speak of a Johannine theology. It is more proper to speak of a Johannine philosophy of religion or Christianity. Where Paul enters into the primary principles of theology, John discusses the necessary elements of religious thought, utterly without reference to their theological interest and bearing. Paul has a definite theory of Christology. John's Christology is that of a speculative mystic who has found the key to the thought-life of the world. Paul's identification with Christ was the heroic assumption of the fellowship of Christ's sufferings. St. John's identification with Christ was the fellowship of a common thought about God and about the salvation of the world. Where St. Peter is ecclesiastical, John is cosmopolitan. Where Paul is theological, John is metaphysical. Where Paul finds his energies expanding in the problem of God's dealings with man and his activities in the world, John is finding his rest in the being of God and the eternal nature of the divine character. Paul gives the outlines of God's personality, and points out the representative character of Christ as revealing the God whom he has portrayed. John feels after the necessary elements of God's nature and accepts Christ as having them. What Paul discovers by argument and inference, John discovers by feeling and the characteristics of reality. Throughout, St. John is a philosopher who has become Christianized and to whom Christ is the center of thought and the satisfying symbol of rest and peace with God. It is in this fact, that John shows such absolute security in Christ and voices the intellectual satisfaction of the gospel life, that there lies the source of the impression that John was a quietist. It was the quietism of an abiding trust. It was the rest of a man who had handled the divine thing and knew whereof he spake. It is the speech of a man who has held in his own hand the true light. But it is also the word of a man who is holding up that true light for the illumination of the whole world.

As the apostle of illumination the very words around which his philosophy groups its thoughts are words of illumination. One of these is light and another is love ; and in these two words we shall find the essential elements of John's conception of a Christian philosophy of the gospel. I say here a Christian philosophy of the gospel, because there is a philosophy of the gospel which cannot be styled in any proper sense Christian. Universal as Christ's mission to the world is, and broad and inclusive as the terms of the gospel life are, there is, nevertheless, a certain exclusiveness about the religion of Jesus Christ which must never be lost sight of in dealing with the life of the apostolic Church nor in finding the sources of apostolic power. While the gospel does everywhere contemplate the carrying of the message of Jesus Christ in its entirety and fullness to the whole earth, there is nowhere the expectation that the whole earth will find itself under the personal dominion of Jesus Christ. There is no such thing as a universalism of Christlikeness taught in the New Testament. John is the disciple who makes this more clear than any of the other expositors of the apostolic Church. Light to him lights every man as he comes into the world. But it is nevertheless true that light comes to the world, as the true Light came to his own and his own received him not. It is not to the world, but to them that receive him, that he gives the right to become the sons of God. The condemnation of the world, according to the same apostle, is that light came into the world, but men loved darkness rather than light because their deeds were evil. It is this same disciple, too, who tells us that good deeds love to come to the light that it may be made manifest that they

are wrought in God.   It will be seen at once that there is no
universalism here.   With all his grasp of the immanence of
God and the pervasiveness of the divine authority and being
in every man and throughout the world, John did not lose
sight of the narrow line of cleavage which separates the
gospel from the rest of human thought and life.   The very
genius and nature of light has as its necessary corollary, both
in thought and in fact, darkness.

It is the failure to recognize this truth which has given us
a very widely accepted philosophy of Christianity which is
not a Christian philosophy of the gospel.   It is willing to
receive the gospel invitation, without pointing out the gospel
conditions of its acceptance.   The gospel itself, the revelation of Christ in a form which is a limited expression of the
will and word of God, would necessarily imply such an invitation as conditioned by the nature and authority of the limitation.   No man who is bidden to a feast in the morning thinks
of coming at noon or in the evening.   Nor does any man in
his senses, to whom the gospel comes as light, imagine that
he can remain in darkness while in possession of the light.
A philosophy of Christianity which is true and which is properly descriptive of the gospel must be at the same time a
Christian philosophy.   It must be as truly representative of
the mind of Christ as the gospel life is a copy of the obedience
of Christ.   The whole trend of St. John's thought keeps it
perfectly clear, that while the gospel says "whosoever," it
also adds, "will."   This light lighteth every man that cometh
into the world truly enough.   But it is only upon him who receives it that the right is conferred to become a son of God.
St. John's philosophy, I repeat, is not merely philosophy, but
Christian philosophy.   It is for this reason, probably, that it
has a place in the divine Word.   It is this that gives it the
singular power which it has always had over the thought of
the Christian Church.   It is this which has made it the place
of trust and comfort which has been its peculiar and distinctive mission among the writings of the New Testament.

Light is St. John's symbol of the gospel life in its substance.
"This is the message," he says, "which we have heard from

him, and announce unto you, that God is light, and in him is
no darkness at all." God is therefore light, and the child of
God cannot be in darkness, because he is of the substance of
light itself. And then he goes on to add, "If we say that we
have fellowship with him, and walk in the darkness, we lie, and
do not the truth." This seems to be plain enough. Notice
how throughout the writings of St. John there is the unconscious confirmation of the doctrine which he thus lays down
for the brethren to whom he writes, and contrast it at the
same time with the spirit of St. Paul. Where the latter is in
perplexity, not to say terror, about his own salvation, St. John
shows no trace anywhere of either anxiety, perplexity, or fear.
His conception of the gospel life as essentially light makes
whatever is obscure to him, for him, not of the gospel at all.
This is really the announcement of the modern doctrine of
the Christian consciousness. St. John seems to teach that
whatever is the gospel to him is by that fact at once clear and
finally settled beyond the region of fears and doubts. This
arises from the doctrine of light which he holds. Such a
view, if made the test of Christian character and discipleship,
would exclude a great many devout and true disciples from
the fellowship of believers. But the same cast of mind which
made St. John capable of holding this doctrine made him
incapable of imposing it upon any of his fellow Christians.
To him the gospel had no darkness. What was the gospel
to him was also light. It was all light. This is the Johannine doctrine of Christian illumination. It is the gospel
Quakerism, if I may so speak. It is a true type of religious
and Christian experience. It was unquestionably John's.
But it must be observed that it has no ecclesiastical or theological significance. It is not a contribution to theology. It
is essentially a Christian philosophy. Christ is the true light.
Christ as an obscure or imperfect light is to this thinker
inconceivable. We beheld his glory, he says. Who can
behold the glory of Christ and be in darkness? The thing
is incomprehensible. Whatsoever is not light is not, for St.
John at least, the gospel.

There lies in this conception of the gospel a most profound

permanent truth of all religion, and especially of the gospel
of Jesus Christ.   This is simply the philosophic way of stating that man's true course lies in the pathway of the truths
which he has made his own rather than in those which he
only dimly and obscurely comprehends.   The ideals of life
are after all the mainsprings of man's inspiration and activity.   The ideals which are known and understood are, according to St. John, the true ones.   God is not the author
of confusion.   The service of the Most High cannot involve
groping around in obedience to what has no rational basis in
the thought of the worshiper.   A rite without meaning, a service without a spirit, a consecration without an emotion, a life
without a sacrifice, these may all give forth a visible symbolism of religion, but they have in them no real religion.   A
rite that brings with it illumination may be crude, but it is
none the less of God.   A service that has in it the Christ-
spirit may be involved and often objectively wrong, but it is
acceptable to God.   A consecration which is unmarked by a
living breath of the Spirit of God in the soul may speak the
language of nearness to God, but it is not the consecration
which marks the kinship of the believer with his Father in
heaven.   It is the truth that really consecrates.   " Consecrate
them in the truth : thy word is truth," was the prayer of
Jesus Christ for his followers.   Truth alone is the spring of
a real illumination, and he who was the Truth and the Way
was the Light before he became either.   It is simply saying
in another way what Christ himself said when he said that
whosoever will do his will shall know the teaching.   It is
the hospitality of the mind to the light of God that makes the
teaching of God effective for righteousness and joy in the
Holy Ghost.   John's conception of the Christian mind is one
that sees.   Indeed, his conception of the Christian is first of
all that of a man with the Christ-illuminated intelligence
which has revealed to him his fellowship with God.

And if light is the symbol of St. John's philosophy as revealing the substance of the gospel, love is his rule for its
practical expression.   The idea which runs through the
whole of St. John's teaching of love is that it is fellowship

and peace, because it is the result of enlightenment. A man
may stumble because he walks in darkness. But if he walks
in the light there is neither reason nor excuse for his stum-
bling. A man may persist in sin who has not seen the
Christ of God, nor felt the light of heaven in his mind, but
if he has seen the light and has fellowship with it he cannot
sin, because he is born in God. Love, to St. John, is not the
strenuous endeavor of St. Paul to be kind and just and forgiving. It is the steady avoidance of conflict and sin against
God and fellow men because there is no occasion for stum-
bling, and forgiveness has made the motive to sinning disappear. Righteousness, which in St. Paul is the result of effort
and suffering, is to St. John the natural product of fellowship
with the true Light of the world. What St. Peter tries so
sturdily and often drastically to make secure by an iron-bound
rule of churchmanship, St. John points out as the inevitable
outcome of walking in the light. There is a sort of eternity
about John's view in this matter which might easily have won
for him the particular fellowship of Jesus, whose own view
he so perfectly portrays. Goodness, says St. Paul, results
only from being crucified with Christ. St. John gives us no
hint of such a crucifixion. On the contrary, he seems to
intimate that one crucifixion was enough, and even that was
accompanied with darkness. Paul is continually pointing out
the warfare between the law of the mind and the law of the
flesh. St. John simply says that sin is lawlessness, but that
Christ was manifested to take away sin, and with the taking
away of sin lawlessness disappears. Righteousness is not an
acquired habit. It is a necessary condition of existence. To
be a child of God is to be righteous. Light has made moral
darkness impossible.

All love, St. John seems to teach, is an emanation from
God, and where love is there is God. There are for him
none of those fluctuations of faith which give us such a vivid
insight into the spiritual struggles of St. Paul, and for this
reason we have little to show the stages of St. John's
development in the faith of Jesus Christ. That he did develop we know, and some of the different points of view

remain in the writings which he has left. But the same spirit which made the apocalyptic glory his favorite theme of hope made his confidence and security in Christ Jesus appear almost at the outset of his gospel experience. His was the mind and the faith of a philosopher. His exposition of the gospel was that of the thinker and the seer. It was not that of the man of passion, of tempest and storm. Where the great apostle to the Gentiles was in the *Sturm und Drang* of faith-making and faith-breaking, the man whom Jesus loved was calmly pursuing his course in the path of the just that was simply shining more and more unto the perfect day. There is no such human, passionate interest about him as there is about Paul. There is no such rugged likeness to ourselves in him as there is in St. Peter. But he, too, was one of the many diverse minds who brought their life and their message to the service of Jesus Christ, and inspired by him wrought out their fraction of the total truth in which men alone may be free. There is an intellectual amiableness about St. John which has always made him the resort of thoughtful, inquiring minds for comfort and for solace. It is he who reaches with greatest penetration into those truths which his colleagues were unable to grasp. It is he who sees and depicts the future glories of the redeemed in Christ Jesus, and hears with ecstatic soul the mighty chorus that around the throne sings, " Hallelujah : for the Lord our God, the Almighty, reigneth." It is he that sees the glassy sea mingled with fire, and the hosts that stand by it with the harps of God, saying, " Great and marvellous are thy works, O Lord God, the Almighty ; righteous and true are thy ways, thou King of the nations." It is he, too, who, through all his sense of completeness and repose in the gospel, nevertheless has yet a larger life, even for his mind and his thought, when he says, " Beloved, now are we children of God, and it is not yet made manifest what we shall be. We know that, if it shall be manifested, we shall be like him ; for we shall see him even as he is." Satisfied, but hopeful and expectant, John to the end knows if there is yet a part of the divine will to be manifested that it will be light, and light will be love, and the soul will find both in Jesus Christ.

ST. MATTHEW THE PUBLICAN APOSTLE.

MATTHEW ix. 9.

Tax-collectors as a class have never been a popular set of men either in ancient or modern times. But the wisdom of this world has not yet been able to devise a plan of human society by which the tax-gatherer can be eliminated from the roster of necessary public men. So long as government exists, it will cost money. So long as money must be paid for public services, it will have to be collected from those who are governed. This much seems to be self-evident. Yet obvious as it is, as a necessary truth arising from the structure of society itself, tax-gatherers have been universally unpopular. Even when taxation has been obviously for the welfare of the whole community and the benefits equally distributed throughout the body politic, it has been shunned and, when possible, avoided. There is not in history, I believe, a single instance of a tax which was received with satisfaction by those upon whom the levy fell. On the other hand, many a tax, like that on Boston tea, has made a nation drunk with fury and resistance. From that intoxication we have not yet wholly recovered.

It has been said on this account that Jesus showed a singular disregard for the dictates of worldly wisdom when he called Levi from the collectorship of Capernaum and made him one of the apostolic company. And yet I venture to say that Jesus was never so worldly wise as on this very occasion. Leaders of new causes are very prone to seek help of those who are powerful or popular, or whose names for any reason are catchwords with the multitude. Great business establishments are fond of informing the public

49

that such or such a one buys at this house. Benevolent societies are very prone to place at the head, as honorary president or what not, some great name as a pledge for the stability and excellence of the charity. But it is rarely the case that any one in any enterprise brings to the front the fact that the most unpopular or the most unscrupulous men in the community are allied to it. Respectability and position have always carried great weight. The Christian Church has not always been above this plea, and has not infrequently sought to keep in touch with the respectable classes simply as a guarantee to its prosperity. But this was not the method of Jesus, nor would it have been, in the work of Jesus, worldly wisdom to employ such a method. It was from the standpoint of the deepest worldliness the wisest thing that Jesus could possibly do to call such a man as Matthew to the apostleship. Every one was willing to have the fellowship of Respectability. But who would have the fellowship of Disreputability? This was precisely the issue which Jesus wished to raise in the world. Nowhere did he raise it more clearly or distinctly than in the call of Matthew the publican.

If tax-collectors are unpopular in the nature of things, they were doubly so in Palestine in the time of Christ. A more odious set of beings probably did not exist anywhere in the world. No considerations of humanity appeared to have the slightest claim upon them. Their taxes were often gathered at the expense of the deepest misery and shame to the helpless wretches from whose very life-blood they were wrung. In this they were most closely allied to that species of the modern corporation treasurers who reply, when the methods of their institutions are under fire, "My business is to furnish dividends." That was precisely the doctrine of the publicans. The holders of those tax levies must have their money, if every penny of it had to be squeezed from the heart of the victims. And as Capernaum was a city of considerable importance, and as the revenues were of considerable value, it is probable that there was no man in the entire community who was so completely identified in the minds of the population with all the enormities of the system as the very man whom Jesus addressed at the gate of toll with the words, "Follow me."

Of course Prudence shakes its wise head even now, after all these years, and says, See how unworldly Jesus Christ was. Admiringly, to be sure, but with just a shade of deprecation in the tone. But deeper knowledge of Jesus Christ sees in that visible alliance with Disreputability the clearest appreciation of all the mixed motives of human life, and recognizes not merely the divine insight and wisdom of Jesus, but also his worldly good sense and judgment. For would not that entire class, hated and despised as they were, outcast from Respectability's inviolate cloisters, rejoice that there was one being at least in all the realm who saw even in the deepest shame of man some token of humanity and possibility of salvation? Would not even the suffering ones who came under the lash of the cruel system wonder who this man might be who made a friend of the conspicuous agent of foreign oppression and robbery at Capernaum? And would not all men marvel at the transformation of a publican into an apostle — the weapon of oppression into the instrument of comfort and hope? Was not that worldly wisdom as well as divine insight? Was it not just so when Lincoln allied himself with the common people and persisted in that alliance, while Charles Sumner and the aristocrats of the Senate were poking fun at the English of his public documents?

But whether it was worldly wise or not, it was what the Saviour desired, and in that call he secured a disciple and an apostle who has done his cause noble service ever since. Matthew was despised, of course, and he was a publican, but he was a human being for all that. And the Lord then, as now, was not looking for men with antecedents, but for men with human hearts. If there was a genealogical society in Capernaum, as I have no doubt there was, probably the Pharisees were the most conspicuous members of it. The caste spirit dies hard even in the most advanced civilization. But in the mind and heart of Jesus Christ there was no possibility of such a distinction arising. Matthew was probably not a total stranger to him, nor was he unknown to the receiver of toll. They had seen each other frequently, and Matthew had had occasion, no doubt, to see and hear some of the wonderful things that Jesus did in that city. It is this fact that accounts for the abrupt way in which Jesus calls him and the almost equally abrupt way in which Matthew at once arises and follows him. His heart was already gone out to this young Teacher who taught not as the scribes and Pharisees. He had already been touched by the deep and tender humanity of our Lord. And in our text we have his own simple statement of what was to him the greatest event of his life.

Matthew does not tell us in his own account that it was his own house in which the feast occurred, at which the Pharisees criticised the Saviour for his association with publicans and sinners. It is Luke who tells us all about it. It is Luke, too, who, recognizing the remarkable nature of the transaction from Matthew's standpoint as well as Christ's, tells us that "he forsook all, and rose up and followed him." There is a significant hint in those added words, "forsook all." But Matthew says nothing about it. But the fact was, that in the joy of his new love to Christ Matthew did exactly what Mary of Bethany did. He gave the best expression known to him of his gratitude to God and his loyalty to Christ, and instituted this entertainment, which partook of the double character of an honor to Jesus and a farewell to his associates. The latter, at all events, were there in force, and many of them, publicans and sinners, as Matthew frankly calls them, sat down to the feast which Matthew had prepared. This was too much for the inevitable Pharisee. "Why do ye eat and drink with the publicans and sinners?" they murmured against the friends of Christ. Jesus himself makes the reply, "They that are whole have no need of a physician; but they that are sick. I am not come to call the righteous but sinners to repentance." This, then, is it. Here is a Friend of sinners. Disreputability is still humanity. Respectability is not the whole of the kingdom of God, after

all. Was not this the whole of Christ's message? If not,
how could it have been made clearer?

Never throughout all his ministry does the character of
Jesus Christ shine with a more resplendent luster than it
does in this scene. Nowhere does he touch the heart of universal humanity with greater impressiveness or with a surer
response from all that makes life true and hopeful in a world
stained with sin and trouble. No single bedraggled being,
in whom the image of God still remains, but may lift up his
head in hope when he reads those words or hears that statement of the mission of Jesus Christ. Christ invited no discussion of the publican's past. He brought no humiliating
confessions from the burdened heart of the man who only
wanted hope and freedom. He did not force him through
the mill of exposure and public shame. He did not imperil
what little of manhood there was in the publican by dragging
it to the light, as a victorious charioteer dragged his victim
around the arena. No, none of all this. He simply met
the desire of the man's heart and called him to a higher service. He bade him leave the lower self and embrace the
higher. Every drop of blood, every instinct of returning
patriotic devotion, every kindly human trait, every divine
lineament that was not wholly effaced in the heart and
brain of that publican, thrilled with power and expectation.
Christ's call was the call of God. He forgot the dishonor
and the shame of his past life. He thought not of the evil
he had done, but of the good he might do. He dreamed of
a time when he might look all his fellow men in the face
again and, free from self-reproach, might minister in Christ's
name and with Christ to them. All the joy of the new spiritual birth leaped into strength and exultation when he "forsook all" and rose up and followed the Lord. A poor
triumph, you say, and the world says. A miserable tax-
gatherer converted! What an accession that is to the
apostolic college! Great influence he will bring, surely!
Where was good judgment and where was good sense when
that choice was made? Where indeed? Flung to the winds
of heaven, while only the royal law of God prevailed.

There is something so utterly disinterested and other-worldly about this call that men cannot and do not yet fully comprehend it. It is hard after all these years, even when to minister has become a world-doctrine, to get men to practice it. Theoretically we all admire the spirit which seeks out the lowly and the weak and degraded, but practically few men care to have anything to do with it. Ready to embrace the magnificent moral inspiration of the gospel of Jesus Christ, how few there are that enter into the real spirit and momentum of the Lord's sacrifice for men. Apologists without number arise on every hand to tell us that this or that thing is not to be taken literally. Conditions, they say, have changed. The gospel, they assert, is not practical if it is taken in too absolute a sense. We must be reasonable. We must use good judgment. We must keep within the bounds of good sense and propriety. We know what such people would have been in Christ's time. We have their exact counterparts in the gospels in the faultfinding Pharisees. But thank God we have the answer of Jesus Christ, too. The whole may be trusted to care for themselves. Self-forgetfulness never has been a drug in the market. But the sick, the poor, the wretched, the degraded, who will think for them? Who will minister to these, the offscouring of humanity? Who, indeed, but Jesus Christ and they who minister in his name!

But this is not true merely of the gospel, it is equally true of every movement which has to do with uplifting man and securing the blessings of life. Here in our own Boston, when the soul of Samuel Adams was on fire for liberty, a firebrand that ultimately lighted the entire sisterhood of colonies to an independence conflagration, his Tory fellow citizens were fond of calling him Samuel the Maltster, or Samuel the Publican, in derision of his father's business. The brewing trade was not then what it is now, and the jeer was not one suggested by moral considerations so much as by a caste innuendo. But Samuel the Publican became, by the heroic industry which characterized him, next to Washington the mightiest figure in the struggle for independence. But while

Loyalists and Tories were sneering, this patriot and democrat made friends of the common people. And to make the parallel even more complete, Sam Adams was tax-collector of the town of Boston from 1756 to 1764, too. A historian states that "he began to illustrate democratic simplicity and democratic friendliness long before Jefferson was old enough to know the meaning of those words. Seated by the side of some calker in the shipyard, or pausing on the street corner for leisurely and confidential discourse with any cobbler or hod-carrier who should care to spend his time in that way, he won extraordinary affection from his fellow townsmen by his evident willingness to impart to the humblest of them the political fears, and hopes, and aims which possessed his own soul respecting the Commonwealth."[1] Patient, abstemious, humble and industrious, and above all a friend of the lowly, the American commonwealth stands to-day in part his monument to the doctrine of the worldly wisdom of a disinterested career. The Tory aristocrats who rejoiced in the companionship of the favored and composed jibes at the raw American citizen patriots and soldiers, where are they? But the name and the fame of the man who caused a British cabinet to tremble, and made two hemispheres ring with the might of his unselfish advocacy of a great human cause, they live on forever.

Perhaps some scholar will, when the times are ripe and the leisure for such a task is possible, write for us a history of Christianity as revealed in the vulgar epithets which have been applied to its professors. Such a work would probably be one of the most suggestive evidences of the moral advance of the world through the agency of the gospel that could be compiled. It would begin with the designation of the Son of God as a "winebibber" and "friend of publicans and sinners," a "gluttonous man" and such like, and it would continue through the pitiful attempt to put down the essential principle of Christ's gospel, namely, that it comes to the needy and helpless of the earth, the sinful and the weak, by means of opprobrious names, clear down to our own day, when the

[1] " Literary History of the American Revolution," Vol. II, p. 6.

Church of England, with an insolence almost unmatched in
the history of ecclesiasticism, times and conditions being taken
into account, alludes to the great nonconforming population
of England as "schismatics." What a choice collection of
names they would make, grouped together, that have been
applied to Luther, to Erasmus, to Wesley, to Knox, to Coligny,
to William of Orange and the rest ! But every one of them
would be a badge of honor which any man who feels the
spirit of Christ in his heart might wear to-day with joy and
pride.

Such a history would contain a record of every noble, personal or national spiritual aspiration which the modern world
has seen. In the struggle for religious liberty in the Netherlands it would tell the story of the "Beggars" of Holland.
In the tremendous movement known as Methodism it would
recount the rise of the Oxford nickname which has become
transformed into a crown of glory. In France it would tell
the pathetic tale of the "Poor Men of Lyons." In England
it would have to recount the sad story of our own denominational ancestor, Robert Browne, and the contemptuous designation "Brownists" by which his followers were known. It
would include that noble body of Christians who to this day
are known chiefly by the epithet "Quakers," which was applied to them in scorn. Many other such names will occur
to you. But how has that derision been rewarded and with
what acclaim do we now greet the honored names which once
men bore with fear and trembling and at the peril of their
lives ! Peter Waldo and his "Poor Men of Lyons" have tri-
umphed ; Robert Browne lives in the Congregational brotherhood the whole world over ; while George Fox and his
brethren of the Inner Light have made the name "Quaker"
a standard gauge of character wherever the name is known.
And this whole history illustrates the profound truth of the
words of George Herbert when he wrote in his poem on the
"Church" : —

> Scorn no man's love though of a mean degree,
> Love is a present for a mighty king ;
> Much less make any one thine enemy.

As guns destroy, so may a little sling;
The cunning workman never doth refuse
The meanest tool that he may chance to use.

If even in the judgment of the practical world the call of
Matthew was a matter of wisdom, history should settle it forever. But this is a minor point in the discussion. There are
practical matters contained in it which are of more immediate
interest to us all. One of these is, that the service of Christ
is not to be fettered by the mistakes and failures of the past.
No Christian can ever look with satisfaction upon his life
apart from the love of God as revealed in Christ. From
whatever standpoint he views it, it is full of regret and humiliation. The past is sealed and comes not back again. It
must remain as a part of the record, to be sure, but it is not
to be kept in the foreground, and certainly is not to have
any place in the making of motives to Christian living except
as the City of Destruction was a motive to Pilgrim to flee
from it. The New Testament distinctly teaches that progress
in the life of Christ is on the basis of forgetting the things
that are behind and reaching forth to those that are before.
It keeps in mind the prize of the high calling of God in
Christ Jesus. Each day will bring sufficient failures of its
own to discourage without the burdensome consciousness of
the past failures. The gospel command is, look forward. It
does not drag out the specters of other days to frighten men.
It does not revamp the bitter sins of youth or ignorance, and
keep them forever thrusting their ugly faces into our growing love for Christ. It cannot permit those who undertake
Christ's service to be thus bound. The Christian life is freedom. It is alliance with God. It is forgiveness from sins.
It is hope in Christ. It is the prisoner loosed, not the prisoner
forever clanking his chains after him in a mock freedom.

You and I cannot always be in the valley of humiliation.
Humbled we must be, and the truer our hearts are to Christ
the more frequently we shall be humbled. But humbled before God is one thing. Humiliated and shamed before man
is another. Christ enjoins the former. There is no warrant
in his gospel for the latter. He bids you and me to come into

the fulness of his own freedom and grow in grace and knowledge and fitness for the kingdom.   Matthew could not be ever remembering the miserable acts of which he had been guilty as a publican and agent of cruel tax-farmers.   He could not be binding about him continually chains of enslavement to a bitter and unwholesome past.   No more ought you.   The publican must cease to think publican thoughts, and think those of his new calling, namely, apostleship.   So must you and I cease to think the thoughts, or have in our souls even a habitation for the leaven of destruction and sin that has made for us the misery and anxiety of other days.   Let it alone.   Think Christ's thoughts.   Live in Christ's pure and wholesome life.   Act from Christ's pure motives and bid farewell to the associations of wrong and shame, and come into the companionship of the new manhood ordained of God. This was what Matthew the publican did.   It was thus he became Matthew the apostle.

At the same time there must be a definite and announced departure from the old career and a definite and announced acceptance of the new before we can hope for usefulness in the kingdom of which Christ is the head.   This does not always involve, as it did involve for Matthew, a total revolution of life and occupation.   In general it means a revolution *in* life and *in* the occupation.   As things are, the service of Christ has become so diversified that there are no secular callings.   All life and labor are sacred, the highest and the humblest are alike honorable to him who engages in them and the Lord who ordains them.   But the fellowship of Christ is not a secret brotherhood.   It is not an alliance which is kept in reserve for defensive purposes.   It is a life contract and fellowship.   It is mutually offensive and defensive. Matthew recognized this decisive character of the choice of Christ's service, for, as Luke says, he at once "forsook all." Hard task for a man whose business had been, not in forsaking all, but often taking all that others had.   But he made the choice and gave it its logical effect in action and abdication.   As a servant of Christ he could stay in that place no longer.   Therefore he left it.   But not even here did his

determination to make the new fellowship secure stop. Love
and sound worldly sense again united in suggesting that farewell feast. All his companions in the crimes of old must
know that he had determined definitively to forsake them and
their life. They must see his new Master, and they must
hear from his lips the same wondrous words which had wooed
him into the kingdom. In that act Matthew made clear to
himself, to Christ and to the world the sincerity and the decisive nature of his choice. The plan was wise. It is as wise
and necessary to-day as it was then. Break to-day with the
old associations of vice and shame. Crucify the vicious habits
that are destroying your life to-day. Bring your decision out
into the open. Exalt Christ with your decision, and let all
the world know that you are living in alliance with the Christ
of God. This is both sound sense and the command of Christ.
Godliness is not a hidden treasure. Righteousness is not a
dark-lantern performance. Association with Christ is not
after the pattern of a Macbeth meeting the witches by night.
It is not to be sought as Saul sought hope and relief from the
witch of Endor in the caves of the earth. Christ's life and
Christ's fellowship are in the sunlight and under the blue
skies of God.

Radicalness and thoroughness are the two words in which
the call and acceptance of Matthew of his new mission in life
may be summed up. Christ's call to him was a demand of a
striking and drastic character. It is no less so to other men.
The acceptance of the call was of the same nature as the call
itself. Both required a radical and thoroughgoing departure
from a life which had definite characteristics, into another
life equally outlined in boldness. For this reason the transaction stands out in such vigorous relief. It called for
thorough and far-reaching action. It embraced the whole
outlines of a future career. Not less so is the demand by
Christ upon men in our own day and generation. But the
most cheering thought of all lies in the fact which is brought
into clearness along with the promptness and cordiality with
which Matthew embraced Christ when his call came, namely,
that out of the most untoward material, humanly speaking,

that could be chosen, Christ produced one of his most useful and faithful helpers in the work of his earthly ministry. This gives the assurance to us all that, with all our defects and with all our natural limitations of mind and heart, we may nevertheless add something to the glory of the Redeemer's kingdom, and aid in some measure, how much the Lord must determine, in hastening the rule of Christ in all the earth.

JUDAS ONE OF THE TWELVE

LUKE xxii. 47.

THE story of Judas Iscariot is, without exception, the most melancholy in the history of human life. Approached from whatever standard we may see fit to choose, this man's career can be regarded only with humiliation and shame. Sometimes the depth of his degradation moves us even to the profoundest pity. But however viewed, no matter what emotion is for the moment dominant, the life story of Judas is the most melancholy of which human history has any record. This arises, of course, from the associations in which he was placed, the height and dignity of his opportunity, and the great consequences that issued from his actions. The Christian world has followed the example of the gospel historians, and has remembered Judas only with shame and contempt. The conspicuous fact of his life, the betrayal of Christ, is the one striking thing that is associated with his memory, and not infrequently men have thought that they did Christ added service when they multiplied invectives against him, and sought to blacken the memory of this fallen apostle. But this is not only unnecessary but very unprofitable. Likewise is it wholly misrepresentative of the spirit and example of Jesus Christ. It must never be forgotten that in the mystery of God's purposes out of that act has come the salvation of the whole world through Jesus Christ's death. We may, I suppose, take it for granted that if the redemption of the world could have been achieved without the death of Christ, it would have been secured in that way. It is totally repugnant to Christian feeling and the spirit of the gospel to suppose that God arbitrarily chose the hateful death of crucifixion in order to impress the world with its

sins. It is equally antagonistic to the Christian thought
and sensibility of the gospel to suppose that he chose death
at all. It is true enough that the path to life lies through
death. There is probably such a relation between sacrifice
and redemption that, as a part of the moral law of the universe, death and life are inseparably associated together, and
the human life of Jesus Christ was subject to this law. The
part which Judas had in the operations of that inexorable law
is a matter for God's judgment alone. We cannot wisely approach the life-story of such a man with bitterness and wrath.
Rather should we come to it with a quietness approaching
awe.

The New Testament records of Judas Iscariot are very
much mixed, and full of perplexities. The evangelists were
doubtless moved with deep and heartrending emotions whenever the mention of the betrayer of Jesus was necessary.
This of itself would tend to make it very difficult for them to
keep their minds perfectly clear whenever they tried to tell
the story of his relations with Jesus Christ. Then, again,
their knowledge of subsequent events would very likely color
unfavorably all their recollections of any earlier events in his
life. It would tend to make them forget all that was excellent in Judas' character and deeds. Moreover, the final acts
of Judas' life were so startling and tragic in their interest
and outcome that the remembrance of these would be more
or less confused. So that as a result all mention of Judas
in the New Testament presents us a perplexing picture. If
we had in the surviving records the whole story of Judas, it
would be difficult to understand why Jesus ever chose him
for discipleship. If he had all the hateful characteristics,
and these alone, which the evangelists give, it is very certain
that he could not have been a member of the apostolic band
long, and certainly could not have been its only important
officer. No, in this we have most strikingly brought out the
human element in the Scripture. Justice, even the men who
wrote as they were moved by the Holy Spirit could not do
to the man who had sold their Lord for thirty pieces of silver.
It was a natural failing. In some respects it was an honora-

ble failing. They did not see, as we see, that the wrath of
man was in this case the redemption of the world. They
could not see the vast moral influence of the lifting up of
Jesus on the cross. They could not see, in the vastness
of a twenty-century horizon, that the contrast of light and
shadow which is afforded by the treachery of Judas and the
humiliation of Christ would be the most majestic scene in the
whole sublime drama of God's effort to save mankind.

It is not my purpose, therefore, to try to unravel the difficulties which the gospel records present about the actions of
Judas. My desire is to present the character of the man
fully, justly and faithfully, that we may see what his place
in that company was, what his work was, and perhaps find
a message for modern life in the study. Judas was probably
a man of Kerioth, and therefore a Judæan. This seems to me
the simplest of the explanations of the term Iscariot, though
there are a good many others. This of itself makes Judas
a rather exceptional personage. Being the only Judæan,
he was the only countryman of Jesus in the whole number of
the apostles, a matter which naturally gives rise to some very
interesting reflections. Then, again, Judas must have been a
person of marked executive and administrative talents, which
was probably the reason for his selection as treasurer of the
band. At various times this office was of great importance.
The administrative method of the men who followed Christ
was probably one of pure communism. Everything was kept
in one treasury. The keeper of the funds made all the
needful purchases, and to him was given the entire income
of the apostles. This was no trifling task, as any who has
ever tried even the simplest experiment in communism knows.
And from what we know of the remaining members of
Christ's college of apostles there were not wanting the usual
critics and faultfinders with whatever Judas may have done.
All this naturally would not find a place in the records concerning him. But the men who tried the patience of Jesus
himself, who constantly quarreled among themselves, who
kept a sharp eye upon each other as to who should have
the first places in the coming kingdom, which they fancied

Christ was going to establish in the earth, were probably not
men who accepted without any single word of interpellation
or criticism every administrative act of their treasurer.   Of
course we know nothing about it absolutely.   But we know
enough about human nature in general, and about the apostolic human nature in particular, to know that Judas' office
of treasurer was no sinecure.

Then, again, as De Quincey remarks, speaking of Judas
Iscariot, he came into daily contact with the shopkeepers of
Palestine, the most petty and demoralizing of all people,
especially in the Orient.   De Quincey thinks that this gave
Judas the impulse to the betrayal of Christ, because he
thought he discovered among these sure echoes of popular
opinion that Christ's cause was externally a hopeless one,
and that he might possibly gain popularity and honor in
being the instrument of a downfall which seemed to him
certain in any event.   That seems to me to be modernizing
too much without warrant.   The Oriental shopkeeper is not
a factor in determining the action of his rulers.   Especially
was this not the case in Jesus' time.   He may have known
more or less about tumults that were impending and something about planning insurrections, but on the question of
knowing anything about the movements of the governing
classes, especially the priesthood, he knew little and cared
less.   But this is true, the daily purchase of supplies and
the daily meeting of the petty, sordid motives of the average
shopkeeper, particularly the average Oriental shopkeeper,
must have been a moral draft from which any man might
well shrink.   It could not have been without its influence
upon Judas.   The everlasting haggling and overreaching
which belongs to all trade and which reaches a point of
Satanic aggravation in the East, might well have been a
counter-influence in the development of Judas' character to
which adequate recognition has not been given.   Moreover,
such activity and service would keep him away from Christ
and the evangelistic work of Christ and his fellow apostles to
a considerable degree.   To be a courier, going in advance to
make the needful preparations for food and lodging and all

that was involved in such preparation, must have kept Judas apart from the apostolic fellowship for a large part of the whole time. In this way much of what Christ impressed upon the disciples who were with him constantly was denied Judas. Much of the kindness and tenderness which Jesus showed to the various men who were around him was thus unquestionably lost to the man who filled the only administrative office which they established. Let this not be forgotten. Men who have seen their salvation through the death of Christ can afford to be generous and just to the instrument whom God permitted to bring it about.

All this is not said in extenuation of anything that Judas said or did. There can be no apology for sin. The freedom of the human will and the promises of Almighty God give no man the right to complain at the conditions in which he is placed as these affect his moral actions. But we very well know that seemingly slight circumstances do affect the human heart, and that the gravest moral consequences flow from what seem on the surface to be very trivial things. What if Judas did not hear some of these sublime promises which have been the consolation and hope of the world? What if, cumbered with practical matters about the physical needs of his fellow disciples, he was too occupied with the material things over which he was set to feel the full force or appreciate at their real value the teachings which the other disciples were eagerly and continually drinking in? We know how little even they got from some of Christ's addresses. We know that to the end even they hardly comprehended what Christ was seeking to accomplish. We know that after his death they thought it was all over and Christ only a remembrance. We know that after the Church was organized and the Holy Spirit had come upon them all, there were struggles and bickerings and disagreements almost without ceasing. Now if this was what the men who were continually in Christ's presence did, what of the man who was only occasionally, certainly one who was very much less frequently privileged to hear his gracious words? That all these things did have their influence on Judas is seen in a single instance. When the alabaster box was broken and the costly ointment poured over the Master's head, Judas' mind at once reverts to its value. Do you notice the exactness of the appraisal? Three hundred pence! There is a specific calculation about that which shows that these things were always on his mind. It was easy enough for John *after the event* to say that he was a thief. But let it be remembered that there is not a syllable that the disciples could remember and record of the previous history of Judas in which Christ had aught to say of rebuke to Judas for anything that he said or did. This of itself indicates to me that he was absent much of the time. If there had been such incidents, we may be sure that they would have been recalled and recorded.

On the contrary, if any inference is to be drawn from these circumstances, it is that they show the remarkable confidence in Judas which Jesus had. Here again the absence of recorded criticism of Judas by his fellow members of the apostolic company becomes significant. There is nothing that men quarrel about so readily and easily as about money. Most of the quarrels of the world, at their base, involve money. Now the disposition to find fault is just about in a ratio inversely to the amount involved. Under Oriental conditions this disposition to find fault is immeasurably greater than Western people can understand without actual experience. But there is no charge in the New Testament that Judas was dishonest. No gospel historian dares to say that the bag was not faithfully kept. His treasurership, so far as we have any record of it, is perfectly secure. John, who says he was a thief, does not specify in the matter, and is writing, it must be remembered, after the events of the crucifixion. During the whole three years of Christ's ministry we do not hear one single word of criticism on either the method or the efficiency of the apostolic bookkeeping, if I may so speak. Why do we not hear a word about Judas in this respect? Simply because in all probability the executive skill of Judas was providing the best preparations that could be made, and the ministry and journeys of Christ were greatly facilitated thereby. If, as is supposed, Jesus had a permanent residence at Capernaum, it will be seen that the duties of Judas were even greater than we would naturally infer. Now to pass the years of companionship that Judas did with his brethren without adverse criticism, or at all events with the ability to so effectively silence it that, after his fall, nothing could be remembered against him, is evidence of great thoroughness and great fidelity. It is, in fact, the highest confirmation of Jesus' choice of this man, not only for discipleship, but also for the treasurership.

But the water wears the rock. Daily contact and thought concerning the petty and sordid things of life soon wore away the higher aims and purposes of Judas' life. It is here that his downfall probably began. I cannot think otherwise than that Judas began his service of Christ in precisely the same way that the other disciples did. A strong mind and a strong will, possibly an earnest and passionate nature, all these seem to have belonged to Judas. Probably he thought, as did the others, that he had made the supreme sacrifice for Christ's cause, and was willing to follow him to the death. But great responsibility did not cause him to exercise great caution. Gradually he began to lose the finer touches of the spiritual nature which first attracted him to Christ and Christ to him. The bag becomes the one object of superlative interest. His mind, instead of thinking about righteousness and truth, is thinking about to-morrow's bread and the balance when the Sabbath day comes. He ceases to think spiritual thoughts. He forgets his spiritual duties. He becomes, as the modern man does, absorbed in business; and even though the business in this case was actually that of providing for the physical wants of Christ and the apostles, in arranging for that bread, he neglects the bread of life. Is that unique? Have you not seen that happen over and over again? Have you never seen a man begin his Christian life earnestly, faithfully and painstakingly, and gradually begin to think more and more of his work and less and less of Christ? Have you never seen such a man lose the finer edges of life, the higher inspirations of service, and fall by the wayside a victim to greed and the love of mastery in trade? Every day sees just such descents into death as probably formed the easy path for Judas from the real service of Christ to the utter degradation of absolute betrayal. I cannot think that Judas fell in a moment to his lowest level. I can make the fullest allowances for his loss of opportunity; but I cannot leave out of the sight that he neglected to watch and pray lest he should enter into temptation. Nor did he have the tender solicitude of struggling fellow disciples. There was not much fellowship and comparatively little sympathy in that assembly. But Christ was there, and the tempted Judas could at any moment seek and commune with the Saviour of the world.

It is here that we find the real secret of Judas' character and career. Like many another strong man, that is, administratively strong, he is weak when it comes to the matter of bringing his occupation into subjection to the higher law. Like many a man, he, too, deceived himself that he was serving Christ acceptably when he was neglecting the higher things of life and immortality. Judas might well have employed the argument, common enough in our day, that he was doing his part faithfully and well. But he was not doing all his part, certainly not the most needful part. Jesus, as it was, had often to go hungry and thirsty, as we know. Better that Jesus should be hungry than that Judas' soul should be lost. And what was true of Judas is true of every man. Better that we lose money and lose lands and have less comfort physically, than that we lose the moral perceptions and the spiritual life itself. What shall it profit a man if he does gain the whole world and lose life itself? What if a man be a great statesman and a moral imbecile? What if he make a great name in journalism but be without moral power? What if he lead a great army and win the mighty conqueror's name and fame, if history's verdict upon his life be that he was a remorseless tyrant and devastator of the homes of men? We can but think how speedily the administrative difficulties of the young Church would have been solved and the whole energy of the apostolic Church practically organized had it had the administrative skill of Judas at its command. He was the practical man of business and the bursar without whose efficient aid much of Christ's work must have remained undone. Alas, that he allowed his work to supplant Christ! A thousand pities that the skill of management should have cost him the one thing most desirable. Nor is he alone in this great and enduring loss. The names are legion of those men who fancy that business is life and that a man's existence lies in the abundance of the things which he possesses. Even when not moved by the greed of gold, they are moved by the love of action and achievement which often is at the cost of eternal life. This is the impressive secret of Judas' fall.

The strength and thoroughness of Judas' mind appears even in the final great tragedy of his life. There is a devilishness about the betrayal which must command intellectual admiration. Whatever Judas may or may not have known about Christ and his mission in the world, he knew that here was the most loving, self-sacrificing creature that the world had ever seen. He knew that this being was daily showing to the world a spectacle of loveliness in life, gentleness in intercourse, profoundness in discoursing on the things of God, helpfulness in ministering to the sick, the needy and the dying, and revealing hidden powers of God which marked him as the Christ the Son of the living God. He knew, too, the emotions of his own soul when he accepted the call and the commission of discipleship. He was the sharer in at least some of the deep and tender emotions of the gospel life as lived under the eye and in the companionship of Christ. Remembering all this, the deliberate plan of going to a chosen retreat of Christ at the head of a band of soldiers, and walking into the presence of Christ and embracing him fondly with a "Hail, Rabbi," and kissing him—it passes comprehension how any man could have had the intellectual hardihood and the strength of will to proceed in such a manner. This was no weakling who did not know his own mind. This was a man of a strength and power of will that are remarkable even at this distance. Great is the fall of great natures. And there is no weakness like the weakness of strong men. Nor did this forsake him when the inevitable reaction came. The wrath of the sounding silver thrown upon the temple floor is likewise magnificent in its passion. Nor is this all. Foiled, beaten, burning with shame and remorse, the courage of the suicide was also his, and to the last we have the evidences that Judas' was a strong nature perverted from its natural strength and become the plaything of a resistless greed.

Can there be a more practical lesson for our own time and hour than this? We live in the era of strong and masterful men. It is the boast of our generation that it is independent and brave. It challenges the elements of nature, and often the powers of God. It looks the severest problems in the face with a deathless daring that is amazing and terrible. But great as is our strength, there is a greater strength which is made perfect in weakness. It was another magnificent nature which said, "When I am weak, then am I strong." Peril is never so near nor so dangerous as when in the plenitude of our strength we are rejoicing that we are not as other men are. It was St. John who said, "I have written unto you, young men, because ye are strong." But true strength is the power that can hold hard to the higher ideals of life, and bring itself into subjection to Jesus Christ in the hour of its supremest glory. If your life is full and fruitful, if it is yielding the glorious results of labor well directed, and industry suitably and persistently maintained, far be it from you to challenge the providence of God and the powers of darkness by forgetting where the secret of man's greatness and power really lies. It was another great nature which said, "My soul, . . . hope thou in God." The deepest natures, the mightiest characters, the most enduring services are, after all, not in the subjugation of what is without us, but in the holding under the will and purpose of God what is within. Keep the will for Christ. Hold true to the first great demand of God upon man, "Thou shalt love the Lord thy God with all thy heart, and with all thy soul, and with all thy mind, and with all thy strength." This is the first and the greatest achievement of a man. All else is dross, if this be wanting. To establish firmly the rule of God in the heart, and in the midst of service to remember the sacrifices of a broken and a contrite spirit, this is man's greatest act of heroism, as it is also the act of his highest glory. It is when he loses himself that he finds himself. The downfall of the traitor Judas lay in the failure to remember just this fact. He could not lose Judas. He must keep the efficient treasurer and the admirable administrator in the foreground. He must exalt his task. Alas, his real task was the simple duty of all men to become obedient to the will and the word of God.

Moreover, Judas was "one of the twelve." There is a wealth of suggestion in that phrase, which is the common one in the synoptic gospels. There is the revelation of the fact that the greatest opportunity arising from nearness to the sources of goodness and love does not necessarily mean the improvement of such opportunity nor ultimate success in the battle of life. Life under almost any circumstances is a great opportunity, notwithstanding much of the complaint of modern agitators against the prevailing social and political conditions. But life lived under the eye of the incomparable Son of God, and with the easy access of the apostolic fellowship to the Saviour's person and conversation, it would seem should have made the loss of such opportunity well-nigh impossible. But the "Satan" that entered into his heart could baffle the efforts even of the Son of God, and, after all, the redeemed man must come to God rather than to be dragged into eternal life. With Christ at his side and with all the great openings for spiritual life and spiritual knowledge, Judas went to the death of a traitor-suicide, leaving to the whole earth the most melancholy exhibition of wasted opportunity of which the world knows. "One of the twelve" has yet another significance which is not entirely creditable to the apostolic college apart from Christ. It is a very singular fact about the company of Jesus, and that is that we have almost no report of any kindnesses which they did to each other or sympathies which they felt for each other. We have not a single word, so far as I know, that shows conspicuously that the personal touch of helpfulness and sympathetic fellowship was exercised in any unusual

degree.   We have the record of the faultfinding and the
criticism.   We have the statements of ambition and selfish
worldly purpose.   Striking acts of courtesy, kindness and
helpfulness are absolutely wanting.   Not that there was no
such fellowship there, for there must have been.   Warm-
hearted men who had made the sacrifices that Jesus' apostles
had made must also have had common sufferings enough to
bind them together with fraternal and helpful feeling.   But
no such acts were sufficiently unusual and impressive to have
secured a place in the minds and memories of those who
have given us the records which we have of that fellowship.
It seems strange enough when we think of it, but it is true.
Being even "one of the twelve" did not secure to the
unhappy betrayer of Christ the highest delights of human
fellowship and association.   Perhaps in the very Church of
God, Christ's "twelve" of to-day, there are yearning souls
sinking into shame and death because the words of life are
not spoken.   Let not only Christ but his Church as well
speak the words of hope and of life.

SOCIAL AND POLITICAL

THE LOSSES OF CIVILIZATION

LUKE vii. 25, *seq.*

SUMMING up a mighty and impressive chapter on the "Decay of Character," in a recent book, Mr. Charles H. Pearson, after reviewing the advance which civilization has made in all the branches of human effort and achievement, the increase in luxury and the distribution of the benefits of larger knowledge and culture, secure government and more stable social conditions, has these impressive words : "Summing up, then, we seem to find that we are slowly but demonstrably approaching what we may regard as the age of reason, or of a sublimated humanity ; and that this will give us a great deal that we have been expecting from it — well-ordered politics, security to labor, education, freedom from gross superstitions, improved health and longer life ; better guarantees for the peace of the world and enhanced regard for life and property when war unfortunately breaks out. . . . On the other hand, it seems reasonable to assume that religion will gradually pass into a recognition of ethical precepts and a graceful habit of morality ; that the mind will occupy itself less with the works of genius and more with trivial results and ephemeral discussions ; that husband and wife, parents and children, will come to mean less to one another ; and that romantic feeling will die out in consequence, . . . and generally that the world will be left without deep convictions or enthusiasm, without the regenerating influence of the ardor for political reform and the fervor of pious faith which have quickened men for centuries past, as nothing else has quickened them, with a passion purifying the soul. . . . The world is becoming too fiberless, too weak and too good to contemplate or carry out great changes which imply lamentable suffering.

75

It trusts more and more to experience; less and less to insight and will." [1]

That the qualities which this author ascribes to our civilization have to a very considerable degree been acquired, no one will think of questioning. There is no calling in life which has not become immeasurably simplified by the advances in the industrial and constructive arts and sciences. Labor never was so secure, and the maxims of morality from whatever source never were received with such universal consent as they are at this very hour. And yet we seem to be travailing as never before in the world's history. These words are literally descriptive of the moral and spiritual lethargy which is stealing over us in almost every department in life. At the point where it would naturally manifest itself first it is already most conspicuous. The wealthy classes care for money, not that they may benefit mankind or rear families, but that they may indulge in all kinds of vulgar ostentation. They talk loftily of the disdain which they feel for the national feeling and spirit of the less favored classes. They are chiefly absent from their native land, and not in sympathy with its masses when they are in it. All that the country knows about them is that they carry on elaborate social functions which are characterized chiefly by prodigality and luxuriousness beyond the understanding of most men. Further than this they do not figure in the national or social or religious life. Nor is this all. They are proving with an absoluteness that admits of no denial that the classes who are by reason of opportunity, wealth and station best fitted to ameliorate the world's ills are those who are least touched by them and do the least to remove them.

But this could readily be endured were it not for the other facts which our author impressively brings out. Our civilization has lost some of the most glorious possessions of humanity — enthusiasm, passion and faith. Conviction seems to be steadily declining, and the ardor for human uplift taking the form of petty pink tea discussions rather than vigorous democratic movements toward a larger life. Fear of suffer-

---

[1] " National Life and Character," pp. 355, 356.

ing and the other fears allied to it are among the most characteristic signs of the times. Plenty of money and plenty of
zeal can be found for the things to which our energies are
directed, if only they are pleasurable and nice ; if we can go
into them without soiling our clothing and without damaging
our entrance into the society of the cultivated and the wealthy !
The natural result is that we are ever robbing Peter to pay
Paul. We are writing beautiful essays on pure religion and
the enforcement of laws on the one hand, while, on the other,
we are violating good faith and levying blackmail. It is this
that makes the anomalies which we see in the great cities of
this country. It is that men can listen complacently to a
moral exhortation one day, and go and dig their hands deep
into their neighbors' pockets the day after. No wonder that
we are producing a set of men who are described as " fiberless " and " weak," and, with an irony too much justified by
the facts, " good."

This seems to me to be something of the feeling that moved
Jesus Christ on the morning when the messengers from John
the Baptist in prison had departed, and he interpreted to them
the character and work of that godly man. "What went ye out
to see ?" asks the Saviour. This man was among the greatest
in the kingdom of God. He was not a reed shaken by the
wind. He was not a gilded lordling clothed in soft raiment.
He was no dabbler at petty reforms and after-dinner purveyor
of glittering generalities. No, indeed ; with him the ax was
laid at the root of the trees. Pharisees, scribes, or priests,
yea, even Herod on the throne, all were one to him. Righteousness was to John the Baptist not an occupation but a
passion. Repentance, to him, was not a compromise statement of shallow ethicalism, but a stern forsaking of sins.
The kingdom of God was not an idlers' paradise for simper-
ing religionists and ephemeral discussions of popular follies,
but an earnest enthusiasm for humanity and for God. This
is why he was great in the kingdom. This is why Jesus singles
him out for such conspicuous and distinguished praise.

That civilization has suffered grievous losses in the direction indicated cannot be denied by any one who feels the

chill hand which is laid upon the man who endeavors to give his life to a noble cause. A genuine enthusiasm is received with something like amazement by one part of the population, and with something like a sneer by another. The young, still uncorrupted and susceptible to unselfish appeals, can still be touched and moved to earnest action. Note how universally the great movements of our time are labeled " young." And yet age, with its knowledge, with its power and its discernment, ought to be more capable than youth. But there is no sign among these experienced philosophers of the enthusiasm by which the great changes of the world are made. And the task is made harder because our civilization has no such picturesque accompaniments as were always found in the mediæval battles for liberty, human rights and the kingdom of God. We have to fight in the hard, cold atmosphere of reason and rational scrutiny. We have to prove every step before we get assent, and then it comes grudgingly. The very gospel we preach is constantly subjected to criticism and reexamination, notwithstanding that its case has been successfully argued before the world for nearly twenty centuries.

Now, the possession of enthusiasm is a necessary condition to the success of any undertaking, whether it be social, religious or political. But it is especially so in the matter of religion. Religion would have no enemies, some one has said, if it were not the enemy of the vices of men. It is for this reason that the expounder of religion and the leader in religious work must have his soul filled with the fire of God, and move in an atmosphere which admits of no restraining admonition. Imagine Elijah standing before King Ahab and measuring his words! Think of him on Mount Carmel offering honeyed words of appeal to the priests of Baal. No; instead, he tells the sinning and licentious monarch to his face, Thou art the troubler of Israel. He mocks the prophets of Baal with their pretenses and their helplessness. He organizes the slaughter of the agents of misrule in Israel and the corrupters of the morals of the people. Nothing weak or fiberless about Elijah! No lack of conviction with him! And as soon as the people in Christ's own time heard the commanding voice of John the Baptist, they knew that another Elijah had made his appearance among them. He was a rude man. Clad in rough raiment and living in the caves of the desert, he was yet the voice of one crying in the wilderness, Make ye ready the way of the Lord.

But civilization has put its veto on enthusiasm. You may indeed be as anxious as is consistent with good taste to make ready the way of the Lord, but your anxiety must be carefully tempered and must be marked by the distinguishing qualities of the age, namely, calculation, coolness, and with a due regard to the consequences. A distinguished college president was reproved in the public prints recently because he was accustomed to expressing opinions that the public did not approve. This is one of the most curious symptoms of moral sterility that can possibly be imagined. Think for one moment of Jesus Christ refraining from the expression of his opinions because the public did not approve of them! Think of any of the heaven-inspired enthusiasts of history pausing in their heroic careers to ask for public approval! Did John Wycliffe and his Lollards wait for approval before going out to give the Bible to the poor and ignorant of England? What did St. Paul on the great personal question of his own conversion? Happily we have his own words. He says, "Immediately I conferred not with flesh and blood." And in this disregard for human approval we have the genuine source of an enthusiasm which is begotten in God and is sustained by the Holy Spirit of God. The trouble with our age is that it is forever conferring with flesh and blood. It is saying experience when it should say duty. It is asking what the human consequences will be, when it should be inquiring what the will of God is. The natural result, inevitable as the flow of the tides, is that the heroic qualities disappear and we generate a race of time-servers and apologists.

"Heaven," wrote Alexander Dumas, "has made but one drama for man — the world, and during these three thousand years mankind has been hissing it." The great elements of that world drama are the eternal issues of the battle between righteousness and sin. Mankind has ever tried to get away from that drama and substitute some weak and tasteless composition of its own. But revolution and counter-revolution, battlefield and dungeon, short sword and canister have forced it back to the old theme, and required it to face the perennial questions of character and destiny. There has been no escape, and there will be none while sin is in the world. As well try to pacify the hyenas in the jungle as bid men to be calm when the great spiritual interests of life are at stake. In no one thing does the singleness of the mission of Jesus Christ appear with greater effectiveness than that he is standing continually as the central figure in this one drama which God has given to men. Men may hiss it, as they have for thousands of years, but their hissing is of no avail. Christ is still the commanding figure in God's world, and man's enthusiasm in the cause of Christ is still the one magnificent passion which excites the admiration of all mankind. But in this drama there are no moments of repose. There are no minutes when we sit stupidly wondering what will happen next. This is a drama of passion and feeling. This deals with life. This makes our hearts burn and our brains reel with the power and awfulness of the issues which are at stake. Painfully we follow every syllable as it falls from the lips of the great Sufferer, and in that travail of soul we learn to suffer, too.

But civilization puts its veto on suffering. Make the world better if you can, but suffer no pain in doing it. Become a Saviour if you will, it would say to Christ, but let us have no crosses. Tell us your gospel, but let us have no scenes. Save the weak and heal the sick and bid your followers be careful and quiet ; but let not this pleasant comedy of life be spoiled into a deep and soul-rending tragedy. We cannot have tragedy. Suffering is painful, and we do not wish to contemplate it. Of course not! But the Author of our salvation was made perfect through suffering. We still have the cross and the crown of thorns. We still have the record of the scourge. We still have the Pharisee and the hypocrite.

The disciple is not above his Lord. If they have hated him, they will also hate you. Count Zinzendorf was so impressed with the figure of Christ on the cross with the inscription, " I gave my life for thee ; what hast thou done for me ?" that it changed the whole current of his life and labors. But civilization bids you not to look at that painful scene. It says that suffering is too lamentable to be looked upon. Here again is the antithesis between the civilization in which we live and the gospel by which we hope to be saved. Suffer not, says the world. Perfect through suffering, is what the Word of God says about Jesus Christ. Which shall it be?

There is a relation between enthusiasm and suffering which is not generally understood. We have in the gospels the frequent record that Jesus "groaned within himself," or that he was " troubled in spirit," or other evidences that he was heavily burdened with the sense of the task which, under God's providence, had been assigned to him. But Christ never wavered in his enthusiasm, nor could he probably as a human being have sustained his labors but for the corrective and ennobling power of spiritual pain. Mr. James T. Fields tells a most interesting story about the novelist Thackeray which illustrates the point. No man had a keener shaft for the shams and foibles of society than did the author of "Vanity Fair." He hated frauds with such an unrelenting persistence, that the critic of the *Times* called him the " head cynic of literature " and the "hater of humanity." But Mr. Thackeray was not a hater of humanity; only a hater of its counterfeits. No man responded with genuine interest and emotion to the pathetic elements in life more readily than did he. He suggested to Mr. Fields that they go to St. Paul's and hear the charity children sing. And there, says Mr. Fields, " I saw the head cynic of literature, the hater of humanity, hiding his bowed face, wet with tears, while his whole frame shook with emotion, as the children of poverty arose to pour out their anthems of praise." It was out of that deep sympathy that he could write the cutting, satirical portraitures that made the snobs of London fear him so intensely.

For a high-hearted, courageous, I may even say joyous,

advocacy of the gospel in the world will, of very necessity, involve opposition and misrepresentation. It will involve a great deal of pain and sorrow of mind. It will give anxious days and nights of doubt; but if it be grounded in a supreme trust in God, and founded in a living faith in his Son, there can no man break the force of that impelling power which is the flame of the Holy Spirit in the heart of a noble soul. Pain is needful to it, that it does not become the mere excitement that leaves only exhaustion behind when the conflict stays for a time. Suffering is the sobering draught that keeps us true to the real issues of life and prevents us from being misled and tempted into inertness. It is probably the greatest character-making force in history. But our Sybaritic notions of modern life make us flee from suffering as we flee from Satan. It needs a young heart, however, to take it cheerfully and happily. Andrew Lang says that Charles Kingsley was a man with a boy's heart. So must every man be in the battle for truth and God in the world.

These are some of the losses which have come in the train of our highly organized civilization, and great and serious losses they are, too. But these are not the only ones. The loss of enthusiasm could be endured, possibly, if we had a corresponding steadiness which gave coherence and persistence to the spiritual work which is necessary to keep life wholesome and morally upright. It is possible that we might do the work of God with less travailing and pain than now seems to be the cost, though that is extremely doubtful. But with these is the loss of interest and endurance in life itself. The great human motives have less force, it seems, year by year, and to rally the nature into the current, where one feels the glow and power of a living, active mission, seems to be one of the most hopeless tasks. As Mr. Pearson rightly says, religion drifts into a mass of ethical suggestions, which, interesting enough in themselves, have no motive power. Instead of grasping a situation with will and force, and with the consciousness of innate power and strength capable of pushing into it for a satisfactory solution, we wait the logic of events to give us some opportunity for avoiding settle-

ment altogether. Thus, few men in our day hew their way
into the callings of their lives. They simply move in the
line of least resistance. A man thinks he will be a minister
or an electric engineer, and winds up an architect. A student
selects the studies which will, with least difficulty, lead to a
degree ; and the result is a mass of nondescripts educated
in name, but only half educated in fact.

" Let us remember," said Governor Russell in one of those
moments of rare insight, to some students whom he was
addressing, " that there is one thing more important than
making a living, and that is, making a life." That sentence
strikes the keynote of our greatest loss in civilization. A
living is mistaken for a life, and the whole energy, the whole
brain force, the whole social machinery, are subjected to that
purpose as the ultimate goal of ambition. But what a chasm
there is between making a living and making a life ! Never
was a greater gulf fixed. But life involves these very qualities of which I have been speaking. It needs enthusiasm. It
demands suffering and pain. It rests on insight and will and
the power of maintaining a persistent course in the face of
difficulty and danger. That is how a life is made. Making
a living is much simpler. It involves no courage. It needs
no enthusiasm particularly. It does not call for much heroic
suffering certainly. It does not demand the high qualities of
determination and penetration which are needful to giving life
its proper aspect and crown. But a living is not a life, and
never will be, in the providence of God. Jesus Christ came
to give men a life. Whether they got a living or not in the
same connection was one of those things that had to be left
in the keeping of God. Christ's followers in the world have
been like him in this respect. As a rule they have been
men like John the Baptist. Hardy men, who lived simply
and worked hard. But their lives are the beacon fires of
history which show us the path over which the truth has
come.

Modern life more than all other things needs the restoration of these old-time qualities which the gospel especially
fosters and encourages. It was the gospel romance that made

the missionaries of the early part of this century respond with such zeal and heaven-born delight to the appeal to carry the gospel to the ends of the earth. It is gospel romance that keeps up the appeal now. When we hear the words of a Hamlin or a Paton, when we read the biography of a Livingstone or a Judson or a Morrison, when we hear the tidings of the missionary successes in the darkest spots the world knows, then we know the power of the romance of gospel life and gospel love. Then we can defy natural barriers and discouraging statistics. Then love is supreme, and what happens in the love of man to woman happens also in the love of man to Christ. We know then the meaning of that beautiful symbol of the Church as the bride of Christ. And we link ourselves with the romance of the world beautiful and hasten to bring our treasures to the work of Christ redeeming the world. Jacob A. Riis has done more for the poor of New York City by his sympathetic romantic picture of those perishing classes than all the statistics ever published by the state of New York. After all, is not the gospel itself one long, beautiful romance? Is not the story of Christ's love one of the most fascinating tales that was ever whispered into the heart of man? Do we not ask to be told the old, old story in the sad and heart-sick hour? Is there any word more beautiful or comforting or inspiring than that which brings us the message of the love of Jesus Christ?

> Tell me the same old story
>   When you have cause to fear
> That this world's empty glory
>   Is costing me too dear.
> Yes, and when *that* world's glory
>   Is drawing on my soul,
> Tell me the old, old story,
>   Christ Jesus makes thee whole.

It is this romantic continuous transfiguration of life that keeps the world warm in the love of Christ. It is thus that we are enabled to keep a brave heart in the midst of discouragements and failure. It is thus that we are lured on to larger life and larger labors. Is it not a curious fact that, in

every one of the great denunciations of the prophets against
Israel, after the denunciation there is a beautiful picture of
Israel when she shall have returned to God and found the
Holy One of Israel? For centuries it was this romantic expectation that kept the Messianic hope alive in Israel. And
when it came how romantically it was fulfilled! The Holy
Family on its way to be taxed, the crowded inn, the bed of
straw in the stable, the lowing cattle, the starlight of God, the
gifts of the princes of the desert, the singing angels, the shepherds and their flocks, the visit to the manger, and the little
Lord Jesus in the arms of Mary! Was not that a scene
worth waiting centuries for? Was not it worth the sufferings of Micah and Jeremiah, of Isaiah, and all the rest?
Surely their faith was rewarded when it came to pass. "And
she brought forth her firstborn son; and she wrapped him in
swaddling clothes, and laid him in a manger." And angels
and men have been singing the glories of that Christmas
romance ever since.

Men in the stress of business, and women in the labors of
the home, need to keep constant watch that life does not grow
hard and sordid in spite of all they can do to prevent it. The
natural anxieties of life are very misleading, unless we read
into them their divine interpretation. Hardships often look
like punishments, when they are really privileges. The love
of God often seems to be withheld, when, as a matter of fact,
it is most abundantly given. Let us never lose sight of these
uplifting features of our own service to God, which are, in
fact, the choicest part of human existence. Let us take to our
own hearts the lesson which Christ taught to multitudes about
John, and find the place where the soul awakens and the
mind expands under the generous impulses that lift us out
of the hardness of toil into the beauty of service. The work
of God was not merely the meat and drink of Jesus, but it
was his delight also. It will not be less to any disciple
who takes up his duty resolutely in Christ's name. Let us
not permit our civilization to lull us into listlessness and luxury.
Let us not make the moral order of our lives matters of personal convenience. Let us not wait for events to solve our

problems, but, with the counsels of God, and with insight and will, let us solve them ourselves.   God gives us the raw material of life, as he gave Michelangelo the rude block of marble.   It is for us to say whether it shall lie there uncut and unpolished, or be hewn into a majestic Moses or other leader of life and hope in the world.   We have determined in our civilization that we must have education and art and science, and a multitude of other modern necessaries.   Let us not leave the soul untouched, and in getting a portion of living, fail to find a life.   True life, after all is said, is the knowledge of God ; and life eternal is to know him and Jesus Christ, whom he hath sent.

INDUSTRY AND MORALITY

LUKE ii. 49

THE picture of the youth Jesus in the temple, surrounded by the doctors who are amazed at his understanding and his questions, has been made familiar to the world by Hoffman's famous painting of the scene. The Master was but a youth of twelve, who had been taken to Jerusalem as was the custom, and found himself, for the first time in his life, face to face with the things which had engaged his mind and thought ever since thought had begun with him.

Here, then, at last is the temple. This is the place where so much of all that he had read in the prophets had been enacted. Here was the great high priest, who was to the young boy's mind the embodiment of all but Deity itself. Here were the great courts, thronged with the worshipers from all parts of the land. This, then, is the place which Jehovah loves to honor with his presence and blessing.

Reared as Jesus was in the culture and knowledge of the religion of Israel, there must have been a strange contrast in his mind between what he had imagined and what he now really saw. All travelers have the same experience. Rome seen through the eyes of artists and archæologists is a very different Rome from that which the ordinary traveler sees on the spot. Jerusalem and the temple must have looked very different to the young Jesus from the pictures which his imagination had painted in his mind.

One thing, however, was not disturbed by the contrast. That was the fact that here was the center of the religious aspiration and hope of himself and his people. That remained. And after all, that was the essential thing. Splendid surroundings and imposing ceremonials are interesting enough, but the moral power and impressiveness of the thing, that is the great point to be considered.

Jerusalem was still the holy city and the temple was the Father's house. That was the important thing, and the growing consciousness of his mission and his message all made this the crucial time, when its first expression must be made. Naturally enough, then, he seeks the doctors and the priests, and engages them in the questions which so excited their astonishment and admiration.

Sought by his family, who had missed him from the returning caravan, the reply of Jesus shows what was uppermost in his mind at this time, and it is this which suggests the theme of this sermon. To his mother's query, he makes the kindly but significant reply, " How is it that ye sought me? wist ye not that I must be about my Father's *business?* " This is it. The Father's *business.* The literal statement is "the things of my Father," of which *business* is a fair translation.

That word business is the starting-point for my discourse this morning. That betokened the impulse and the desire for work and occupation. It revealed in the boy's mind the conception of his Father's concerns as labor, and as involving industry. The notion that the service of his Father's house was a dreamy, Oriental indulgence of speculation, is utterly wanting. His Father's business is work, and he who would do the Father's work must be industrious in his calling.

The naturalness of such a thought in the Master's mind may be inferred from what we know of Jewish habits, with reference to their children, in the matter of work. It was a common maxim that he who failed to teach his son a trade reared him a thief, which, if not literally true, was nevertheless dangerously enough near to it to be worth considering. Jesus was a carpenter, Paul was a tent-maker, and all the members of the apostolic college had trades. Not to have one made a Jew a suspicious character.

Jesus' own experience had probably given the doctrine of industry as a permanent feature of righteous life added weight in his mind. As a helper to Joseph, he had no doubt learned many of the lessons which only apprenticeship has to teach. The value and the dignity of work itself had been impressed upon his mind by the occupation of Joseph, and that gave the thought in his mind about his Father's business the turn which caused him to think of it as his work.

Now mere industry is admirable, even when it is exercised for a bad cause. No man can justly withhold his admiration from a man or woman, who, in the pursuit of some idea or end, is ceaselessly laboring until its achievement is secured. There is something positively fascinating in the sight of a man whose energies are all aflame, and who is using mind and hand and strength to bring about some great object on which his affection is fixed.

So great is this admiration that it sometimes tends to obscure the nature of the object, and blur the moral sense, with reference to its desirability. We say that a man who has worked so faithfully and so intelligently ought to succeed! We feel that so much effort ought not to go for nothing. Often we unconsciously turn in and help him, without considering at all what the character of the object is. So great is the attraction of a man at work.

Industry, moreover, makes allies on every hand. Active itself, it requires or induces activity around it, and that makes more labor and new forces and new facts, which only widen the opportunities for labor and invention. So one industrious man makes many, because of the product which he brings into existence. That product, again, requires handling and care. That makes more work, and the workers multiply.

If religion has on hand the greatest task in the world, then religion ought to call for the greatest industry. There is no doubt that the great leaders of religion have been prodigious workers. Calvin produced the "Institutes of the Christian Religion" when but twenty-five years old. The tremendous energy of John Knox was the same, whether a galley slave or the spiritual leader of Scotland. Martin Luther wrote not merely theological treatises, but patriotic ones as well, state papers, manuals of instruction, and hymns almost without number. Paul's activity may be inferred from what he says in his letters, as well as from the letters themselves. Leadership in the Church has always meant work.

But it was not so much to encourage mere industry that I wished to speak this morning. It was to show that industry had an important relation to morality, and that this relation should have a larger recognition in our plans for bringing about the kingdom of God. Intelligent industry may be made one of the strongest forces by which the reign of righteousness in the world is to be secured.

It has always been noticed that where idleness is most frequent, the temptation to wrongdoing is greatest. To have nothing specially to do is to be ready to do the first thing that comes along, which, nine times out of ten, under such circumstances, is something that ought not to be done. The periods of lawlessness among workingmen have always been times when large numbers of men were idle. The idle rich, while not lawless, are usually immoral.

It is found that idleness is so productive of wrong, because idleness is not a normal state of man. Man with his magnificent endowment was made to be productive. His mind was apparently given him to plan and invent, and construct endlessly, that his hands might be as endlessly employed, in realizing what he has thought out. Work is the normal state of a healthy and well-endowed man.

This is not saying, however, that the object of such work is mere gain. Gain does come as a result. But it is merely the love of working that makes a well-made man uneasy if he is not employed and has not the opportunity for giving expression to his powers in whatever direction he is capable of expressing himself. Much of the criminality of our criminal classes is undoubtedly due to the fact that they are forced, while imprisoned, to spend so much time in absolute idleness. It is surely a mistaken idea that the prisoners in our penitentiaries should not be permitted to work at something.

This may not be an inappropriate moment for me to say a word about the choice of an occupation for young men. American young men for the most part have not yet grasped the idea that the mastery of a trade may be both honorable and profitable. They think that what they call menial work may generally be left to "foreigners" and their children, and the result is that there are vast numbers of young men in our country who, except for the class of work called erroneously "clerkship," have no occupation whatever.

Now, while the country is large, and our people indulge in so many extravagances, this style of living may be possible for some time to come. But it cannot last forever. Clerkships, for the most part, are not productive work and call for no training or apprenticeship. And they rarely amount to much as a return for labor. A good carpenter or mason or any skilled workman, on the contrary, can usually command a good price for his work.

Many journeymen would reply to this that their trades are now overstocked with workmen. But I cannot find that a really first-class man is not in demand. I notice that when there is any important work to be done, a first-class man has to be found for it. Of course, second-class men or third-class men, which is the largest class, will be left, until necessity compels their selection. But it is not so with a really skilled mechanic in any calling.

The Jewish idea was a sound one. A trade can never be an encumbrance, and unless opportunity or occasion specifically call for something else, a young man in ordinary conditions of life cannot so wisely serve himself and his generation as by making himself the master of a good trade. The recent enormous advance in technical instruction in Germany, coupled with Germany's tremendous advance in the commercial world, is a sure index of the trend of opportunity.

But my interest in industry this morning is on account of its aid to morality. In the battle for a high moral existence, we need every possible aid that we can get. We need education, and we need art, and we need religion; but education must have a point of expression, and art must be productive in some form, and religion must give us something practical to take into our daily existence.

That expression of Jesus in the temple was a truthful

prophecy of his own life. When you reflect on what Jesus accomplished in the three years of his ministry, and to what extent the ideas and the personal labors of that brief space of time have revolutionized the world, you get some notion of what an untiring ministry it was by day and by night — with the multitude or with his disciples one by one, ever teaching and enforcing the message which was the business which his Father had committed to him.

I have said that work is the normal state of a healthful man. It is also the necessary state for a life of genuine enjoyment. There is no relaxation from idleness. You cannot rest from doing nothing. You cannot get delight and inspiration by turning from doing nothing to the continuance of doing nothing. But when, having labored well and fruitfully, whether with the mind or the hand or the heart, you lay aside that labor, how full of enjoyment the relaxation becomes !

Indeed, it may be said that relaxation and enjoyment are the test of genuine labor. A man may acquire much money and be able to spend many months in the capitals of Europe and among its choice treasures of art. But that does not assure his enjoyment of them. A Raphael or a Rubens will be enjoyed by those only who have put their thought into the thing for which Raphael and Rubens labored.

I have often been impressed with the barrenness of the enjoyment of those who had simply the means of gratifying their desires, without the capability of enjoying what they thus secured. No, enjoyment is a product of work, not of mere opportunity. Such persons are like the African savages who kicked the diamonds about contemptuously, till European knowledge taught them what their possession would bring.

But industry has a moral bearing beyond that which simply keeps us too much occupied to engage in wrong things. It is, that it fixes in the mind genuine things and reality, as objects to be striven for, as against mere satisfaction of self, in trifling and worthless matters. A student may take his pencil, and, if he be skillful, go out into the streets and reproduce many scenes of passing interest or usefulness. But if he does wisely, he will use that skill for higher ends than mere sketches which satisfy momentary vanity.

So, also, a possessor of a good voice may gain applause in some low resort where mediocre vocalism takes high rank. But a much better use of it would be to consecrate it to the reproduction of the classics of musical genius, and to enlighten and uplift the world by keeping it in active touch with high thoughts and noble imaginations. It makes a world of difference to what use a talent is put.

Now, constant industry is impossible in connection with trifles. Life is too serious a matter to be frittered away on things of no account. Even an idle or a trifling mind revolts from bondage to trifles. So there can be no endurance in trifling. But it is different with good, wholesome productive work. No man who sees Trinity Church or the Public Library can feel anything but self-respect, if he did nothing more than to carry the mortar to rear such structures as these.

Labor by divine command should be six-sevenths of life. The commandment says, Six days shalt thou labor, with no less emphasis than it says that the seventh shall be a day of rest. The constant employment of six days is as necessary to a pure and upright manhood as the rest and worship of the seventh. But the labor thus enjoined certainly cannot be identified with the foolish uses of time and strength by which many people seek to shift through life without honest work.

Why is it that in every nation the bulwark of sobriety and morality is the great so-called middle class? Is it not because these are the ones most constantly employed, and whose energies are being absorbed in useful and uplifting callings? Removed, as they are, from the idleness of the rich, they are spared the gross vices of self-indulgence which are so common with these. Too intelligent, and having too much responsibility, to be patient amid the wretchedness and squalor of the very poor, they are saved from the excesses of the listless and the ignorant. But it is, in the main, that they have something to do and are doing it, that keeps their self-respect alive and their moral natures from being corrupted.

What is true in this respect of the middle classes, in industry and national life, is true in religion. The great Christian enterprises are not kept in existence by the gifts of the very wealthy, notable as some of these are. They are fed by the constant additions of those who give from the fruits of patient and earnest toil. In England it is still the fashion to jeer at "middle-class morality," but that Nonconformist middle-class conscience has taught more than one prime minister of Great Britain that brewery-made peers and titled debauchees are not the true types of British life.

Discontent and rebellion against the order of society is also least where industry is greatest; namely, among these same middle classes. They, better than others, know that a social order is the joint product of all working together. They are doing their part, and have no time to harass others. No light ailment can lead them from their accustomed places to engage in revolt. But when a cause *is* strong enough to divert them from their ordinary callings, the result is not discontent merely, but revolution.

It is a common complaint that we as a nation work too much already, and that working people, meaning by that, not merely those who are technically wage-earners, but all who need to labor at any fixed occupation for a living, have too many hours of work as it is. In some cases this is true. But in the main I do not find that men work too hard. I am very certain that no wage-earner would submit to the number of hours which are required of scholars in their studies. The great artists and sculptors, the great editors, and captains of industry, spend many more hours at actual work than the ordinary wage-earner does.

But I do not believe our nation as a whole works too much. It engages in too many things that take energy and strength, which are not work, and which are not productive in any way. The work for which I am arguing, as an aid to morality, does not destroy the vitality of a people, nor its power of recuperation. On the contrary, it keeps both safe and unimpaired.

The conception, however, must be the conception of Jesus Christ. It must be the Father's business, whatever it is. It must have a value which will justify it, in the sight of God, as a fit occupation of one of his creatures, who bears his image. No work like that ever destroyed a man's enthusiasm for life, or made him want to limit the number of apprentices either. Rather does it make him glad, if any one can be induced to take the same high estimate of himself and his abilities, and help on the Kingdom, by being about the Father's work.

There passed away a man in New York the other day, who was thought to possess a fortune of several millions of dollars. In connection with his death, two things specially were noted; one that he was the leading figure in the Sugar Trust, and the other that he was a great patron of the game of golf. To the average man, this was a fit combination. One occupation was a synonym for dishonesty and embezzlement, the other the peculiar pastime of the idle rich.

In that illustration one may see what it is wise to avoid. Any labor which, when it is named, suggests such moral defects as come to mind when we think of the operations of the Sugar Trust may well be avoided. The speculative habit, whether in great or small measure, is the ruin of honest toil. On the other hand, the sport which is identified chiefly with the ability to lay aside the ordinary cares of life, for an indefinite period, merely to indulge in play, cannot present any rational idea of social or personal relaxation.

The idea lacking in both these extremes is the idea that man is a social being, who has responsibilities to his fellow men and to his God. That he cannot think about himself alone, nor even first. That when he is rightly using his life he has an eye out for the common welfare, and assumes his proportion of the social burden freely and honestly. Few men are unwilling to bear their own burdens. They become resentful when they are compelled, unjustly, to bear the burdens which belong to others.

It is in the reflection that the business to be done is the Father's business that the relief for the complaint lies. If

God is our Father, then we are a family, working together
for the interests of the whole family. We cannot make our
own pleasure supreme. We cannot even demand blindly our
rights. Rights give place to responsibilities, and we see that
every just claim against us is satisfied before we think of
asserting what we conceive to be ours against others.

The business of Christian service is no less absorbing, in
its picturesque features, than it is in its bearing upon the
moral welfare. We hear that men consider their work dull
and commonplace, and that each man thinks his own calling
the most uninteresting, and longs for something else. How a
thorough man can feel thus I am unable to understand.
Most work properly carried on has features of interest which
are peculiar to it alone.

But Christian work is far more interesting than any other
possibly can be. For one thing, it is more inclusive and takes
in the whole range of humanity from almost every conceivable point of view. All charity and philanthropy is included
in it. All that can possibly give vitality to men's moral
energies is a part of it. With so many branches of service,
what an interesting picture the whole is!

The existence and the continuity of the Christian Church
is the best evidence of the truth of this statement. Try to
gather in Boston an audience consecutively, for a year, or six
months even, to hear addresses on Astronomy or Botany or
Natural History, and see what the result will be. Try to
interest the public for any continuous length of time in anything other than the gospel, and you will find that the gospel
of Christ is still the most vital thing in the world and the
newest.

And yet it is simply the same message which Jesus began
to preach centuries ago. Christians about their Father's
business, with skill and energy, afford the world the most
wonderful field of human action that ever could be desired.
It is probably not inaccurate to say that the largest part of
the literary and mental activity of the world, at this moment,
is the direct result of movements inspired by the industry of
men, alive with the zeal of the gospel message.

And then, after all, it is the only work that remains as the final test of the real use and power of living. A great scientific discovery may revolutionize the outer life, but it cannot affect permanently the inner life of man. A great poem or a great play may even stir the emotions, and leave the will untouched. Jesus Christ alone taught the moral message to men, with the power of affecting the will of men for righteousness.

But, like every other worthy work, this work has to be well and thoroughly done. It has to have the whole man enlisted in its cause. It requires the brain of man to think, as well as his hands to work, and his lips to speak. It requires its just distribution through the entire life, rather than to be made simply the characteristic of a part. Religious thought and living are too much already made simply a Sabbath accessory to a busy worldly life.

It is sometimes said that extreme spirituality cannot survive extreme activity. That if a man is very active, he cannot, by reason of that fact, have the repose necessary to deep spirituality. That of course depends upon what spirituality is supposed to be. If merely to contemplate spiritual truths is to be spiritual, then possibly it is true. But spirituality is not considered any longer after the type of the monastic in his cell.

The truly spiritual man, in our day, thinks less about himself and his own states and more about the effectiveness with which he is attaining the things which are dear to him, as a laborer in the Kingdom of God. He is not the dainty gilt-girted cadet on dress parade, whose main thought is about his appearance at the grand stand. He is rather the dust-begrimed soldier, who is storming some battlement of the enemy, and thinks only of planting his regimental banner on the walls above.

We are sometimes told to have more faith in God. But it is also well to add that we should do something more for men. Man is more peculiarly the representative of the Father than ever before. We know in our generation the force of the saying, that if a man will not love his brother whom he hath seen, how can he love God whom he hath not seen, better than any other generation has known it. It is for this reason that we are trying with might and main to respond to every human call, whether it is in Greece, India or the Dakotas. The religion that will not work is now generally held to be worthless.

The religious life and the moral life are thus seen to be inseparably linked with industry, which alone can give them power and effectiveness. We must be about the Father's business with the same enthusiasm that moved Christ when he began his ministry. We must continue it patiently to the end as did he. We must not falter when the hard places come, nor be discouraged when misfortunes overtake us.

How many a man would suddenly find his own life enriched and glorified if he permitted the Father to give him his task in the work of saving the world, and cheerfully took that work as the particular subject of his thinking and doing! Would not many a commonplace become radiant with new meaning and many a dark spot become wonderfully bright? Would not the world become transformed to him because his labor had been transferred to the Father's house, instead of merely ministering to his own selfish need?

Life being what it is, wherein so many of us must work with tools that are not fitted to their use, and at times which are not productive, and under conditions which are unfavorable to the largest growth in ourselves or our professions, there is no happier moment for any man than the moment when he turns from all these things to the work of God, and feels the companionship of Jesus Christ in the undertakings he plans for him. Every man may feel that happiness and that inspiration. The boy Jesus, in the temple, a product of right training, was a true prefiguration of the man Christ Jesus. " My Father worketh even until now, and I work," — these were his words. May we be able to make them our own !

THE WEALTH OF MAN

I CORINTHIANS iii. 21, 22.

THIS is a very remarkable declaration. Put that statement up in the factories of the land, in the working-men's
assembly rooms, or in the public courts, and men would look
at it as a sort of ill-timed joke upon their ills. It would make
very much the impression that was made upon the man who
saw for the first time the motto on the Royal Exchange in
London, "The earth is the Lord's, and the fulness thereof,"
which he thought might be true enough, though there had
evidently been some mistake in the distribution of the
same.

Yet Paul was not a very irrational kind of a man. He was
not a dreamy idealist who knew nothing about real life. He
was not even a bloated bondholder, as the phrase goes, simply
clipping coupons when they came due. He was a workingman. He knew how to support himself with his own hands
and did it more than once. Indeed, Paul was even less favored
in his undertakings than the average wage-earner of to-day.
The latter at least has a claim on his employer and on the
thing he produces. Paul, on the contrary, had no earthly
sponsor, and must sustain himself by reliance on other than
earthly sources.

But Paul was a rich man if we may trust him to tell us
what he thought of himself. He had nothing, yet he possessed all things. He was poor, yet he made many rich. He
was able to glory in tribulations and could rejoice in suffering, and appeared to think that he was most favored of men
in being able to do just these very things. Modern cynical
mammonism, I dare say, thinks that Paul was a fool. Fool or
not, he certainly was very happy and prosperous in spirit

99

in his foolishness. A man can afford to be the subject of cynical comment if he is happy in himself.

Was Paul mistaken in this assertion then? Was it merely the rhetorical outburst of a mind religiously aglow? Are we to take the modern spirit and trim down this enthusiastic statement to proportions which political economy would indorse? According to this doctrine there are no poor men. Every man is wealthy beyond the dreams of avarice. No multi-millionaire ever began to be as rich as Paul here describes the Christians to be. Is it true? That is the question before us this morning.

Well, let us first of all contrast the world in which Paul lived with the world in which we live, and see what that reveals. In Paul's day travel, for example, was a dreary and perilous hardship. In ours it is a delight and a continually unfolding panorama of new things. In Paul's day education and knowledge were the possibility of only the very smallest fraction of the race. We live in the light of widest information and the broadest intelligence. In Paul's day there was only a half a globe to know. In our day there is only a North Pole left to discover. This is simply an elementary contrast.

Think of the primitive conditions of life and action prevailing when Paul wrote these words. Think then of the enormous transformation which the world has seen since then. What would have been thought if Paul had in so many words described simply what every child among us has as his daily possession, — free institutions, rational government, education, art, culture, religious freedom, and all the products of Christian civilization, challenging men to get all out of life that possibly can be gotten out.

Suppose Paul had told on board the ship that carried him to Rome the story of the Lucania's last voyage across the Atlantic. Suppose, while he was standing on the Acropolis, he had told the Athenians about the telephone and the kinetoscope. Suppose, while in conversation with Luke the physician, he had suggested to that astute man the discovery of broken bones by the Roentgen ray. I see not Festus alone, but all who hear him, shouting with derisive laughter,

" Paul, thou art mad," and possibly putting him under bonds to keep him safe. Yet no one thinks these things strange to-day. They are ours as really as though we had them in our own possession.

Let me go further still. Suppose he had told the Epicureans, delighting as they did in the joys of the table, that some day a physician would find out whether a man had a cancer in his stomach, by having him swallow an electric light bulb, and then turning on the current, as was done with the Count of Paris not long since. Suppose he had said that the same process would be carried on in studying the anatomy of fishes. Suppose he had told them that there would be such a huge structure of steel as the modern battleship, and that from her bridge a slight whisper from the commander into the telephone, amid cannonading above and shrieking machinery below, to the bowels of the great monster would turn it completely around in twelve minutes.

Yet that would all have been true. There is nothing so very marvelous about all these things to us. What Paul did say was, All things are yours. Those four short words seem very tame beside what I have outlined as already the possession of every man. Yet I have not told a tithe of the remarkable things which the mind of man is achieving, and the height toward which invention and discovery are yet to climb. Does it not begin to look as though all things were ours ?

The luxury of modern life even among the simplest classes of the people is one of the astounding features of it which a student of antiquity never can fully make real to himself. We have often seen old people come from the country towns and look with wonder and amazement upon the sights of the city. But all the world looks like that to a man who has made himself even slightly familiar with what the conditions of life in the ancient world were.

The curious thing about all this luxury is that it has not brought what would seem to be its first product, namely, contentment. People seem to be more disquieted than ever. We hear more about not having what belongs to us than we ever did before. There is more clamor about injustice than at any period of the world's history. The unequal distribution of wealth seems to be the great cross which the multitudes are bearing. No one apparently seems conscious that we are personally and individually wealthier than the mightiest princes of antiquity, and have resources at our command beside which the wealth of a Midas is a mere bagatelle.

But some one tells me these things are for the rich alone. I ask them is the Public Library for the rich alone? Is the City Hospital for the rich alone? Or are these experiments and these new results made at once the possession of the whole race as soon as discovered? There was never a greater folly than this. Do not the poorest as well as the richest cross and recross the Atlantic these days to see friends and visit relatives? But they go in the steerage, you say. The cabin of the Mayflower had not half the comforts of the steerage of a modern ocean flyer!

Now it is well, occasionally at least, to meditate on what we have, and treat ourselves like the princes that we actually are. Let us recognize that a lightning express train is as much our servant as it is that of the greatest millionaire. That we will travel as quickly and as comfortably as he, and probably with more comfort, having less at stake. Let us see the tremendous proportions of the wealth of a man in our day just as we see him living in the nineteenth century.

The Mind that planned these things was in the world when Paul wrote, and already there were the signs of the revolutionary changes which were impending. The gospel itself was one such revolution, and Paul was carrying the germ of that revolutionary life everywhere. Personal freedom in religious life and the democratic aspirations of the religion of Jesus Christ made it as certain that modern life would come forth as we know it, as that daylight follows the dawn.

Goethe, in discussing the character and philosophy of Hamlet, has a beautiful and striking figure of an oak seedling planted in a beautiful vase. The oak grows, and finally the costly vase is splintered and broken and its beauty destroyed, because it could not contain the giant thing that was grow-

ing within it. That is a fair illustration of the relation of
the mind to the world. The world is fair and beautiful, but
the mind of man in it keeps on expanding and developing
until it bursts beyond the limitations and environs of this life,
and stretches out into the life which is to come.

Paul's prescience discovered this, too. Mark you how he
says that all things are ours, not merely in this world, but also
in the world to come. Life is ours, but death is ours, too.
Things present are ours. But things to come are not less
ours also. Everything is ours, and we are made the custodians of the boundless wealth which the mind of man in its
continual growth will bring forth for the uses of man. All
things are ours.

This is true even in the lowest physical sense of the term.
A man invents a new and beautiful toy. Well, to make it
profitable to himself, he must have children to play with it.
And so, beautiful as it is, costly as it is, he must study the
process of cheapening its production so that he can afford to
make it the possession of the many. Hence his brains and
his skill are ultimately the property of all. The toy must
have the children to play with it. Nothing in this world can
be made profitable until it has been made essentially the property of everybody.

A Shakespeare may write plays. But people must go to
the theater to see them, and the printers must print them, and
the costly first editions must soon become the countless cheap
editions which every one can own. Every invention in electricity, in medicine, in mechanics, has thus been made the
property of the very poorest. All are yours. Shakespeare,
Milton, Darwin, Gray, Pasteur, and Edison, — all are yours.
They may not work a day but they must give to you what
they have learned and produced ere they can fairly enjoy it
themselves.

I suppose a man might have planned out the cathedral at
Milan, and kept the sketches and plans to himself, and gloated
over them in secret. But the same Power that gave him the
talent made him want to see it in stone, and then every one
had to see it. Raphael might have kept his Madonnas in

his brain, but God made that talent to be seen in color and majesty on canvas, and now it is yours. And so it is of them all. Sculptors and painters and architects and poets and inventors! — all are yours, and they must be yours to be themselves.

This idea was the one which Paul wished to impress upon the Corinthians in the matter of religion also. The church had its Apollos party, its Peter faction, its Pauline caucus and its Christ coterie. But Paul brushes away the distinctions with that broad, inclusive touch of his. All are yours, he says. Christ is yours. Paul is yours, and so is Peter, and so is Apollos. And then he sweeps beyond the confines of the mere earth and sees the Lord in his glory and majesty on high, and then the world grows little to him and he adds life and death and the things to come. And why? Because ye are Christ's, and Christ is God's. God is the all in all. Being in him ye have all things.

But what I have already said about Goethe's illustration of the oak in the vase is especially true of the soul of man if he fixes his thought on this world alone. And this accounts for the general discontent amid our opulence. Man is like the oak seedling that needs the broad earth to develop and grow in. No petty view of life can contain a being made for immortality. If he thinks of himself merely as the economic man, of course he will be discontented. If wealth to him is merely gold, then he will surely be disappointed.

If life to a man means merely that he shall be able to feed his body and satisfy the cravings of his lower nature, then he will surely find the world pall to his taste very soon and will feel that he is circumscribed by many limitations. The trouble is that he has not horizon enough. His outlook is not far-reaching enough. He does not go into life deep enough. He has not made himself competent to deal with the great destiny which is the portion of every rational being in the world.

Such a view must naturally make us feel that we are being defrauded because we *are* defrauded. The higher nature is suffering from starvation and resents it. The soul is dying

and wants to be rescued from the death which is closing
around it. The immortal man is like the oak struggling to
be free, that he may be himself for his own highest uses and
ends. We may well in such a case say with Hamlet : —

> What is a man
> If his chief good and market of his time
> Be but to sleep and feed? A beast, no more.
> Sure, He that made us with such large discourse,
> Looking before and after, gave us not
> That capability and godlike reason
> To fust in us unused.

Man's resources are so splendid in their character and
variety that, as we think of them, it seems as if heartaches
must be banished and there must be happiness and peace.
So wonderful has the world become! So abundant are the
agencies which minister to comfort and power! Yet the very
splendor of this equipment shows us how helpless it is to
minister to that which most makes man. The great pains
of man are not of the kind which can be remedied by the
surgery of the physician of the body. The great problems
which agitate man's mind are not those which have to do
with the distribution of material wealth. What about the
medicine for the soul? What about the healing of the spirit?
Are these also ours?

Let me answer that question by asking one. Is it reasonable to suppose that the Being who has taken such extraordinary precautions to secure the development of the mind of
man has not made equally abundant provision for the needs
of his soul? Did God make a splendid vase and then leave
the oak without strength to grow? Which was the greater,
the oak, or the vase in which it had been placed? The oak,
you answer. So I say of God's provision for the soul.

The humblest man soon arrives at the point where he sees
the beauty of the earth to be merely the shell in which
only external life can reside. His mind speeds on to
thoughts of God and immortality, to the life to come, to
eternal justice, to infinite pity, to divine compassion. All
these, he sees, are too great even for the wonderful, beauti-

ful earth. The oak expands and finally breaks forth, and he must see another world and a larger destiny than the earth can provide for him by itself.

And he need not look far for it. Indeed, it is looking for him. He looks on the face of Jesus Christ, and then he sees life in the finely rounded outlines of completeness and symmetry. He sees his own nature glorified. Earth then is merely the antechamber to the palace, not the palace itself. Life here is but the beginning, and a small beginning at that. What he has here is but the merest pledge of what he is to have. But better than that, he sees what the true wealth is and knows that the kingdom of heaven is within him and not outside of him.

Great is the world, but the soul of man is greater. Great are the thoughts of poets and philosophers and the sages. But the thoughts of a man seeking to know God are greater than them all. Mighty is the wealth of this world. But the peace of God in the heart is above it as a diamond is above the pebble. This is true wealth. This also is ours, and the best of all that the heart can desire or the mind conceive. " My peace I give unto you : not as the world giveth, give I unto you."

The genuine wealth of a man is thus revealed to be the genuine worth of a man. Apart from all that can be acquired is the moral nature behind it all which can give it character. That nature is itself the priceless thing. And it has characteristics which belong to it which do not belong to any other wealth the world knows. It never fluctuates. It is not subject to stock operations. Supply and demand do not affect it. It is standard the world over. It needs no syndicate to float it. A good name is riches that no trust can corner and an investment that no panic can depreciate.

But such wealth is inseparable from the spirit of Christ. It is not to be gained by self-seeking or even by the closest application to details. It comes of self-forgetfulness and self-sacrifice. We have it most when we are least conscious of it. It shines in the darkest places most brilliantly. It grows as it expends itself. Most freely given, it most freely renews itself. This is a wonderful wealth, the wealth of the spirit of Christ.

But here the cynic appears again. "Ah," he says, "that is what I thought was coming. You tell me that virtue is wealth, and that to be good and true is to be rich. But I may starve for all that. I'll take my heaven now. Never mind what may come hereafter! Let me have my portion now!" You all know that speech.

In the face of that cynicism I repeat the words. Virtue *is* wealth. To be good *is* to be rich. Satisfaction in the heart and soul *is* above rubies. And the compensations of self-denial and self-sacrifice are above the choicest treasures the world can give. It is true! Let us not be browbeaten out of it. "My kingdom," said Christ, "is not of this world." Let us not forget that. The world by wisdom knew not God. Let us not forget that. Let us not forget that in the sight of the tragedy on Calvary the most impressive thing to the Roman soldier was the mysterious influence that made him exclaim, "Certainly this was a righteous man. Truly this was the Son of God."

But there is a wealth which every man has which is, I believe, more precious to him than even the satisfaction which he may be able to have in himself. It is the delight and joy which his friends may justly have in him. No man who has ever performed any task which brought him the pleasant messages of approval from honest souls who appreciated or were helped by what he did can fail to know what I mean. There are few things a man can call his own which are so precious to him.

This wealth of moral approval of friends is more than mere acknowledgment that some work has been well done. It is rather a statement of obligation that something has been added to the lives which thus express their gratitude. That means that you have built your own thought and nature into the thought and nature of others. You have made your life contribute to the enrichment of some other.

What by the side of this is the building of a great cathedral or a wonderful monument? We may thus have our wealth in the living flesh and blood of men whom we have wrought upon out of the fulness and freedom of our own labors. When a man dies who has done this kind of amassing of wealth, what a revelation of power it is! When the great preacher of Trinity Church died and the vast surging crowd filled Copley Square, how insignificant the great stone piles that adorn that square seemed! But how puerile and ridiculous beside that demonstration would be the reading of a millionaire's list of houses, stocks and lands!

Not in so great a measure, possibly, but to a degree that will be as creditable to our opportunities and our abilities, we may build up for ourselves these vast fortunes of love and good-will and interest. To give one's life unselfishly for the good of others, and to gain a place on some pedestal in the soul of a living, breathing being, is to win a greater glory than can be found in any earthly pantheon. It is to put our treasures where moth and rust do not corrupt and where thieves do not break through and steal.

Here is a field where the freest of competition may be indulged in without the slightest possibility of wronging any one. To wage the contest of making ourselves loved for what we are able to be and do in the world is in all respects honorable. All the motives which Jesus brought to men were motives which tended to make men love him and to love God. In a similar way we are encouraged to endeavor to multiply the reasons why men should love us.

But how shall we gain this treasure of being loved? Just as we gain the wages of service in our secular and worldly callings. The doctrine that love gives itself is not true of the love that endures through life and into immortality. Love must be earned as all other things that have value or worth. Men give a bronze statue much more readily than they give the innermost regard of the heart. The statue can easily be paid for with things that perish. A man's heart cannot be paid for other than with the heart of another man.

And what a vast field of operations there is open to us in this gathering together of our treasures! There is the field of human ministry to the needs of the body. That is the lowest form of the treasure. Then there is the sympathy of mind which sees with kindness and encouragement every struggle for enlargement and self-development. That is higher still. Then there is the fellowship of character which makes us respect every being because he is in God's image, and hold him in honor because of the fact. And then there is the spirit of sacrifice which offers the best there is for the poorest and lowliest. That is the spirit of Christ.

Many of us will to-morrow think with emotion of the brave young soldier, Robert Gould Shaw, who gave in his brief young life so fine an illustration of this highest wealth of man. Bearing in his body the best blood of a proud commonwealth and reared in those traditions which have made the Puritan name the symbol for righteousness the world over, at the head of his black fellow soldiers storming the walls of Fort Wagner he fell richer than if he had held in his hand the gold supply of the world. It was not his blood or his breeding that made Robert Gould Shaw a great young man. It was that the humanity in the highest culture could respond in him to the humanity in the deepest degradation that made him a prince in the possessions of a noble soul. That was true wealth.

There are many such heroes in this world who will not have their monuments dedicated with impressive ceremonial and military display. Their lot is not cast in such a dramatic time or the manifestation of their devotion wrought out in such brilliant coloring. But almost every household has one. Some have more than one. But most have at least one in the patient, loving mother-soul that broods over and bears the sorrows and ills of us all. Think of the most splendid monument you know. Where is it when you look upon the face of mother?

Have I made you feel richer this morning and made it more easy to believe the great words of Paul that all things are yours? Is not your own life, with all the harassing things that make you uneasy in it, much better after all than you thought? Is there not still a great treasure for you that only needs to be garnered to make you the happiest and the wealthiest of beings? While there is a heart that can be touched by a single note out of your own life that treasure is yours. And with it you have all things.

But central in this great treasure-seeking enterprise in which we must all engage stands the one thing indispensable to our happiness and our joy. It is the love of God in the gift of Jesus Christ. He who has made so many millions of hearts love him will best teach us how we shall make ourselves lovable in this earthly life. He will keep burning in us the fires of his own holy sacrifice and enable us to respond quickly to all the high demands of our calling in God. We must be Christ's as the prerequisite of being aught to others.

What has not the world been willing to do to prove its devotion to Jesus Christ? To him it has built its most costly palaces and cathedrals. To him it has consecrated its most beautiful paintings and its most delicate sculptures. To him it has reared universities and hospitals. For him it has organized armies and navies. For him it has destroyed governments and created constitutions. For him it has penetrated unknown seas and braved nameless dangers. From the breaking of the alabaster box to the heroism and devoted sacrifice of Father Damien, the leper priest, it has offered all that it had, to prove that it loved him.

Yet of himself he said, " The foxes have holes, and the birds of the heaven have nests ; but the Son of man hath not where to lay his head." All things were his none the less. The whole world is his monument. Passionate zeal could do no more. He had not where to lay his head, yet he was the head of all principality and power. Let us remember that. Not in the way of the envious and selfish world do we gather our eternal treasures. But in the oft unspoken gratitude of a sinning soul that has been through us taught to look up again we rear our choicest altar to the Father in heaven. And through the glistering of repentant tears we look as through windows into the heart of God.

THE BATTLE AGAINST GREED

MALACHI i. 10.

THE prophets of Israel were a peculiar order of messengers of righteousness, ordained and inspired by God and commissioned to Israel, apparently because the regular agencies of religion had failed to secure the ends for which they were established. They were religionists, but they were also reformers. They ministered in worship and were loyal to the established faith and institutions of Israel, but they were bitterly opposed to institutionalism without life and worship which was only form. With the priesthood they had generally little sympathy, because they usually found them inert, unspiritual attendants upon the ordinances of God, who served merely for the bread with which it supplied them. With the nobles and the ruling classes they were usually at variance, because these gathered the priesthood around them for flattery and comfort, while they plundered the poor. With the cultivated and learned they had little communion, because these ordinarily were opposed to violent measures of public reformation.

For these and other reasons the prophets became, almost of necessity, the chosen champions of the poor and the leaders in all causes affecting the public and social life of Israel. Social burdens fall most heavily upon those who are least able to bear them, as a rule. To the common people, therefore, the prophets went, and by the common people they were loved and honored. It may be noted in the lives of the prophets how often they spring from the humbler classes and how much of their association is with them. It was because of this loyalty and coöperation of the common classes, that they were able to hold at bay the wrath and the hatred

of kings and nobility, when without it they would speedily
have been destroyed.

The condition of religion in Israelitish life which brought
forth the prophets had not passed away in Christ's time.   It
was on this account that while the chief function of his whole
life was to be his sacrificial death, yet the whole trend of
Jesus' life on the earth was not priestly but prophetic.   He
did not perform a single ecclesiastical ceremony, so far as we
know.   He did not give utterance to a single ecclesiastical
formula except in connection with some minor matter of personal religion.   In all the ministry of Jesus the prophetic
element stands out with power and boldness, and more than
once the priestly element is almost, if not quite, obliterated
by the determined assault which he made upon its empty
sanctions and its profitless worship in the temple at Jerusalem.   It has ever been observed that the greatest tenacity
of form is always found where the living spirit is most conspicuously absent.   Christ's ministry is in logical succession
to the prophets rather than to the priesthood of the temple.

In the time of Malachi this state of religious inertness and
formal service had reached an acute stage.   It had especially the distinguishing characteristic that always appears
when service is rendered not for the love of it but for what
there is, as the modern saying goes, in it.   The worship of
the priests was merely a hired service.   Men did nothing in
God's service except by agreement and under contract.   Pay
was exacted for every service, and in the midst of it all,
though there was the most formal offering and the most impressive ritual, glaring social faults and monstrous social
wrongs were passed over or utterly ignored.   The usual im-
pressions and solemnities of religion had become altogether
a matter of jest.   When a man did evil they said he pleased
the Lord.   They delighted in him apart from the question
of righteousness.   Judgment had no hold either upon their
faith or their imagination.   And the prophet, endeavoring to
express the divine wrath or disgust or both, puts into the
mouth of Jehovah the indignant speech which I have chosen
for the text.   The doors referred to are the doors leading in

the temple to the place where the offerings were made. And seeing all around the spirit of self-seeking and avarice, tried and angered and utterly impatient with the greed of them all, where no single man will do one thing from a pure motive and with a willing heart, Jehovah exclaims, "Oh that some one would shut even these doors without expecting compensation of some kind! Oh, if there were but one soul that would kindle a fire on mine altar without the hope of gain or reward!"

And it was a pitiful condition indeed. Yet not a novel one in Israel, nor one with which we are ourselves utterly unacquainted. Service to-day is getting to be paid service, and no other kind. Voluntary helpfulness, in the church or out of it, is rendered much more by tradition than with a spirit of love to God and with a genuine desire to bring in the reign of righteousness in the earth. It is still true that a large part of the service which is given to the cause of Christ is voluntary and unpaid. But it is becoming more and more true that there is a desire to shrink away from such service; to shift off duties upon our neighbors, and to demand that if such service is rendered there shall be compensation for it. Not compensation in money always. Far from it. But it is true, and it is becoming more so, that when service is rendered, he who renders it must be flattered and petted or praised or rewarded for it, and when such rewards as are expected are not promptly delivered, there is unhappiness and discontent. Nor is this all. When such service is unselfishly rendered, it is often made a subject of criticism and unfavorable remark. Many a whole-hearted young person has begun the service of Christ with a fresh, unspoiled spirit, who found before long that the crass, sordid spirit around him had made the task too heavy, and forced retirement from loving and successful labors. Analyzed to its root, this is but a part of a prevailing vice of such colossal proportions that it threatens to engulf the Church, the State, and society in general in one grand moral and spiritual ruin. It is the vice of greed. It is the arrogant, stalking self-consciousness that everywhere rears its ugly head.

Greed is the colossal fact of our time. In commerce, in the social life, in literature, in science, and in religion there are present the full-developed germs of this unhappy condition, which has been steadily growing for years. When greed is mentioned, most people think of money first, and often of money alone. But greed is more than of money; and often the greed for money is not the worst form of it at all. The greed of money is the vulgarest and probably the most widespread of the various forms of the vice, but it is not the most dangerous or the most malignant form. Money has a way of reacting upon the people who love it better than life or truth. And it is the irony of fate that a millionaire, who can lay up vast masses of money, cannot often beget love which will prevent it from being tossed to the four winds of heaven through litigation and fighting heirs. But nevertheless the greed of money is the most prevalent.

But there is the greed of recognition as well. Literature never has been cheapened as it is to-day. Authors uncover the loveliest and most sacred portions of family histories for gain and for literary reputation. Wives sell the love-letters of their famous husbands, partly for the money, more for the name of the thing. Nothing is too sacred, nothing too dear, nothing too highly cherished, but it may be brought forth to satisfy a kind of greed for recognition and name. Scientists are not immune from the disease. Our scientific departments at Washington are as full of chicanery of a refined character as the purely political offices are of the more vulgar types. Valuable knowledge is withheld, if discovered by subordinates, because it will detract from the luster of the superior's reputation. In a great university a promising and brilliant young man was dismissed not long ago, manifestly and confessedly, as it was divulged in private, because he threatened to overshadow the man who was at the head of his department in the learning and brilliancy of his services. In politics I need not tell you the facts. One of the most famous politicians of New York City, a man with a national reputation as a *reformer*, said to me not many months ago that his chief reason for going into politics, and staying in and wrecking the candidacy of a certain other reformer, was the determination to make them "recognize" him. In religious circles this same practice is not entirely unknown. Almost every denomination has its cliques and its governing rings, and the weapons they use for the furtherance of their aims are sometimes not of the most sanctified character.

All this is greed. Whether it is greed for recognition or place or power or money, it is greed. And it has all the hideous and deforming features, whatever it be. No complacent optimism can wipe away this unpleasant fact of our modern life. We are all familiar with it. It makes us compromise in religion, in politics, in government, in business, and, shall I say it, in law and in art. Yes, I may say in art. For a true history of the public art works in the city of Boston and the motives by which they were secured, and the various methods that were used in connection with them, would prove this true even in art. True in law? Yes, there is a widely diffused belief that even the courts of the land are not entirely free from the tainted touch of greed. Certain it is that an eminent authority on the law of carriers has not hesitated to state that the decisions of the Supreme Court of Pennsylvania were not worth very much as law, because that court seemed to be merely a department of the Pennsylvania Railroad, like its general freight office. The profoundest sanctions of humanity and love are constantly violated by this insatiate desire for the particular form of possession which we all long after. Nobody is wholly free from it. It has infected us to such a degree that we call evil good and good evil. We never think of the judgment to come. We mortgage the happiness of future generations as though it were no concern of ours at all. Righteousness, liberty, truth, honor, and the joy of an untrammeled service of God Almighty are all laid at the feet of this monster vice of civilization. Grasping avarice touches the very sacred songs we sing. It compasses the very Bible from which we read the divine word.

This eagerness to possess by fair means or foul means the thing which lies nearest to our hearts is corrupting the finest feelings of which human nature is capable. There are many things in this world which are valuable only because they represent toil, industry, self-denial, and a capacity perfected by long and patient discipline. The reason why twenty-five thousand people will go to and enjoy a football game is because victory there, in general, represents superior skill and alertness and training, and all these show qualities which are not gained in a moment, and which are not easily counterfeited when eleven determined men are looking for every weakness and anxious to make the most of it. But even here the delight is often corrupted, I may say usually corrupted, by the vulgar desire of beating a foe irrespective of merit or genuine superiority. Many of the higher things in life are also of such a character that the possession of them in a measure proves that certain disciplines and self-denials have been met and vanquished for the higher pursuit. They show usually that something lower has yielded to something higher. They show effort and patience, and most of all real worth and quality. But the vice of greed is changing all that. And the evidences are multiplying that genuine capacity is being thrown aside for advantages gained by unlawful and unfair means. In business it is the victory, not of skill and industry in an open field and in a market unfettered by fictitious quotations, but a victory by under-billing and secret freight compacts. In literature it is not the prize gained by genuine ability, but the exchange of favors between rich amateurs and sordid publishers. And so on through the whole list. To be sure, genuine worth will win. But it often wins after the man is dead in his garret and another eats the fruit of his genius and travailing. No man can have aught to say against the most earnest desire to succeed. But every man should protest in his own life first, and after that in all that concerns the general welfare, against the triumph of mere greed over righteousness and true merit.

Leave aside that form of greed to which I have already alluded and the vulgarity of which is commonly recognized, and which therefore need not much be spoken against here.

Let the mere money-lovers go. They have their reward.
But take the subtler forms of the trouble as they affect all
classes of society. Take the greed of favor, for example. It
is curious what a man will surrender for some visible token
of favor, especially of public favor. The man who would
not be corrupted by a thousand dollars cash will have his
vanity aroused and his sense of self-importance so stimulated
by some slight token of public favor as to throw overboard
in his greed for favor and appreciation nine-tenths of his
principles. Have you ever known a man to quietly crush
all his ideas of religion, of righteousness, and public rectitude, because some government publication was sent to him,
or some thieving alderman had put a lamp-post in front of his
driveway, or caused to be improved, without any cost to
himself at all, a public highway that was a disgrace to the
community ten months in the year and was patched up just
three weeks before election? How important he felt!
How impressed with the majesty of his free-born American
citizenship! How full of complacent self-love, because his
presence was recognized and his *own* money was spent for
him by the industrious politician who was laughing in his
sleeve all the time because he was rejoicing in the vote to
come!

A Secretary of Agriculture repeatedly called attention
to the utter waste of public money in the annual sending
out to the farmers and others of the country of vast quan-
tities of seeds; but do you recall with what a storm of
protest this manifest economy was met by the congress-
men who knew their constituents? They knew that that
little ten-cent package bearing the congressman's name
would mean worlds to the greedy, self-important individual
who needed no seeds indeed, but who wanted to be "recognized" by his congressman. They saw, with the shrewdness
with which politicians sometimes see things, that lack of that
package would mean forgetfulness on the part of the voter
when the time for reëlection came round. Have we not
known such things over and over again in all forms of our
social and religious life? The desire for favor, for recogni-

tion, utterly apart from all principle and worth, is among the most deeply rooted of all our greeds. No social class has an exclusive mortgage on this form of the vice. All want it, and often for lack of their dues, as they consider them, in this regard, they will batter down and wreck the enterprises which are nearest to the heart and life of a community. Half of our public life is based on the geographical theory. And almost as much of the church life and the social life is also based on a theory of geography utterly apart from merit and intrinsic excellence.

Contrast all this with the ministry and public service of Jesus Christ, and how paltry and mean it all is. Contrast it even with our own highest ideals, and feel the degradation of it. Yet this is a practice so common that it has ceased to excite remark, and is hardly recognized as a thing vicious in itself. Recognition without worth is the curse of civilization both in religion and life. It is akin to the meaningless ceremonies of the temple from which the spirit has fled. It is holding up the empty shell in which there is no kernel. It is degrading real strength, real power, real usefulness and real service. No honorable man can compete with a dishonest man if such a system is to prevail. An honest man must move in response to the public weal independently of how it affects the individual. Christ's rule of self-sacrifice cannot be squared on the theory of constant recognition. Many things in this world have to be done without recognition and often in the face of great hardships. A man must do his duty whether somebody is giving him credit for it or not. Only a fool or a knave will wait for a carriage on election day, if he has a good pair of legs and reasonable ability to use his wits. And yet our streets will be filled with hired vehicles when our next election day rolls round.

Closely allied to this greed for recognition is the greed for applause. It is certain that at least one great figure in our national history sacrificed the ambition of his life for the approval of a certain portion of the public. And since his time there have been many such, and the number seems to be increasing. How delightful it is to hear the shout of

approval and the applause of the unthinking multitude!
How grateful to the ears, the flattery and gracious smiles of
men and women whose vices are left untouched and whose
brutalities are glossed over, while deep under this veneer of
smoothness and smirking satisfaction there burn the volcanic
fires of social and industrial and moral wrath! The theory
of preaching has come to mean that the preacher must
please his audience as the actor must please his audience.
Yes, that is the term. It is not a worshiping congregation,
it is an audience that fills the house of God. And they
must be *pleased*. Fancy the Son of God coming into our
modern life and trying to please three hundred masters as
the modern minister vainly tries to do. Fancy him trying
to recognize everybody and pleasing everybody. Fancy him
enjoining courage upon Christians, but with the proviso that
it must be a courage which will *please*. Fancy all this, and
then think how far we have bedimmed the exaltation of
genuine leadership to mere time-serving as men-pleasers,
when as servants of God we ought to have launched out
into the deeps of eternal and unchallenged truth. Stilled
are too oft the voices of noble spirits that see the truth
indeed, but are hushed into silence by the threatening voices
of demons that encourage the love of applause rather than
the love of truth.

It may, I think justly, be brought as an arraignment of
modern life, that it judges success very largely, almost exclusively, by the applause which it receives, rather than, as
stated before, because of the real value of the thing itself.
Let the mob shout and the demagogues hearken. Nor do the
demagogues alone stop and listen to the verdicts of applause.
The universities do it also. Will the public approve? is the
question. Not the eternal question, Ought they to approve?
And the love of applause has played more havoc with vital
affairs of our nation than many people dream of. Foreign
policy, currency reform, tariffs, civil service and the multitude of other concerns have not in times past been regulated
by the desire for the equitable distribution of taxation and
other burdens, but with a view to the issue whether the

people would throw up their hats and shout in applause. There are many people who distrust the ministry for this same reason. Thousands who believe and hope in Christ are nevertheless alienated from his Church because they believe of his ministers just what Malachi said was true of the priests of the temple. Therefore they follow prophets whose activities are directed against the Church and organized religion. For one I cannot often blame them. And if we have come to a place like that in which the prophet stood, when the accredited representatives of religion are unfaithful to their trust, then for one I hope that in God's providence there will arise mighty voices and inspired natures that will bring us to the throne of God in humiliation and remorse for the deeds we have done and those we have left undone. They loved the praise of men more than the praise of God, is one of the saddest epitaphs in Holy Scripture.

Greed of power and knowledge are also forms of this all-absorbing vice. Mere wanton use of opportunity to crush men and women, competitors and associates, is constantly growing more common and is being taken as a matter of course. We often hear it said that the altruistic spirit is increasing in the world, and that there is a more general disposition to give due regard to individual rights than ever before in the history of the world. This may be so, and in general I believe it is so. But it is also true that there have rarely been times in the history of the world when power was so wantonly used as it is to-day. And a vast multitude seem to be yearning for power for no other reason than to use it wantonly. Hence lusting for power is now exalted into a fine art. To govern the mightiest city on the continent we now go to the race-tracks of England. And the general feeling is, that though of course as Americans we must disapprove of a government gotten from the turf of a foreign land, yet we secretly admire the power of the man and envy him, too. Most of the men who make outcry against the illicit use of great power would make the same use of it if they had it. In this respect they are like the people who would do wonderful things with money if they

had it, but are little, mean, selfish creatures with what they
have, giving the most accurate foreshadowings of what they
would be if they had more. The same spirit applies to the
lust of knowledge. The most amusing illustration of this
is in the triumphant boast of a great newspaper that it
exceeded its rivals in the publication of the news by getting
an extra edition on the streets a few minutes in advance of
the others. The greedy public demands to know. Not that
it must use wisely its knowledge or must be moved to loftier
ideas of service and higher conceptions of character, but that
it must know. It must be taken into confidence in every
trivial detail, whether it concerns the President's cabinet or
the latest murder trial.

This is the outline of a tremendous foe to pure and righteous living that the Christian Church has to face. It is the
selfishness of man, never a trifling thing, working itself out
in social, industrial and religious forms and life. It is the
colossal and ever growing lusting for satisfaction in the
desire to possess the particular thing wanted, irrespective of
right, truth or honor. It is in violation of every Christian
and rational truth. It is in opposition to every human and
kindly instinct. It is animalism pure and simple, applied
to the state of civilization in which we find ourselves, ignor-
ing the obligations of brotherhood, fellowship and Christian
love. It is the practical nullification of the gospel itself.
It is a vice which, plastic enough to take on refined forms,
enters every department of life and corrupts the very sources.
Universities are not more exempt from it than the slums.
Knowledge is as much affected with it as ignorance ; and,
changing its form to suit every condition of society, it steadily
obscures the operations of conscience and the law of God,
and works iniquity and demoralization. In business we call
it competition. In science we call it advancing human
knowledge. In government we play that it is statesmanship.
In political campaigns we call it skill. In religion we call
it wisdom and tactfulness in administration. But in every
one of them, it is simple, unvarnished, sordid, selfish greed
of power, of applause, of knowledge, of reputation, or of gold.

In such a battle there is nothing left for honest and upright men but the method of the prophet — stern, unyielding truthfulness and vigorous fighting against the false ideals that prevail with might and main; a larger appreciation of the power of Christ, and the successful matching of Christ's power of righteousness against all the natural predispositions to the greed which I have described; this is the sovereign remedy for the disease. Let the unselfish take heart and find in the promises of the Lord comfort and hope. Let the men who feel the prophetic function in their souls, who revolt from unrighteousness and from false triumphs, possess their souls in patience, but at the same time keep an arm free for the service which the times require. Let us have truth without veneer. Let us have an honest emulation which shall seek to the utmost to develop our resources and our abilities. But let us hold them under a stewardship which shall make them the weapons of righteousness under the leadership of Jesus Christ. We war not against favor nor against applause nor against power or knowledge; but the favor we crave is the favor of God, whatever else may or may not come with it. Our approval is the approval of Christ; our power, the power of God for salvation; our knowledge, the knowledge of life eternal through Jesus Christ.

THE MANY-HEADED MULTITUDE

MATTHEW v. 1.

WHETHER the Sermon on the Mount was actually delivered to a large crowd of hearers or not, it was the sight of the multitude that inspired it. It was the compassion which Jesus had on the mass of mankind that moved him to many of his noblest emotions and gave the point to many of his most pregnant sayings. But he was not on this account unconscious of the failings of the crowd. It did not cause him to underestimate the value of the individuals who composed it. It did not make him forget the quality of man in the vast numbers of men. And, as a result, individualists and socialists have both claimed Jesus as their representative leader. It is probable that he was both, with a higher aim and a larger purpose than is expressed by either term. Every man was to him a child of God with redemptive possibilities. Mankind as such was to him full of divine suggestion. In both he saw, not merely the materials of a new and better social order, but the raw material of the kingdom of God.

Nor was Jesus without knowledge of the weaknesses of the mob. When their passionate enthusiasm seeks to make him a king, he hides himself. When their greed leads them to a devotion manifestly inspired by selfish ends, he rebukes them and exposes their folly. He knew what was in man. Then, too, the prophetic and reforming spirit in him probably foresaw the natural culmination of such a purgative career as his on the earth. It is a great mistake to suppose that religious and social reformers do not know the consequences of their actions. Many of them see the end long before the multitude suspects it. They know the fickleness

of the crowd. They know the dangers of popular encomium. They know the desperation of foiled greed and ra-
pacious power. But their reliance is on the rectitude of
their intentions and the determinate counsels of God.

Even in the apostolic period the problem of the multitude
was present. Jesus saw it when he saw them as sheep without a shepherd, and was moved with compassion. The disciples saw it when they contrasted the size of the audiences
which were addressed by Jesus and those addressed by John
the Baptist. The Jewish religious oligarchy saw it when
they noted that all men had gone after him. All Jerusalem
saw it when they were moved by the songs of the triumphal
entry on Palm Sunday. Pilate saw it when, with Roman
penetration and the instinct of a machine politician, he preferred the favor of the organized religious machine of the
temple to the righteousness of Jesus' cause, in releasing
Barabbas rather than Christ. The question of the multitude is not a new one. It is a very old one, and has been
with us from the beginning.

And opinions about the multitude have been various.
Tribunes have arisen in every age who have believed in
the people. Wiser leaders have sometimes believed in the
"people" without meaning by that the multitude. Cynical
rulers have seen the fleeting character of the popular ideals,
and deliberately sought the satisfaction of passions rather
than the inculcation of ideas. *Panem et circenses* has been
the real motto of many who did not dare to avow it openly.
Shakespeare makes Coriolanus call it the "beast with many
heads." And while it would not be just to call it a beast,
that it is many-headed is beyond question. The multitude
is not a single thing, as so much discussion seems to assume.
It is a many-headed thing. It has not a heart, a brain and
a conscience. It has many hearts, good, bad and indiffer-
ent. It has brains, but of varying quality and no quality.
It has conscience, but only a fragment of it is active, and
some of it is seared with a red-hot iron. It is a many-
headed problem, the problem of the crowd.

Christianity has always followed Christ in this, that it has felt a peculiar solicitude about that class of the population who are supposed to be included in the term "the masses." The largest part of Christian activity has been in ministry to the least favored of the sons of men. This has really been at the base of all the so-called magnificence of Christian self-indulgence. The building of great cathedrals has really been in exaltation of the fundamental idea of the gospel. The splendid worship and the beautiful ceremonials which have accompanied them have had the same ulterior object. Sometimes the spirit has left the temple barren, in spite of its splendor. But, taking the Church as a whole, it has been true, absolutely true, to the fundamental idea of the gospel. To this very day, with so much of the world's wealth included in it, the major portion of its exhortation is of duty to the poor and the needy.

But with us here in America the problem of the multitude has taken a special and technical form, and one which is calling to us for the most careful and thoughtful attention which we can bring to it. Our multitudes are in possession of a freedom and self-regulative power which have never been seen before in the earth. They have opportunities which seem almost beyond belief when the conditions of other ages are considered. With a suffrage free enough to be polluted almost at will, with an educational impulse which places the child of the millionaire by the side of the pauper, with a political system which is at once divine and ludicrous in its suggestion and working, and with a religious liberty that makes thoughtful minds of other countries reel with fear of moral anarchy and confusion, our multitude is unlike any that the world has ever seen. There are no precedents for us. We must be pioneers or perish. The older orders have no word of counsel for us, and we ourselves must work out our salvation. Not only must we devise the method, but we must at the same time persuade the masses to accept it. This is our problem.

This apparently impressed that keen and kindly student of our institutions, Mr. Bryce, for in his chapter on the "Influence of Religion" he closes with these words: "So, sometimes standing in the midst of a great American city, and watching the throngs of eager figures streaming hither and thither, marking the sharp contrasts of poverty and wealth, an increasing mass of wretchedness and an increasing display of luxury, knowing that before long a hundred millions of men will be living between ocean and ocean under this one government, — a government which their own hands have made and which they feel to be the work of their own hands, — one is startled by the thought of what might befall this huge yet delicate fabric of laws, commerce and social institutions, were the foundations it has rested on to crumble away. Suppose that all these men ceased to believe that there was any Power above them, any future before them, anything in heaven or on earth but what their senses told them of ; suppose that their consciousness of individual force and responsibility, already dwarfed by the overwhelming power of the multitude and the fatalistic submission it engenders, were further weakened by the feeling that their swiftly fleeting life was rounded by perpetual sleep. . . . Would the moral code stand unshaken, and with it reverence for law, the sense of duty toward the community and even toward generations yet to come ? . . . History, if she cannot give a complete answer to this question, tells us that hitherto civilized society has rested on religion, and that free government has prospered best among religious peoples." [1]

Thus does a sympathetic Englishman muse upon our future as a nation on the religious side of our development. The best among us have had thoughts like these for many years, as we have seen many old ideals apparently vanish, and the spirit of consecration and simple-hearted service give way to an easy-going cynicism and unthinking belief in the rightness of things themselves. What shall become of the multitude, and us with them, depends on what that mass of human beings shall think about God, life and duty, and the remaining symbols of religious responsibility. This is more than anxiety about mere social betterment. It is the application of the message of Jesus Christ to human life in its

[1] " American Commonwealth," Vol. II, pp. 598, 599.

entirety, and the practice of the professions to which the New Testament calls honorable Christian men. It is this that lies at the base of the problem of the multitude and their welfare. And, as stated, it is a question with such varied interests and of so many different turns of thought and feeling, that the entire energy and Christianized sentiment and conscience of the whole Christian Church cannot too soon be directed to it. It is not a matter for sentimentalism and dreamy speculations. It is a time for vigorous and resourceful activity.

Mr. Bryce touches a very sore spot and one which is vital to this whole matter when he alludes to the "sharp contrasts of poverty and wealth." Indeed, I have the impression that a large portion of the social discontent is caused precisely by such contrasts. I do not think that any one especially resents the possession of fine things and the luxuries of life to any one, as these things go in themselves. Even here, however, there is a danger which was voiced long ago when the secretary of the Anti-Corn-Law League of Great Britain, seeing the new building of the Reform Club in London modeled after the Farnese Palace, said to John Bright: "John, John, how can we remain honest if we live in such palaces as these?" showing an appreciation of the inherent danger in magnificence itself. But when the contrasts take on the forms of social and industrial mockery, and when with the loftiest sentiments of humanity and brotherhood on our lips we have the most degrading examples of misery and wantonness, there is bred a spirit which does not readily yield to exorcism.

Luxury in America does not withdraw itself from the public gaze. One might live many years in some of the European capitals without seeing the displays of personal luxury which are common in America. The passion for display is almost as great among us as the passion for wealth by which the display is made possible. We want, not the luxury alone, but we want every one to see us in the enjoyment of it. While it would not be just to say that we enjoy the sensation of having what our neighbor cannot afford,

there is a touch of satisfaction in seeing his manifest amazement that we ourselves are thus able to indulge our own
tastes without regard to consequences.   It is this that brings
the anguish and pain to the less favored and creates the
fierce feelings of resentment which, properly nurtured, result
in violence and destruction.   Then, too, it takes the most
offensive forms.   I have never heard of any mob orator
resenting the possession of fine books or fine paintings or
rare editions of old authors, or literary treasures or classic
remains of one kind and another.   Whenever I have read
or heard such men speak it has been against dress, jewels,
and the paraphernalia of wealth which require the least culture and the least taste for their acquisition.

Now, such feelings touch the moral nature.   They arouse
the sensations which affect the thought of the brotherhood of
man, and by implication the fatherhood of God.   Thus what
was originally, as I believe, a not very culpable feeling, perhaps only a kind of childish feeling of joy in pretty and
costly things, becomes the instrument of moral damage
and disruption.   The loss is the loss of the moral interest
and solidarity of mankind.   The ways are seen to be not
one, at different stages of the journey, but two, and leading
in opposite directions.   If such an exhibition were always
confined to men of mature life, who by industry and application had earned the day of enjoyment and rest from their
labors, all would be well.   But the most virulent form of it
comes from the very ones whose own labors have not produced the wealth which they so lavishly and so vulgarly display.   The simplicity of life is thus destroyed, and the moral
appeal is always of the simplest kind.   A high moral purpose does not live in the atmosphere of constant explanation
and interpretation.   Neither does human brotherhood survive where it has always to be vociferously asserted lest it
be forgotten.

Then there is in this country an exaggerated confidence
in personal force and individual power which is very destructive, not only to a sound national and religious feeling, but
to the moral development of the masses of the people.   Like

Nebuchadnezzar we are constantly saying, "Is not this great Babylon, which I have built?" Our great fortunes and our great industries and our great universities are all more or less associated in our minds with some man who stands out conspicuously in their organization and management. One gets the idea, and gets it easily, that Almighty God has little to do with things. One comes to believe that the moral order is not the final or the essential order. One feels that if there is individual capacity and strength to battle down opposition, the game of life is won. But is this true? Suppose we did try to assume that God was merely a quiescent spectator of this life of ours? Suppose we all came to the conclusion that responsibility was only a name handed down from other times, but which had no meaning now?

It seems monstrous to suppose that any one would deliberately rob the poor of their belief in the existence of God and the sanctions of morality and uprightness which spring from that belief. But forgetfulness of duty to God is having just this result. The vast number of well-to-do people who never go to a church and never give any outward assent to the influence and authority of the gospel are the real anarchists, from whom the masses stand in danger. In a community a God-fearing and church-going population is infinitely to be preferred to a wealthy and non-church-going one. A churchless respectability is one of the most devilish forces in society in my judgment. It is not that the people themselves are useless in the religious life. That might be endured. They might be permitted to descend to their hades of uselessness and religious death. But their example teaches many who are not thus favored in a worldly way that the possession of wealth brings with it immunity from religious duty and obligation. This is the sad part of it. They are not properly entitled to such influence. But it is in human nature that they have it.

This many-headed multitude, which is thus moved alternately by hope and fear and envy and greed and passion, cannot be dealt with on the human side by any one method which will answer all its needs at once. Indeed, all its needs are not demanding attention at the same time. Sometimes one thing is uppermost and sometimes another. But one thing and one only is always present. And that is the need for the spiritual impulse and the saving power which springs from the person and authority of Jesus Christ. This, being the only constant factor, is the only real mode of approach to the people. When the people are full of bread, they are not moved by the discussion about the distribution of property. When they are busy and fully employed, they do not care much about questions of labor and wages. When they are well and hearty, the matter of sanitation and tenement houses does not make very much impression upon them. But the need of forgiveness for the sins of their life is just as real as the need for forgiveness for the sins of those who are not, technically, the multitude.

The gospel is what the multitude must have. That is not, in my view, mere exhortation to sobriety and pious talk about heaven and the hereafter. The whole gospel of responsibility and life is what I mean. A poor man has a duty to society as really as a rich man. Demand his duty from him no less than from the other man. The poor people in a church have just as much duty to give to its support as the rich people. The young men have as much duty as the old men. Nobody has any business to assume that he is a part of a class in society which must be forever coddled and babied. Men resent the activities of the rich, and then shirk the measure of responsibility which they can control. Men say that the rich own and control the church, when they will not come forward and speak according to the measure of their own authority and power. The fact is that such men have already damaged themselves by making money their own god. They are afraid to speak to the rich because they know that they would be tyrants themselves if they were rich. I say to the poor man in the church or anywhere else, you have your duty no less than others. Do your duty, and then you can with better grace demand that others shall do theirs.

There has been entirely too much talk about the woes of the multitude and not enough about its responsibilities. All

men have woes, and it is the sheerest nonsense to suppose that
the possession of money gives happiness and satisfaction, in
spite of the foolish assertion of many that they are willing to
take their chances. An able-bodied man who is upright in
life and industrious and sober in habits will not be free from
difficulties and troubles. But the chances are ninety-nine to
one that he will be able to take care of himself in a rational,
reasonable way, and be a useful and helpful member of
society. But he will need the uplift of the gospel of Christ
to remain such a man, and to renew his strength by the
observance of the rites and ordinances of religion. He will
need the help of God over the hard places, and he will need
the fellowship of the Church of Christ to make him keep on
believing in himself. With God and his fellow believers in
God, under the common law of service in Christ, he will be
the ideal man in the social order. Then God may call him
to the stewardship of riches or not as he may see fit. But
if he does, the man will be then just what he was before, a
self-respecting, honorable child of God and a man among
men in the spirit and life of Jesus Christ.

The note of dependence has been struck in dealing with
the problem of the multitude almost to the exclusion of every
other note. It is here that the change must first be made if
we are to reach and uplift the masses of men to the contemplation and practice of higher ideals. Man was made intellectually and morally capable to deal with his own life under
the providence of God. The kindly, genial sympathies which
are the choicest fruits of Christendom were not intended to
be the playthings of all kinds of foolishness nominally intended to give help to men. Man needs help and will need
help as long as he lives. But the help he most needs is the
help that refines his nature and purifies his life. He needs
not to be told that he is the victim of circumstances and bad
laws and bad men and a host of other things, true as these
are at times. Man is primarily a victim of his own selfishness and self-indulgence. Charity rarely finds a case which
has not in it, as the root of the evil, vice, or lack of moral
strength in one form or another.

With all the sympathy for the masses which Christ had, with all the compassion which he felt for them, he did not leave a single utterance which could encourage any man in dropping voluntarily into the ranks of a dependent class. In fact, the Sermon on the Mount itself is a call to manhood. It is a call to earnest and passionate pursuit of righteousness and true living, and crowned with a trust in God as the sufficient completion of man's personal activities in his own behalf. Let us sound that note. There is no room in a Christian society for a permanent despair. Overcome by misfortune, men may sometimes find themselves in the valley. But not permanently, nor with satisfaction while they are there. Christianity has ever taught that responsibility lies at the root of character.

Then, again, no amount of rhetorical gloss can obscure the fact that the real troubles of society are moral and spiritual rather than social or industrial. Sin is the disturbing element in society, and the scheme of saving the world which overlooks this fact might as well prepare itself for failure at the beginning. Righteous men make a righteous world, and no others. If a man forgets Almighty God in his life, he is likely also to forget his fellow men, and be in turn forgotten by them. Then he curses society and his fellow men when he could with greater reason curse himself. Let us not permit this fact to be obscured in any discussion that may take place. We owe a duty to all men. But they owe a duty to themselves. Let us do the one and demand the other.

It is a source of growing wonder to thoughtful men that the ministry of Jesus Christ contains so few temporal expedients. It has always been known and noted. But as society develops and the perplexities of dealing with vast masses of men increase, more and more it becomes evident how divine was the wisdom of Christ in all that he said and did. There was no roseate picture of a sensuous Mohammedan heaven or earth in that preaching. There was no self-complacent congratulation on freedom from difficulties and responsibilities. No; on the contrary, he said, "In the world ye have tribulation." The price of the gospel life is labor and travail. All must have it, no matter what their station in life. The forms vary, but the thing is one. Life is itself a matter of limitation and restraint. Order and authority are not creatures of caprice. And life must be rounded out in order and authority. The multitude needs to learn this, and to learn it needs to have it frequently and emphatically told.

Is there a nobler title in this world than the title "workman" or "laborer"? Yet most people think of the "working" classes as people who are in especial need of sympathy. I think the sympathy belongs to the miserable idle classes. To me there is no nobler title than that of workman. It is a New Testament designation of the laborer with God. "A workman that needeth not to be ashamed" is what each is enjoined to be. Nor need a true workman in any calling be ashamed. But a shiftless, quarrelsome, pettifogging, selfish, envious man with a handful of tools is not a true workman. A true workman is a man of God, no less than the priest at the altar. He works in the fear of God. He tries to turn out an honest and well-made product. He is faithful to the implied contract between him and his employer. Life has no grander name than that. The multitude needs to know it and learn to honor itself.

Christ was a workman in the actual and spiritual sense. Every Christlike man will be the same. Each man must contribute something to the social health and the social wealth. It may be little or it may be much. But he must contribute to it, and share its responsibilities, and respond to its necessities. Dependent classes properly can be those only who are physically or mentally unable to bear a part in the social responsibility. But we have made dependent classes in thought of a vast mass of men and women who are not properly such, and whose moral sense and character have been impaired by the inculcation of the false idea that they were subjects of peculiar care and sympathy. Let us correct that error before it is fatal.

Happiness and contentment on the earthly side rest on

industry, frugality and integrity. On the spiritual side they rest upon faith in God and love for men. They rest upon forgiveness for sins and encouragement to new life and effort for personal character and self-expression. When God controls a man's life he can be himself, as God intended he should be. When some one else controls it, he can neither be himself nor anything else that is satisfactory to himself or the world. It is the battle between moral and spiritual order, which is salvation, and moral and spiritual chaos, which is destruction and misery. There is no middle ground. Let us love mankind with the discriminating love of Christ. Let us give them the help that makes helpful. Let us not give them the help that will make them spiritual paupers. Let us enforce the thought of an all-present and overruling God in human affairs, and an equally ever-present and imperative duty to minister to ourselves and each other. That is the kingdom of God. Nothing else ever can be.

THE DAILY DUST OF LIFE

2 CORINTHIANS xii. 4.

THIS statement of St. Paul's has usually been assumed, and correctly I think, to refer to an experience of his own. Precisely what that experience was, or what it was designed to teach Paul, is not certain. All that there is to say about it is, that it occurred, and that the apostle refers to it in such a way as connects it with his " thorn in the flesh." But even of that we are in doubt. There are many conjectures. But no man can positively state just what that thorn was, nor what its relation to Paul's ecstatic spiritual experience was. It must have been very impressive, and probably to Paul was very illuminating. But this is inference in the absence of any exact knowledge. We know who St. Paul was, and we know that a statement of this kind from him would be valid testimony. But there our knowledge ends. The interesting thing about it is something which does not concern it at all. Wonderful as that vision in Paradise may have been, sublime as the third heaven, if it was the third, into which Paul had temporary admission, the singular and striking thing about it is that no matter how splendid it was, how impressive its lessons, how inspiring its suggestions, Paul brought back to the toiling sons of earth not one single word about it. Of all those unspeakable words, there was not one that was lawful to utter.

That was the astounding thing about Paul's great ecstasy. From the glory of that Presence and from the thrilling eloquence of the words unspeakable he brought back not one for his fellow man. It must have been beautiful, yet he gives us no description of it. It must have been soul-compelling in the searchingness of its moral purity, yet he does not allude

to that.   It must have given a vision of God that to a man of
Paul's insight and susceptibility to divine influences was
hardly less than transforming, yet he is absolutely silent
about it.   What shall we say to such a strange phenomenon
as this?   Paul was certainly ready enough to communicate
his experiences to the churches.   There is none of the apostolic college of whom we have such familiar knowledge as we
have of him.   He is apparently always ready to refer to himself in whatever mood he is.   We see him in dejection and
despair as well as exultation.   We see him with the troubles
of church regulation and discipline upon him, showing a very
human temperament and habit.   We see him battling with
the other apostles for the apostolic recognition.   Always
human and easily approached, on this great experience of
his life Paul has nothing at all to say.

The words were " not lawful to utter."   But what does that
mean?   Does it mean that he was expressly enjoined from
telling what he had seen and heard?   Did the Almighty lift
Paul up to a wondrous view of the Eternal only to deny him
the privilege of inspiring others with the narrative of the
vision?   That seems incredible.   Or was the knowledge thus
gained of a nature that made its utterance unlawful in the
sense of unprofitable for the average man?   Did it present a
picture so roseate that the man in the daily dust of life would
give over to settled despair when told of it?   Perhaps this is
the true interpretation.   But whether it is or not, let us settle
down to this : that the great Apostle Paul, when lifted out of
himself and into the company of seraphim and angels and
into the sight and hearing of the eternal things of God, came
back to his toil not a puffed-up semi-god, a halo-crowned saint
divested of his humanity, but a thrice humanized laborer for
God, and more than ever a workman in the dust of Christian
service, for the glory of Jesus Christ, his Lord.

There has been and is still a great deal of idealization in
the matter of religion, and it must be confessed that we are
often lured on to noble acts and heroic sacrifices by the hope
of a future which to the imagination is free from the cares
and anxieties which envelop us here in the present.   But as

the anxiety about a future punishment has lost much of its force to make us good, the hope of a future heaven has lost much of its power to make us happy. Both goodness and happiness are not affairs which require a particular location. They are conditions of the moral nature and the will. Goodness is goodness anywhere, but especially on earth, where many people are bad. Happiness is happiness anywhere, more especially on the earth, where most people appear to be unhappy. It seems, therefore, that we might with much more propriety give ourselves to the solution of the question of how to become good and happy now, rather than in some ideal state hereafter.

There is, I think, a' growing disposition to find both the highest good and the highest happiness in the known life rather than in some other. Not that we shall not have the beautiful anticipations of heaven left to us for inspiration and occasional comfort. But in general we must find our inspiration in the things that are, not in those that are to be. If some one had told Columbus that men would actually cross the Atlantic Ocean in seven days, four hundred years subsequent to his own attempt, the only result that I can see to his mind would have been increased misery at the limited nature of his own equipment. It does no good to a starving man to tell him that in other climes there are abundant harvests. On the contrary, it adds to his exasperation and distress. After all, the present demand is the most imperative, and the present need the most urgent. This thought has recently been beautifully expressed by the poet Stephen Phillips in his "Marpessa," in which she tells Apollo why she cannot be his companion, preferring to the various moods of the gods and the changeful conditions of the godlike life

> The pastoral fields burned by the setting sun.
> And he (Idas) shall give me passionate children, not
> Some radiant god that will despise me quite,
> But clambering limbs and little hearts that err.

Even when the first joys of human love and delight have passed and the soberer and more somber side of life is experienced, she sees no reason for changing her opinion : —

And though the first sweet sting of love be past,
The sweet that almost venom is, though youth,
With tender and extravagant delight,
The first and secret kiss by twilight hedge.
The insane farewell repeated o'er and o'er,
Pass off; there shall succeed a faithful peace;
Beautiful friendship tried by sun and wind,
Durable from the daily dust of life;

which seems to be a faithful presentation of our better
thought and judgment, as well as a beautiful poetic picture
of the fact.

This seems also to lie at the base of the lack of reference
by the apostle to his wondrous experience in Paradise. The
passionate delight which almost blinds the sight and turns
the brain, painful in its very exultation, which comes to every
man in his first grasp upon the power of Christ in his soul, is
after all not the norm of Christian living and hope. The
"tender and extravagant delight" of youth is not the sum of
human life and human love. But the truer and finer feelings
of friendship and security which spring from the community
of suffering and the joint sympathies of a common pain,
these make the strength and power of life, and are the real
treasures of Christian faith and hope. And these fall, not
from the clouds, but rise from the "daily dust of life." Out
of these very throes and passions which are the burden of
each day's triumphs and losses comes the sublime life, the
life of reality with self and with God. The process may be
slower than that of ecstatic inspiration, but its fruits are for
all.

Paul's own life furnishes us the most illuminating contrast
between the appeal of the things celestial and those terrestrial to the human heart and soul. If there is a single man
whose earthly experiences are more eloquent and full of
pathetic pleading for the Christian life than his, it would be
interesting to know who it is. Paul never seems to appeal
by the authority of his higher-life ideas, though he evidently
had them. He never seems to be actuated by the power of
an extra-earthly demonstration, though he was familiar with
these. In all such matters Paul is amazingly reticent. Just

as he is with this experience in Paradise. But he is never
weary of telling the story of his sufferings for Christ's cause.
In this very letter he tells the pitiful tale of his own personal
hardships. And what a record it was! Perils of divers
kinds, beaten with rods, stoned, shipwrecked, hungry, thirsty,
weariness, fasting, and the whole catalogue of human trouble.
He had them all. Yet it is of these very things that he
speaks. He seems to think that in these lies the strongest
motive power in his preaching to bring men to the gospel of
Christ.

Not that Paul forgot the rewards of the divine life or that
he did not have the eager anticipations of the crown of rejoicing. Not that at some times he did not feel the doubt of
wondering, which was better, to stay and fight it out or to
depart and be with Christ. In this feeling Paul showed distinct traces of Hamlet's skepticism about life itself. But these
were moods. I am glad we have had the glimpses of them
that Paul's letters give. It shows a human being under all
the moods of life clinging to a profound and austere purpose,
the one thing worth living for, the glory of Jesus Christ. No;
Paul did not forget the power of the celestial life and the
glorious anticipations which it brings to hard-pressed men in
the fight of life. The man of toil knows what rest is. The
man who has been sitting in darkness knows what light is.
Paul knew what heaven must be like from what his own sufferings showed him earth could not possess. But he remembered that what the Christ came to save was on the earth,
not in heaven, and to earth his thought and attention must
be given.

Yes, and out of the earth his true joy and delight must be
garnered. Did he not remember the prophecy of Christ which
said, " He shall see of the travail of his soul, and shall be satisfied " ? What could that possibly mean but that the Saviour's
own joy would be secured in the triumphant sacrifice of himself
for all mankind ? Did he not write to certain of his converts
and call them his " joy and crown " ? Surely heaven has nothing better to offer than the souls of redeemed men. Surely
the crown of rejoicing and the " joy and crown " in the life of

saved men and women were not two, but one. It was the same joy and the same crown on earth and in heaven. This made Paul's daily conflict of the supremest interest to him. It gave a sort of eternal earnestness to all his efforts. It threw the light of the kingdom of heaven into the darkest spots of his daily life and made them radiant, even in suffering, with the brightness of redemption glory.

The obvious lesson of all this is, then, that out of life's daily dust must life be realized, and out of the hardship of daily labor must the true satisfaction of life be gathered. Some men may have supernatural visions and dreams. The average man has his work. Some may be called to the brilliant companionship of angels and archangels, but most men must live and act with men. An occasional man may find the happiness of his soul in the life of constant contemplation. Most men have neither the time nor the equipment for a purely contemplative career. Work is the normal order of human existence. Toil is the blessing which brightens most lives. Labor is surely transformed into a joy since it has been hallowed by holy thoughts and sacrificial pain. Blessings on the life of work, and blessings on the workman who sees in his work the hope of his life that now is, as well as that which is to come.

Even the poetry of life lies hidden in its daily dust. Who writes of the gilt and tinsel which form the edge of humanity's great woes? Who has ever made an epic or composed a poem of passion or power that was not born out of those deeper human experiences which are everywhere and always the same? When Homer writes his immortal epic, 'tis of war and men, of wrath and slaughter, of jealous warriors and the clashing ires of gods and men, but all upon the battlefield of Troy. What makes the gods in Homer interesting is that they act like men. What makes the quarrels of Olympus so full of fascination and gives the stimulus of dramatic interest and movement to the sublime bard's portrayals is that they banter and battle just like the sons of earth whose enlarged figures they really are. And is this not equally true of the story of the wanderings of Æneas and the sounding pæans of the Augustan glory? Even the immortal poetry of life is in its daily toil and trouble. When some gifted man takes our own sorrows and with winged words transfigures them into the materials which appeal to the imagination, we hold up reverent hands and say, How divine! Nay, brother, but these are thine own sorrows and thine own sufferings. Not more divine now than when from thy sorrow-burdened heart they sprang, fresh with the willows of thy grief and woe.

This daily dust is golden. Only, like the miner in his distant camp, we must find its precious part and gather its stores, its wealth of treasure, and fill the mind and soul with the knowledge of the goodness of God. "Who are these?" said the Apostle John, when he saw an immortal company around the throne, brighter than the rest, and apparently standing in places of honor. "These are they which come out of the great tribulation," was the reply. But they had washed their robes and made them white. They had toiled well. They had suffered much. Out of the perils and griefs of a genuine discipleship they had found the golden rewards of God.

But some one will say that even now this is idealization of life. No, far from it. Life is full of all the interest that we can give to it. The choice by Christ of a life full of sorrows and grief must forever settle the question as to the nature of the most abundant life. An easy-going and cynical age may well feel that it is alien to the Man of Galilee with his thoroughly human and sympathetic appeal. But mankind feels it, and has felt it ever since it was first revealed. It saw a man whose deep and tender affection for his fellow men was not obscured by the passing show, nor dimmed by the hope of temporal or eternal reward. It saw the splendor of the life of meekness and self-abnegation. It saw a visible demonstration of that strange axiom of the spiritual life, that a man must lose his life to save it. It is not an ideal Christ who is saving men, but an actual, passionate, human Christ, one touched and tempted in all points as we are. It is not a Saviour in heaven that calls to men; it is a Saviour on earth and filled with the knowledge and woes of earth.

Has it ever occurred to you that of all the divine communi-

cations that must have been Christ's during his earthly ministry, we have no single hint of their bearing and message to
men? When the transfiguration scene is reached, all that we
know is that Moses and Elijah talked with him concerning
his decease which he should accomplish at Jerusalem. Christ,
who knew if any one did, gave us no hint of the splendors of
the eternal mansions, only that they were there. That was
all. When legions of angels were at his bidding he used
them not. His was to be life for men, not a campaign for
angels. His was to be a perpetual glorification of the anxious
existence of the sons of earth, not an exploitation for celestial
beings. In all Christ's ministry there is not a single instance
of a theophany having a purpose for men in any special sense.
Only the simple humanity of it all! Only the daily life, with
all its limitation and constant questioning!

Can we fully enter into the depth of the meaning of this
great fact? Jesus never says to men that he is authorized to
address and command them by reason of his celestial knowledge or heavenly experiences. He does not ask men to become his disciples because he has what they have not in the
way of supernatural illumination and light. The reason he
asks them to follow him is that they may become, not angels,
but greater men. The life that he gives them is a more
abundant human life, not a rarefied heavenly existence which
the average man cannot understand. Discipleship with Christ
is not the muttering of mysteries, but to seek and save the
lost. He is the companion of all men. Some even scorn
him because he is the friend of sinners. The phylacteried
Pharisee who thanks God that he is *not* as other men are
stands at the polar opposite from Christ's own position.
Christ comes because he *is* as other men. The divinest life
is the most human life that can be, not the life most removed
from men. The one being capable of telling men what
heaven is, and reciting out of his own knowledge what its
joys and delights are, has nothing to offer of that joy and
delight in his quest for the souls of men.

Perhaps for him, too, these things were not "lawful to
utter." We can easily believe it. If this life is the period

in which the eternal issues of life and death are solved, then
this is the life that must be sweetened and purified. If these
are the men who have the possibility of eternal hope in them,
then as soon as possible we must awaken the life of God
within them into power and strength. Not by visions of
things to come, but by the moral force of things that are.
The whole round of daily life must be filled with the energy
and moral vigor of a holy purpose. We must make men
believe, and believe ourselves, that the possession of life
itself is a holy trust to be administered for God and men.
This daily business is my contribution to the world's salvation if it be filled with the purpose and love of Christ. This
trivial round, this common task, is neither trivial nor common.
What God has sanctified let no man call common. Nothing
is trivial that brings bloom or blight to the heart of a human
being.

Slowly but inevitably the great world forces are feeling
their moral import and power. Trade and industry gradually find that the leverage for power and the condition of
security lie in the observance of the moral relations of man.
A passing storm proves that after all the Almighty is on his
throne, and that he is still the Sovereign of the earth. To-
day we sit boastful and defiant, proud in our achievement
and triumph over the powers of heaven and earth. Then
the Lord of the universe drops the silent flakes of snow for
a few hours, and lo, our defiant house of boasting falls to the
ground, and we are reduced again to the elementary dependence upon each other that really never left us, even when our
lips were most full of boasting and vainglory. Yesterday we
harnessed the lightning and made it our beast of burden.
To-day the helpless steed from the skies waits the pleasure of
Him who sits on the circle of the earth. Then they cry unto
the Lord in their troubles, and he saveth them out of their
distresses. No more defiant, we hasten to help each other,
and render the kindly offices to our fellow men in their isolation and need.

Human life, then, is the real place where the kingdom of
God is to be revealed and exemplified. Into every type of

life and into every calling by which men must earn their daily bread there must come the majesty and the suggestive hope that spring from the life of Jesus Christ. Whatever thy hands find to do, do it not only with thy might, but do it also to the glory of Jesus Christ. Do it unto the glory of humanity in its dust and grime, that out of it may come a purified hope and a spiritual grace that make for light and truth among men. This is the only sound and enduring approach to humanity's future. Let us assert the solidarity of mankind at whatever cost. This seems to have been one of the most important of the lessons that Jesus came to teach. Mankind is one and is kept one only by the assertion and proving of the divineness of life itself in the possibility of its scope and spiritual glory. Christ's life is itself a heroic presentation of the dignity and impressiveness of a life utterly devoid of the symbolism and trappings of human greatness and station. It is simply unadorned life. It is simply plain humanity. It is the sinless picture of a common existence.

It is said that in the diplomatic complications in the far East England is fighting the world's battle when she contends for open ports with equal rights of trade to all nations. In the world of commerce this is probably a true contention. And in a similar way, to keep open the life of every man to the influences of God by asserting the authority of God in every life, and the divine character of every human interest, we keep humanity's ports open to the possibility of redemption and salvation. Once assert that any part of humanity has an experience or a capacity for spiritual exaltation which is not open to every man, and you close the ports of many hearts to the appeal of God and the universal humanity of Jesus Christ. Men may be caught up like Paul into the third heaven, but it is not lawful or wise to utter what they have heard or seen. God gives his personal message to each man in his own way and time. But he is not singling out some men as more divine than other men, nor giving glimpses of heaven to some men for the purpose of exasperating other men with the meagerness of their own knowledge of the limitations of their own spiritual experience.

On the contrary, what God is daily doing in the lives of Christian men is giving proof that the commonest experiences of the daily life are the richest in their messages for the human heart. They contain all the essentials of the most exalted life, because we have seen that life thus exalted through Jesus Christ. Your own life, with its dust and murkiness, gives the widest scope that any man can desire. It contains all the happiness of this life in holy contentment and the security of human love. It contains the possibilities of a holiness that can make us children of the Most High. It had for Christ all the possibilities of becoming the Prince of Life and the Saviour of the whole world. What it had for Christ it has for you and for me. Surely the world has not grown smaller since that Judæan ministry two thousand years ago. Surely its capacity for energy, for service, for light and helpfulness, has not grown less but more. Christ-likeness, if it was so wonderful in that diminutive world, is to-day even more wonderful because of the greater opportunities which the world's growth has created. Common Christian living is the most powerful force in the world to-day. Simple Christian service is the mightiest productive instrumentality that has yet been discovered. All other things give the accessories of life. This gives life itself.

When we fight this battle we fight not our own merely, but the battle of every man. The history of Christianity, indeed of religion itself, is a history of the departure of privilege and the opening of the holiest places to all mankind. Priest-craft and redecraft have yielded to the power of our expanding humanity under the guidance of the Spirit of God. There are no more holy classes and saintly offices. All life is holy and all offices are the ministry of the good. Christ has in this accomplished his greatest work. Unlocking the gates of privilege and opportunity, out into the fields of God humanity has come for larger and riper experience and a fuller breath of the winds of spiritual life and freedom. At the head of this vast procession is the Son of God himself. Before him crumbling lie the remains of superstition and fear. Not less have fallen before him the tools of license and anarchy. Freedom, but freedom for service has been his rallying cry, and all human hearts have responded to his call.

To this impulse, which begins and ends in Jesus Christ, literature and art are responding, as well as trade and industry. The life of the lowly has now a passionate interest for literary men and women which it did not know a few years ago. Instead of forever dwelling in the halls of the castles and the festivities of the great, literature is finding its newest and greatest inspirations in the renewed discovery of life itself. And thus it comes back to the greatest literature of all, the world's book, the Bible. "When I think," says John Oliver Hobbes, "that Almighty God was willing to come down from heaven and sit anywhere in order to tell a lot of vulgar people the most perfect stories in creation — I refer to the Parables — I own I cannot tolerate the gifted beings who can only bring themselves to address a little circle, who are not, by the bye, especially anxious to be addressed." Christ's world is the whole world. Only man cares to make an aristocracy or an oligarchy. But be of good cheer, Christ has overcome the world.

EDUCATIONAL

UNIVERSITY RELIGION

John iii. 10.

NICODEMUS was what might appropriately be called the university man of his time. He was a gentleman, a scholar and a religious and social leader. His attainments as a scholar made him a suitable companion for the religious leaders of Israel and caused him to be chosen a member of their leading assembly, while his qualities as a man and a fellow citizen doubtless made him a familiar and popular figure among the less conspicuous of the people. His qualities of mind, so far as we have them revealed in the New Testament, are those of a trained and tolerant intellect. Even his visit to Jesus by night, which in its harsher aspect resembles cowardice, in another view shows the natural conservatism of a well-balanced character. Religious radicals would probably call him a coward. More thoughtful men would probably say that careful inquiry should precede discipleship and the evening call upon Christ was in the nature of an endeavor to interview and understand Christ away from the crowd. Many a man is a hero in a mob who shrinks to very diminutive proportions in a private interview. Wise men do not accept mob standards of heroism. Nicodemus was a wise man. He sought to know Christ in the only way in which to a man of his type Christ could reveal himself with the power and fullness which appeal to the trained and sumptuous mind. That was the method of personal interview. Whether his coming by night was the result of fear or not is purely a matter for conjecture. Christ's days were busy days. Perhaps the evening was the only time in which a personal interview could be secured.

Christ, it will be observed, did not reproach Nicodemus for

coming in the night.   On the contrary, the record of the conversation seems to show that he was glad to be sought out
by the learned ruler, for the talk that resulted bears the evidence of careful comparison of ideas and explicit effort on
Christ's part to make Nicodemus understand the fundamental
idea of the gospel, namely, the doctrine of the new birth.
Only once does Jesus give any sign of surprise in anything
that Nicodemus says or does, and that is when the new birth
is announced.   Struck by the greatness of the ruler's surprise,
Jesus exclaims, "Art thou the teacher of Israel, and under-
standest not these things?" apparently himself surprised
that this should be so utterly novel to his interviewer.   Jesus
does not seem to have been greatly astonished at the ruler's
general ignorance, but when that individual breaks out with
the astounded, "How can these things be?" showing that
the thought was absolutely foreign and new to his previous
life and thought, Jesus in turn is also astounded and expresses
himself as the text relates.   It was a curious scene.   The
university man was amazed at the idea which Christ offered,
and Jesus was amazed that he should find it so new.   That
the multitude could not understand did not surprise him.
Popular education was not then the great distributer of knowledge and intelligence that it now is.   But that an educated
man, the university man of the time, should find the doctrine
of the new birth so utterly alien to all his life and thinking
gave to Christ a shock of what seems to have been a very
unpleasant surprise.   If the educated and intelligent are so
dense to the idea of experimental religion, what can we possibly expect of the rest?   This seems to be a fair interpretation of his words.

And yet knowing what we know now this was not strange
after all.   We expect educated men, the university men of
our time, to know a great many things which they do not
know.   Indeed the "practical" man of the world has had much
occasion for amusement at the innocence and ignorance of
really highly cultivated men when they have given themselves to the reformation of the practical ills of society.   Experience has changed it considerably, but the early efforts of

the university men of this country to reform politics were
very ridiculous, no matter how well they intended. The
academic habit once acquired is very strong and not easily
thrown off. It is well known that Charles Sumner ridiculed
in the United States Senate the English of Mr. Lincoln's
messages to Congress. It was certainly poor taste and worse
manners to add to Mr. Lincoln's troubles in this petty way,
but Sumner was simply following out the academic habit
from which he could not extricate himself. So the efforts of
educated men in the political contests since the war were
marked by an uneasiness about details which often obscured
the main principle. It became the habit among the lower
strata of political workers to jeer at the efforts of the "literary fellers," and though many non-academic intelligent men
declined to join in the jeer they did share in the amusement.
One of the most cultivated governors of Massachusetts not
long since openly derided a young clergyman for speaking of
the voting body as the "electorate." And yet that is exactly
what the voting body is. But the distinguished governor and
Harvard overseer had learned, or thought he had learned,
what the young minister had not, that the term was too clas-
sical for the American political platform.

We are not surprised, then, that the scholastic habit was
strong enough with the distinguished Israelite to obscure the
experimental idea of religion. Nicodemus was but the type
of many of his class then and now. This country is full of
educated men who have no more definite ideas about the
Christian religion than if they were educated in China or
India. Each year there comes forth from the colleges a
mass of men who are absolutely ignorant of what was formerly considered a *sine qua non* of a liberal education,
namely, a thorough knowledge of the English Bible. The
quotation from the Bible by public men reveals this in a
degree that would be amusing if it were not so shocking.
An educated Chinaman who knew as little about the sacred
books of China as some of our alleged statesmen know about
the Bible would be an impossibility. In a recent assembly
in this city a Harvard professor made a speech to five hun-

dred men in which he alluded to the Bible twice and each time misquoted it. Even the scholastic habit ought to have rendered this impossible. But the man knew probably so little about experimental religion or had given to his personal religious life so little attention that the incentive to a ripe and religious scholasticism dominant everywhere else was absent when it came to the literature of religion. He was not scholastic about the Bible because he was not concerned about the religion of the Bible. Thus both religion as a personal matter and the university capacity in the matter of Biblical knowledge and instruction suffered. A university professor of this type is an intellectual misfit in modern life. No greater calamity is thinkable to the youth of our land than that they should attach to the religious ideas of such men the same importance that they do to their special branches of scientific knowledge.

But the university-bred population of this country is very small, some one says. True enough, but small as that fraction is of the whole, it has given the tone and direction to nine-tenths of the culture and thought life of the land. College breeding may not make a man a genius, but no man, or better, perhaps, few men can give four solid years to the habit of book life and book ideals without having certain tones of life and a certain power of penetration into the real essence of things ground into them. And Christianity, let it never be forgotten, is a book religion. The Bible is a book which requires the most careful and painstaking study for its complete understanding. One of the ideas that modern education has driven out forever is that any one can offhand understand and explain the Scriptures. We know better than that now. And while we do not believe in the Roman Catholic doctrine that there can be only one authoritative interpretative power, yet we do believe that the truth of God is not to be gained with that jaunty ease that some people affect in dealing with Bible knowledge. It is of the highest importance, then, that the university population shall receive training of a character which shall make the reenactment of the scene between Christ and Nicodemus impossible. We cannot afford in this country to have an educated class which is totally ignorant on the side of experimental religion. We cannot afford to have the educated youth of the country believe that all there is to Christianity is a scholastic belief in the gospel as a survival of the fittest in religion. We cannot submit to having the educated mind of this land nominally Christian while experimentally it is essentially pagan. And that so great a calamity does not come upon us, we need to demand of those who teach that to all their scholastic and scientific qualities they shall add that of the highest education of all, the knowledge of God in a personal Christian character and communion. Longfellow is said, while a member of the Harvard faculty, to have offered a resolution that none but Unitarians should be allowed to teach in that university. If the poet believed that Unitarianism was the only truth in religion he was logically right. If he had put in the place of the word "Unitarians" the word "Christians," he would not only have been right, but he would have met a necessity the lack of which Harvard has never fully weathered. Not even the fire and religious genius of Phillips Brooks has been able to bind up the wound which the religious looseness of other years has inflicted upon our college.

This opens up the question of the relation of Christianity to the colleges. I am quite aware that the scholastic ideal at once steps in with the statement that the true university presents all religions and lets a man "prove all things and hold fast that which is good." But there was never an application of the university ideal that was so full of blunder, to call it by no other name, than this. Does the department of history present the ideals of civilization prevailing in the fifteenth century as equal with those of the nineteenth and say, "Choose whichever you please"? Does the university say to the students who come to it, "Choose any kind of morality you please"? Would Harvard or any other college submit to the presence of a student who had the Mohammedan ideal of the relations of the sexes, knowing that to be his thought and practice? Why submit to a religious license and anarchy which would not be tolerated in fine arts or in geology? The professors in geology do not teach all things and then tell the students to pick out what suits them. They teach them what they believe to be true. They formulate definite ideas and expect the student in the absence of better ideas to accept them. In fact, in Germany students are in the habit of wandering around from university to university for just this reason. They seek to get the ideas for which each specialist is distinguished. And yet these same people, when Christian people want Christianity made the dominant force in the religious life of the college and expressed in some formal and definite way, talk about "narrowness" and "bigotry" and the rest of that habitual phraseology of scholastic non-religionists, and ask us if we wish to coerce the nineteenth-century mind in the matter of religion. Coerce it just as it is coerced in fine arts. Coerce it just as it is coerced in physics and chemistry. Coerce it just as it is coerced in geology and botany. The nineteenth-century mind in religion is just as much rooted in the history of religion and the Christianity of the nineteen centuries past as the geology or astronomy is. Nobody says to students, Decide for yourself whether you will accept the Ptolemaic or Copernican system. It says, You will accept the Copernican system or be a fool. On strictly scientific and academic grounds we demand of the university that it shall say, You will accept Christianity or be fools. If Christianity has not vindicated its supreme and singular authority to the academic mind by this time, then it is time we threw the so-called academic mind overboard and began at some other point.

It is this feeling which has given the impulse to Christian education in New England and elsewhere. In fact it is this impulse which has given to America the magnificent results springing from New England college life and training. Not a college here but was organized and endowed under the rule of the thought that its ultimate end would be the wider knowledge of the gospel and a greater glory of Christ. Without this belief the toil and the sacrifice and the patient heroism which as much as money builded these schools would never have been forthcoming. It was not a desire to produce learning in itself that made the college ideal in America. It was the desire to inculcate knowledge and develop learning as an adjunct to a higher type of Christianity and Christian service. No one should know this better than the men who assist in turning out of the colleges Bibleless coxcombs and educationally veneered obscurantists. If we have been betrayed in the past, we shall not be betrayed again. The twentieth century will see the Christian churches of this land insisting, with twentieth-century scientific enlightenment, upon religious instruction in the colleges of the land in a way which would be an astonishment to many of the *dilettante* triflers who are now the representatives of solid learning but with no religious experience and with no religious practices. The twentieth century will take its academic infidelity "straight," not under religious and semi-religious endowments perverted from the uses of their pious founders.

You will please note that by Christian education I do not mean education along sectarian lines, though I firmly believe that as between sectarian religious education and no religious education the sectarian type produces the best results. Both result in experimental isolation so far as the religious feeling is concerned. The one produces only one type, while the other produces nothing at all, which is also but a single type. I prefer the former on many grounds. But in urging that education shall be distinctively Christian, I mean to insist that the type and experience which shall guide the college men in their expanding intellectual life shall be in accord with the spirit of the New Testament. The man may call himself whatever he pleases. But his life and the spirit of his work shall be suggestive of the ideals and spirit of the New Testament. Surely this is not an exorbitant demand. But it is a demand. It is not a suggestion. It is not a plea. It is an imperative summons from the organic Christianity of the land as formulated in Christian churches and assemblies that the colleges of the land shall not undo in the academic years of our young men and women what we have laboriously built up in the adolescent years in the home. When we have taught them dependence upon God and habits of prayer, we do not want any one in authority at any college to tell our sons and daughters that God is merely a necessary idea to the completion of thought, and that prayer is merely a reflex kind of spiritual exercise. If they say anything, let them say what the New Testament says. If they want to quote experts on the subject, let them quote the great Expert of the religious life, namely, Jesus Christ. We insist that they have no business to give the young men their diluted notions when they may have the words of Jesus Christ.

You see now what I mean. I insist that the colleges on the matters pertaining to spiritual life shall give Jesus Christ the same place in the curriculum that they do to the highest expert in any other phase of human culture and growth. I want them to take Jesus Christ in matters of prayer and faith and hope and the service of God, just as they take Darwin or Haeckel or Pasteur or Koch or any other expert in their special functions. I object to the instruction of Huxley in spiritual life in exactly the same way as I would regard the New Testament as an absurd text-book in physics. I am perfectly willing when the teaching of Jesus can be superseded that it shall be superseded. Of course I do not expect that time ever to come. But until it does come I want the spiritual authority of Jesus Christ asserted as a part of the educational life just as much as the theories of scientists or the discoveries of explorers. If the words and life of Jesus Christ can demonstrate the hidden things of man's spiritual nature and destiny as the Roentgen ray can photograph substances through bodies hitherto supposed to be opaque, then I hold it to be absolutely logical, educationally and practically, that the one fact shall be taught equally with the other. Christ is entitled to the same collegiate recognition that Darwin is or any other scientific discoverer. I hold that education to be fatally defective which does not teach it. It is one-sided and fatally lacking in the culture and training of those primary instincts of the human race which make the most for happiness and peace in this world.

Such a place in the life and instruction of the college for

the gospel, that is, the history of Christ's life and that of his immediate disciples, will give to the youth in college some conception of the commanding importance of the subject and the power and authority of Christ over human life. If after such a presentation a man chooses to reject the gospel, well and good; that is his inalienable right as a free moral agent. But he should not be left in ignorance concerning what is in the opinion of the Christian thought of the ages the most important fact in all history. I am utterly unable to see how such instruction can in the slightest degree militate against the freest operations of human thought or in the slightest measure interfere with the best development of the world in any sense. Such a presentation of Christ has no bearing upon scientific discovery and can have none upon historical analysis. It is simply the most advanced knowledge of the spiritual life and the most finished presentation of the ethical life known to mankind. How absurd it would be to call that kind of a demand the "dead hand of ecclesiasticism" or any other term of opprobrium! On the contrary, it is the living hand of a genuine spiritual life and nature bearing the message of moral and spiritual greatness to the future world. The college is the place for it. The college is the most appropriate place for it. The college as furnishing the university type of religious life and culture is a cruel and miserable grotesque of humanity and growth without it. If the most commanding fact in the history of the world must be excluded from the college for fear of ecclesiasticism and arrested development, it is hard to see how these dangers will be avoided with that commanding fact left out.

But a larger result than a proper conception of the importance of Jesus Christ to the personal life will be attained if our colleges will meet their Christian opportunity and duty. This is the wider application of Christianity to the concerns of the world. It is beyond all question that much of the education as also much of the commerce of the world is conducted on principles totally at variance with the simplest elements of Christianity. Most of the great commercial enterprises that give type and direction to the world's life are in the hands of the college men. Once out in the world with these vast concerns demanding time and energy and strength for their pursuit, the engrafting of new social ideas or of new formulas for ethical procedure or new ideals of spiritual brotherhood for the race is not quite but almost impossible. If these captains of industry, the great corporation managers and others, are ever to get their hearts and minds trained, it must be during the college period. Afterward they are so wrapped up by their mercantile or speculative obligations that they can rarely be reached for the higher life of the world. Sometimes, rarely, their money can be reached, but the men scarcely ever. This adds to the imperious demand that they shall be properly trained during that period when the mind and heart are still plastic to nobler ambitions, and Christian conceptions of life and enterprise can be planted in the mind. More and more the higher education is to be mingled and allied with the world's commercial and industrial development. For this reason, if for no other, the men who make that relation must be given with positiveness and with New Testament power the Christian conception of the world. Least of all should men, educated men, men highly organized in their nervous and intellectual life, be left to caprice in the matter of religious instruction. These are the men who need to be carefully taught, for they are to be the teachers of others. More than this, they are to be the examples and models for others. Unchristian standards in them mean unchristian standards for the world. Let us never lose sight of this momentous truth.

The religion of the university and the college, therefore, is more than a personal or denominational concern. It is not a question of sectarian interest or aggrandizement. It is a question of the continuance of the knowledge of Christianity in the most cultured circles of our civilization. The danger to Christian institutions comes less from the lower and more ignorant members of society than from the so-called higher and more intelligent. It is from these that we expect the kind of thinking that sees further than the immediate result. When an ignorant man breaks the sanctity of the Lord's day, the danger is comparatively limited, because his example and influence are limited. But when a man of influence does these things, much more is involved. Now Sunday festivities of one kind and another are notably increasing among these more favored classes. The usual excuses of hard labor during six days of the week do not obtain with them. It is not a case of confinement and lack of fresh air. It is a matter of forgetfulness of the sacred obligations of the day and the dangers which are involved in breaking down the sanctities of the day upon the maintenance of which our civilization rests. Many of these people have no knowledge of what the Christian claim for the Sabbath day is. They have never been taught what an involved matter violation of the Sabbath is. In fact, few of them can be said in any proper sense to have any Christian knowledge whatever. The reason is that the college through which many of them passed did not give it, and it ought to have given it. The failure to give it has given us a cultivated paganism which has in it the seeds of social disruption and national dissolution. In a similar way these same people lose the sense of personal obligation by losing their personality in the great corporations of which they often form a part. What they would not think of doing personally they suffer the corporations in which they have invested their money to do in their behalf. Christian training on the persistence of personal obligation wherever the personal ability extends, along New Testament lines, would make this contradiction impossible. The college should teach it.

The religion of a nation irresistibly follows the religion of its educated men, and the type of religion in the universities will undoubtedly be the prevailing type of the land. There is no escape from this result. The educated man has such greater advantages and can present his cause with such greater resources of argument and illustration by the appeal to reason, imagination and history, that it is inevitable that what the educated classes of the nation decree will ultimately come to pass. It may take time and there will be the usual rebellion, parleying, and then surrender by those who are unable to cope with them except in the matter of numbers.

It is therefore of the greatest Christian interest that the college shall be kept the citadel of Christian thought and Christian life; that the knowledge of the gospel, both intellectually and by experience, shall be kept constantly active and diffusive. Therefore we must have Christ preached in the university. We must make the university religion the religion of the New Testament. We must not permit a race of Nicodemuses to come forth to stand aghast or incredulous before the facts of revealed and experimental religion and say with bated breath, "How can these things be?" On the contrary, we must bring out of the collegiate cloister a class of men who, being rich in the spiritual knowledge of Jesus Christ, and whose well-furnished intellects filled with the discipline and information gleaned from all the fields of science and history, shall add to the moral and spiritual capital of the world what they add to the mental wealth of the world. We must have the religious life of the nation and the world enriched as well as the commercial and intellectual life. The college is the natural feeder of all. There is at present great clamor because the education of the land does not seem to fit men for the commercial needs of the nation. But there is a more important need than this. It is that the college shall fit for the moral needs of the nation. The university is in its inception and theory among us an institution for the nurture and culture of the highest possible life. The highest possible life is the life of Christ.

TEACHERS AND MORALS

JOHN iii. 2.

THE offices of which Jesus Christ is the highest exemplification as bearing on the rational and spiritual development of man are many and various. He is the supreme example of spiritual power; he is the finest ideal of mental poise; he is the truest pattern of sane human feeling; he is the most universal manifestation of complete and symmetrical development; he is the most suggestive illustration of the proper relations of liberty and law; he is the most inspiring demonstration of quietude under martyrdom; he is the only example of perfect self-sacrifice known in the history of human life.

Those who were nearest to him saw these things most clearly. Succeeding ages have interpreted him with probably larger light and with a wider and more universal application of the truths he taught, but in general our knowledge has come out of the consciousness of his contemporaries. It was their insight and penetration that preserved for us the record of his words and works. It was their zeal which perpetuated them in the Christian Church. It was their readiness to meet the ethical and spiritual demands which he made upon them that has given to us the outlines at least of his sublime and incomparable life. They said, and they said with the appropriateness of witnesses of his wonderful power and life-interpreting skill, "Rabbi, we know that thou art a teacher come from God." The world has indorsed that judgment ever since.

The special word, however, upon which I wish at this time to lay the stress of this discourse is the word "teacher." Whatever else Christ was or was not, there is no title more descriptive of his mission to man than this. And from his example the teaching office has acquired for Christian civilization an importance which is almost unequaled in that civilization. There is probably no person in the whole modern social structure who plays so large a part in the social and rational development of the race as the teacher. His importance is determined of course considerably by the nature of his surroundings and the cooperation and state of intelligence in the community. But as in the earliest times, so now, the teacher is a person of the highest importance to the community.

Both the Church and the State have taken peculiar cognizance of this fact. The Church has felt his importance so much that to a very large degree it has felt the necessity of controlling both his training and his selection for a particular post. This has survived into our own times and is justified very largely, as I shall show later, by many of the prevailing ideas of the teacher's office. The State has recognized it by making certain standards to which he must conform before he can be allowed in the work of public instruction. To further secure this it builds schools specially designed to fit teachers for their work.

The reason why this importance has been attached to the teaching office — and let me say in passing, as civilization advances there will be still greater care exercised in the training and selection of teachers — has been and still is that the teacher can almost make or unmake the life of the student whom he has in charge. He can instil right or wrong ideas. He can make high or low standards of life. He can teach a high or a low morality. And, what is of infinitely more importance, he can illustrate these, whether he teaches them or not. He can illustrate a high moral feeling or a low one. He can show a cultivated symmetrical nature or an angular and half-developed one. And from the earliest times, even from the remotest periods of pre-Christian education, this peculiar union of precept and example bound up in the personality of the instructor has been watched with special anxiety and solicitude.

Next to the parent and, when sustained and allied to the

enormous power and wealth of the State often more than the parent, the teacher is the most powerful personage in society. It is therefore of greatest importance to all who are interested in right living and high ideals, who wish certain aims and types of life and standards of behavior impressed upon their children and dependents, that they know to whom this task is committed. Life is literally at stake. No parent can compete in these days with the well-equipped instructor who, with all the modern appliances of knowledge-getting and knowledge-dissemination, takes the lad in hand. During the formative period of life the teacher has actual charge of the child or youth more hours than the parent. He has that charge without the parental responsibility and the parental personal anxiety. That is, according to the theory of some he has, but that is a point to be discussed.

As to the whole question of education, after all, what is it other than the question of how we shall live? And in this connection I cannot do better than to quote a memorable passage from Herbert Spencer's essay on Education. He says: "How to live? — that is the essential question for us. Not how to live in the mere material sense only, but in the widest sense. The general problem which comprehends every special problem is — the right ruling of conduct in all directions under all circumstances. In what way to treat the body; in what way to treat the mind; in what way to manage our affairs; in what way to bring up a family; in what way to behave as a citizen; in what way to utilize all those sources of happiness which nature supplies — how to use all our faculties to the greatest advantage to ourselves and others — how to live completely? And this being the great thing needful for us to learn is by consequence the great thing which education has to teach. To prepare us for complete living is the function which education has to discharge; and the only rational mode of judging of any educational course is to judge in what degree it discharges such a function."

That is the best statement of the aim of education that I am acquainted with. I think it comprehensive enough and inclusive enough to embrace the most liberal and the most conservative views of the subject. It is broad enough to include all religious instruction, and it is wide enough to comprehend all knowledge of every description. Life is the standard of judgment. How to live is the aim not merely of education and religion, but of life itself. It is life to learn how to live. That reaches out into immortality.

But all apparently do not accept this standard notwithstanding that it comes from the source that it does. You observe that a large, indeed the largest, part of the function of education as here described is moral. "Right ruling of conduct," that is a matter of morals. "To treat" the mind or the body is a matter of morals. "To bring up" a family is a matter inseparably connected with morals. "To behave" as a citizen is a moral view of citizenship. Such expressions as "how to use all our faculties to the greatest advantage to ourselves and others" and "to live completely" have a sound which suggests the New Testament very strongly. You observe that the moral element in instruction is here so regnant that strip it out of this definition and there would be little else left.

Now of course there is such a thing as teaching morality. But as stated, the teaching is more in the teacher than in the instruction. What the teacher *is*, is of infinitely more and greater significance than what the teacher teaches. I fear that the modern ideas of education have tended very largely to obscure this fact. After all, the personality of the teacher is the important thing. Jesus Christ as a moralist would have been classified with Seneca, Cicero, Socrates, and other moralists. Jesus Christ as the living illustration of every truth he proclaimed is far more eloquent than the New Testament possibly can be. No eulogy of Christ can compare with Christ himself. No statement of the majesty of his teaching can match the unrivaled and penetrative power of his example.

Morals and the teacher are therefore so inseparably allied that their relation should be a matter of careful and constant scrutiny. The morals of the instructor and the extent to which they are living realities instead of barren theories should be the elementary basis of selection. I do not mean by this that we should prefer a " good " ignorant teacher to one who is not "good " but skilled in the technique of his profession. I mean that neither should be chosen. I mean that we can live without grammar, without chemistry, or without history. We cannot live without the moral inspirations and the moral restraints which make man capable of civilization and spiritual growth. Character first and then capability. Not character without capability. But by no means capability without character.

I referred a moment ago to the feeling on the part of many of the religious people of the community that the prevalence of opinions contrary to this doctrine justified the building and endowing and increasing of the agencies of instruction under religious or denominational auspices and control. Is it not a justifiable opinion when educational leaders are asserting that the teacher has no responsibility for the morals of the student? The old doctrine used to be that the teacher stood *in loco parentis*. When people hear teachers say, as if by authority, that they have no responsibilities corresponding to the ideal of education which I have just quoted from Herbert Spencer, who certainly will not be supposed a reactionary authority on the subject, is it strange that we hear talk about " godless " and "immoral" schools?

The teacher is therefore in the nature of his calling a moralist of the broadest and most inclusive type. He cannot separate himself from those duties which involve thought on the moral aspects of things if he continues in his office as a teacher. Dealing with life, he must show that whatsoever things are pure or lovely or of good report are of the first importance in the wise ordering of life. He must give those things the first place in his own life. " Chemistry not character is my business," said an instructor to me once. Character *in* chemistry is what he ought to have said.

The doctrine that the teacher's personality is more than his instruction is important enough to call for some further elaboration. And this can best be done by bringing to mind certain noteworthy examples which clearly illustrate the point.

I may say that America is peculiarly rich in such illustrations because the history of education in America up to this time has been, for so large a part of it, the struggle to give light and knowledge under adverse conditions. No compact and well-developed public sentiment aided the pioneers of education in our land, unless we except Eastern Massachusetts and possibly Connecticut, and even in these sections, though the sentiment was strong, the appliances were crude. But even here from the beginning the personality of the great teachers was the most impressive thing in the educational life.

My thought is rather to take examples familiar and near at hand. And first of all I wish to cite that of Mark Hopkins, the great president of Williams College. It would be difficult to mark the limits of the influence of that wonderful man. Yet his greatness lies not in the literature which he produced. Dr. Hopkins' books, while suggestive and always showing that clear intelligence which distinguished their author, are not of an epoch-making character. But there was not a student in all the years of that great career, who came under the power of that personality, who did not carry away a life-impression. A roster of the men who would be glad to admit the domination of Dr. Hopkins' mind over their own during the character-forming and mind-making period of their lives would include a very large per centum of the most distinguished names in the cultural life of New England to-day and for a generation past. But the impression was not merely nor primarily mental, though it was an intellectual touch. It was moral. It was spiritual. It was full of the suggestion of the eternal and abiding. Mark Hopkins may fairly be called an incarnation of the intellectual life completely spiritualized.

Another great teacher, and yet wholly unlike the one I have just named, was President James H. Fairchild of Oberlin College. Many of you are familiar with the wonderful history of that unique institution. Of all the chapters of college and community-building in this country the history of Oberlin is in some respects the most picturesque and striking. It was a radical community from center to circumference. It was the most advanced community as a community, on the side of human and moral development, in the early days of its history, that there was in the whole land. It was the first college to admit women, and did it from the beginning. That was a long time ago, in 1833, when such a step in New England would have involved a kind of revolution in social and educational life. Even now in 1897 Harvard University is willing to give women only its *seal*. Besides this, Oberlin was radical in politics. It was as hot a hot-bed of abolitionism as one can imagine. Think of a whole town of Phillipses and Garrisons and you get the idea. Some of this radicalism was not of the most wholesome kind, but it was thorough. Into this community came President Fairchild as a youth from the farm, took his course, became tutor, instructor, professor and president. For twenty-seven years he filled the latter office. In all that period he made not a single false step, uttered no public word that was not based in sound and defensible logic, led the college through its radicalism to conservative and careful thought and administration befitting the changing times, and did at the close of his life the most radical thing in all of it, when he insisted on resigning because he was seventy years of age, over the united energetic and loving protest of faculty, alumni and community. He has not been a prolific writer. He has not been heralded far and wide as a distinguished educator, even as these things are done nowadays. But the influence of that calm, clear, morally balanced man has gone round the earth over and over again in the men who came under the spell of his personality and moral power. It was not a literary influence. It was not an intellectual influence. It was both but it was more. It was the power of a man, of whom his students could say with propriety and after his own great Exemplar and Master, " Thou, too, art a teacher come from God ! "

What these men have done in their respective stations has in a less extended sphere been done in many a community in this land. In every high school and academy, in every grammar school and seminary, there is usually one, often more, but at least one such teacher who is remembered with gratitude and interest by every student whom he touches. The man is the important thing. It may be chemistry or geography, it may be history or geometry that he teaches. But back of all these there is the mind and the character of the man who after all is greater than his theme.

It is a singular fact that when the community becomes convinced of the character of a man, what he does becomes of comparatively little interest in itself. Let a teacher acquire the confidence of his school and the community where he is located, and his methods and his point of view are not a subject of much trouble. His discipline will be sustained even when not understood. All the presumptions will be in his favor and the community will sustain him until it distrusts him. But that is the loss of the man himself, not the mere condemnation of his proceedings. This again is because the man is greater than his calling.

What Christ as a teacher did was to impress men that he spoke for and by the authority of God. May not all teachers aspire to the same office though in a lesser degree? Why should not every student be able to say of his teacher what Nicodemus said to Jesus on that memorable night? That judgment was based upon the signs which Jesus did and possibly this may have reference in a considerable measure to the demonstrations on the part of Christ of supernatural power. But surely these are not necessary. If there had been no such manifestations would not that life coming to us as it does have proved by the moral power which it exercises that it was from God? And did not Christ promise his disciples that they should do greater works than his own because he went to the Father?

How wonderfully that promise has been fulfilled! By the authority and under the inspiration of Jesus Christ what vast clouds of ignorance have been lifted from the world! Into what darkness have not the teachers of the gospel gone for the love of Christ! What knowledge have they not spread over the earth, and how they have bound in ties of love and communion the most distant nations of the earth! Teachers sent from God! Surely they have been, and the promise of

God has followed them every step of the entire journey. Where the darkness has been densest there they have caused the light to shine most brightly.

But knowledge shall pass away. The world by wisdom knew not God. It became vain in its imaginings, and its foolish heart was darkened. It thought knowledge was a desirable thing for its own sake. It thought that the arts and the sciences were of more account than the brain which comprehends and arranges them. Professing themselves wise they became fools and changed the glory of the incorruptible God for the likeness of corruptible man and four-footed beasts and creeping things. Love is greater than knowledge. Character is mightier than talents. Moral power is the seat of authority in life. To know is important that we may know how to live, but for life living is the best text-book. Happy and blest the teacher who seeks first in the heart of the student that imperial scepter of the soul of man, the moral source of service.

But after all the very best instructor in the world is nothing without students. The teacher who is most learned in anything, even if it be the art and manner of living, is an isolated and comparatively useless being unless there are those who seek to make his knowledge their own and to make the standards which are exceptional in him common property. The students are also a part of the teacher. Indeed they are the completing part of his function, as the capital completes the column. Teacher and student form, so to speak, the solution of human living and progressive development.

There is a reciprocal relation between the mind that is seeking knowledge and that which is conveying it which is of the highest importance to both. It is not, however, merely the relation of capacity for understanding the terms employed and the instruction offered. It is a relation of personalities joined by common interest and aim. It is a relation born out of a moral impulse to perfect the nature and enrich the life for service. In consequence, at the very bottom the first relation of student and teacher even on the intellectual side is one profoundly saturated with moral meaning.

This is specially true of the gospel which Jesus came to teach. The thing which the people around him noted was that he spake as one having authority and not as the scribes. The truths themselves were important enough, but the striking thing was that he *was* the Truth. Christ was anxious lest men should ally his power with something temporal and human about himself. For this reason he was ever reminding his auditors that it was not himself but the Father that was the effective agent of his words and works. That meant, I suppose, that he wished them to observe and dwell upon the eternal and infinite aspects of his mission. In like manner every wise teacher will seek to create the same impression. Faith in the mediate agent will ultimately prove disappointing because he is only a secondary source of knowledge and power. The learner should be directed to the unchanging sources of truth and power.

In Christ as a teacher this consciousness of identity with the Eternal was the preeminent element of his method. " I and the Father are one." No one will ever be able to say that with the confidence and the consciousness of its truthfulness and confirm it in life as did Christ. But every man who sees about him less favored sons of the earth and endeavors to teach them in the ways of life, and every instructor who is called by professional service to give the minds of young people their direction and bent should be able to say of the mind and purpose of Christ, " I and the Master are one." He should be able to rest his authority as a teacher upon those fundamental sources of light and strength in life which are as unchanging as the law of gravity.

Moral power in the teacher is usually allied in method with four things, — moral clearness, moral directness, moral suggestiveness, and moral unity. Search through the discourses of Christ and you cannot find a single obscure note. All is as clear as day. Duty is read in unmistakable terms. It was this which brought his life so swiftly to its tragic close. He presented the moral issues of life, death and immortality with unrelenting clearness. Sin was labeled sin in large letters. Hypocrisy, formalism, vanity and pride were appropriately denominated. There was no veiling his meaning under obscure paraphrases. If there is ever to be moral power in the world it must be done in a similar way by the leaders of opinion and the instructors of the young.

The Bible is the most powerful book in the world because it has the largest number of things in it which can be directly applied to life. What the Bible is to literature Christ is to humanity. He touches life with direct and non-mediate energy. Moral power of the first order comes in no other way. Duty done suggests duty still to be done. Mankind is ever asking when it is still learning. Humanity is an unending mine out of which gold for eternity is to be brought. Each new find reveals the larger possibilities yet to come. Suggestiveness is peculiarly present in every effort that touches the moral nature of man. So, too, the moral life is a unit wherever found. Truth is one, not many, whether in science, in art, in literature, or in religion. All when they are true are true as related to life. And where life is there is something that must be dealt with as actual and real.

Every disciple of Christ is a teacher by the very terms of his discipleship. Taught himself in the good tidings of the gospel he must go forth to teach others also. His instruction must be after the model of the teacher who by his contemporaries, by history, by experience and by the consensus of the judgment of mankind has been a teacher come from God. He came as teacher from God that he might lead men and teach them the way to God. For the consummation of his task every man of good-will and with a consciousness of latent immortality will rejoice to lend a helpful and encouraging hand.

EDUCATION AND LIFE

DANIEL xii. 3.

NEXT to the love of liberty it may truthfully be said there is no idea to which the American people are so fondly attached as the idea that a liberal education is one of the best things that can come to any man. It is this idea which has made the wonderful faith in our public school system endure, even when it was not producing results which warranted so confident an expectation. It is not much of an exaggeration to say that Americans very largely rely upon the public schools to keep the nation true to the original doctrines upon which it was founded.

Nay, they have even gone further in their idolatry of education as a saving factor in life. They have for the most part heaped upon the public school functions which properly never belonged to it. Parental discipline is now generally the discipline which the parent administers by proxy through the school-teacher. The cultivation of manners, instruction in habits of obedience and patience as human qualities are taught more in the schools to-day than they are in the homes, as many believe. The fact that the school commands thus and so is usually sufficient to make the parent satisfied that it is for the best without any further thought on his part.

The business of civilizing the young has been given over to the schools. Uncouthness and gruffness must be unlearned, not at home and through the kindly influences and examples of the home, but from the training and mutual restraints which the school imposes. Public school education is openly advocated on the ground that it will smooth off the rough edges and make the boy a better member of society and, in short, civilize the youth so that he will not become absolutely intolcrable. It is true that the edges are thus worn off. But they are not worn off the boys alone. They are worn off the nervous organization of the teachers in the schools as well.

No argument is therefore needed to convince any one of the value of a liberal education. Perhaps there may be some doubt as to the attachment to a "liberal" education, but it is certainly true that common school education is a cause that needs not to be argued since it is championed by every one. But what of the education thus gained and the estimate of education when pushed to its logical extremity?

Now if educating a man is a useful thing, then he ought by reason of that education to be something different in the social body than he would have been had he been left without it. Has our idolatry of education in general, and common school education in particular, made us ready to accept the logical results of such processes when they are applied to life? Indeed, has education itself realized for us what we have been supposing was inseparably connected with it?

There is no fairer test of the value and power of education than the political life of a nation. Here there is an open field where the whole people are in active participation and where the ideas that control them may be seen in actual operation. The home perhaps is a little fairer, but obviously it would be impossible to get the data from the various homes upon which a sound argument could be based. But with politics it is different. Here everything is in plain sight.

Assuming now that we are so firmly rooted in our conviction that education is a good thing as fitting a man for life, what part have educated men played in the nation's life, and what part do they take in the political situation to-day? We may say, I think, that every important idea in our governmental policies since its foundation has been the product of a broadly educated mind. So much is probably true. But what of the carrying out of those ideas?

Looking over the country, there is no department where comprehensive training and careful mental discipline would naturally seem to be more needful than in the administration of the government. But what are the facts? It would not be true to assert that the mass of our legislators are illiterate persons. It would be monstrously false, however, to say that they were persons of education. The men of highest intelligence, of broadest training, of most liberal cultivation and widest knowledge, are no more in touch with the mainsprings of the American government than if they lived in Timbuctoo. On the contrary, in the metropolitan city of the continent a few years ago, a majority of the public officials were men with criminal records. Within the year past a leading newspaper of that city gave it as a reason for congratulation that the reform administration had brought it about *that there were no criminals holding conspicuous public places this year.*

This is the condition of the relation of education and government in our largest city. If we step over into the capital, we are not comforted with a much better state of things. With the highest and most cultivated public sentiment in the country vainly appealing in behalf of the arbitration treaty with Great Britain, that document was rejected after being indorsed by two presidents and commended as the longest step onward in international civilization this century had seen. In the meantime belligerent resolutions and Sugar Trust gambling furnish the chief characteristics of the upper branch of Congress.

Now where lies the trouble? These men are the government *pro tempore* because the people have made them such. Did the people deliberately reject the counsel of the educated, and did the people deliberately choose criminals for their rulers? Something may be gained if we can find out what causes these things. With one breath we shout our adulation of education and with the next we cheer and vote into office men who cannot be suspected of having had the slightest knowledge of it. Why is this?

The view of education which prevails is one reason, and the habits of the educated in accordance with that view is another. Let us see what is the prevailing view of the real value and uses of a liberal education. Ask any man who meets you why it is a good thing to have an education, and he will answer at once without the slightest hesitation that it is because it gives an enormous advantage in the race of life. You will get along better. You will have more money. You will live more comfortably. Education is a great tool for fortune-building.

Now see how the view works. The moment a man finds that by reason of his education he has an advantage over his less favored fellows, what does he do with that finely trained mind? He immediately sets to work to bind and enslave them to the uses to which he wishes to put them. Instead of helping them develop themselves he helps them to develop him. He uses the knowledge that he has gained to organize trusts, create monopolies, pack caucuses, subsidize legislatures, and finally, if he has any yearning in that direction, he buys a seat in the United States Senate.

Is it any wonder that the people have no affiliation with the educated classes in political action? It is only a few years ago that educated men striving for a great reform were contemptuously dubbed "silk stockings" and openly jeered at because of the high character of the principles they advocated. But they were themselves to blame in no small degree. They were the people who never participated in political struggles and scorned to make the acquaintance of the wage-workers in the common sympathies of the political rally.

Surely education is entitled to little respect if this is to be the result. People need not be educated if the use they make of their advantage is to destroy the sympathies that bind man to man, and jeer where they should cheer those outbursts of feeling and faith which lie dormant in every man's mind ready to be called to the surface when a sincere and truthful voice speaks.

The process I have described here at its culmination begins, however, a long distance from that point. It begins even in the public schools. Many a grammar school or high school graduate will go home from his graduation exercises this month and pity in his youthful swelled head the humble father and mother who brought him into the world and who have paid all his bills to make his success possible. More than one young man will go home with his bachelor of arts degree in his pocket and patronize the village folk where his childhood was spent. He will sneer at the grammar he once used himself and will smile contemptuously at the open demonstrations of kindly interest and regard which the young people indulge in, which far be it from his dignity to manifest.

The highest education of course is not the companion of snobbery. But education and snobbery have gone hand in hand so often that common people must be made to feel that there is sincerity in the education before they will give it the implicit confidence which they give to homespun integrity. Let every youth remember that. Education should not be the veneer of an arrogant self-seeker. It should be the garment of wisdom to make a man more human and brotherly, not less so.

But if education is not a money-making tool, neither is it a toy for luxurious idleness. Getting knowledge and the ability to know and see things is not for the purpose of merely having the resources with which to pass away spare time. Mere pursuit of knowledge with no practical aim in sight and no end to be achieved is not an occupation worthy of a man. I have no quarrel with the speculators who are digging deep in philosophic caves for some gold the world has need of. But no one can have patience with people who are forever learning and never adding to the sum of human happiness and joy as the result of their labor.

The relation of education and life is a far more serious matter than these things which I have outlined. And I would not have you get the impression that all of the educated have perverted their educational advantages. There is a large part of the educated class in our country which tries sincerely to employ its culture and training for the highest good of all. They try to instruct the ignorant. They try to defend the weak. They protect those who are unable to protect themselves. They make innumerable sacrifices for the common good. But many of these have just the experience which John Wesley had at Oxford. His idea is born in a university, but it has to leave the university to get its growth and development.

An education should make him who receives it first of all more human. It should ally him to all that interests humanity. It should fit him to be the companion not of the cultivated alone but even more of the uncultivated and the ignorant. Knowing better than the ignorant themselves what is moving them, he should address himself to the real life and sympathies with which his superior knowledge has made him familiar. Grammar and pronunciation are important, but they are not the vital necessities of life. A man may be a good citizen and a worthy father and a thoroughly useful man without ever having heard of the Odyssey or the Æneid.

It is at this point that modern education has signally failed. It has been a point of departure from humanity rather than a step toward a larger one. It has been the point from which a man has often wandered farther and farther from his ancestral home and become more and more strange to those who knew him in the days gone by. No such education really meets the uses to which a well-trained mind should be put above all things. It was the characteristic of Jesus Christ, gifted with superior knowledge, superior sympathies, and a superior destiny above all other human beings that he remained in closest touch with them all. The learned members of the Sanhedrin and the outcast woman alike felt the power of his abundant human sympathy and life. Nothing that breaks the continuity of the healthy associations and memories of life can truly minister to the progress of our race.

There is no better illustration of what I have just said than the manner in which the progress of thought has been brought about in the Church of Christ. Fostering education as the Church always has, she has nevertheless received the truths which her own offspring have discovered with a slowness that often seems very discouraging to real lovers of truth. But the reason has been plain. Many scholars have been willing to break utterly with all past tradition and feeling and practice and have been so sure that the new was not only true but all the truth, that the common heart, which knows that no isolated fact or experience can invalidate what the years have proved, has preferred to limp along in semi-darkness rather than be shocked to death by the electricity of immature revolution. And the common heart was right.

A true education keeps close to humanity. A truly educated man, though gifted with the insight which mental discipline and extensive knowledge necessarily bring to him who has them, remembers, nevertheless, that he must be a man among men and not allow the healthy associations of humanity to be broken in his life. He must not seek to get away from the ignorant. On the contrary he must not let them get away from him. They need him. But he needs them, too. It is the teachers that shine above the brightness of the firmament. Where they are he must be. With great patience he must instruct those that are their own worst enemies. He must be patient with the most difficult thing in this world to endure, the self-confidence of ignorance.

Surely the deformity of men confident in their ignorance presents a task which should appeal to the best-trained man in the world. Jesus once said to his disciples, Blessed are your eyes for they see. So we may say, Blessed is the man who can see in the vast clouds of ignorance the signal for duty and proceed to a vigorous attack upon it, rather than a discouragement that makes him seek the cloisters of selfish enjoyment amid congenial associations. It is a poor exchange, the world for the private club.

The education whose characteristic note is a jeer is like the patriotism whose chief expression is boasting. Neither of them ring true and both are probably hollow and false. The business of the man who has had advantages in life is to demonstrate that they make him more loyal to all good and true things and make him more capably a servant of the interests in which all mankind have a part. Giving him a primacy it should remind him all the more that being the chief of all he is the servant of all. Life being itself a trust, education and knowledge only make it a sublimer one.

But while there are and probably always will be those who show the unloveliness of the highly educated mind, ignorance and mediocrity have also their duty, for education carries with it some rights as well as obligations. On a matter of which a man has no personal knowledge and is not competent from training or experience to speak, he is bound to listen with deference and respect to those more qualified than he when they offer the results of their investigations. We are sometimes in our self-satisfaction likely to let profound matters from competent lips fall upon unheeding ears, as the Jews sneeringly asked, Can any good thing come out of Nazareth?

The scholar, the man of books, may not know a great many things that men of action know. He may make ludicrous mistakes about the simplest things. But he is not to be judged by these alone. He is to be sought for what he knows, not for what he does not know. But the secret of his education lies in the fact that, not knowing, he has the discipline which enables him to find out and be taught. That is the supreme test of a really educated man. If he can be taught, as long as it is true of him that he is willing to learn, he is exhibiting the best fruit of a trained mind. Education stops when the mind refuses further light.

But, after all, the purpose of liberal training in science and the arts is ministry. A man learns a language that he may more perfectly communicate with his fellow men. The extent of his association and fellowship with them is determined by his ability to communicate with them on a common platform. He must serve them to the extent of knowing their tongue before he can have dealings with them. So a man makes the most of his own mind that he may more perfectly understand the operations of the minds of his fellow men.

Formerly when a man was obstinate or rude in a discussion the matter was settled by an appeal to blows. Now we appeal to his mind. If his mind does not understand the nature of the thing discussed, we do not fight about it. We explain what we are trying to accomplish. That makes us minister to his ignorance. Incidentally it stops warfare and bloodshed. It also saves money and time and trouble. Ministry is thus found to be profitable as well as godly.

It is not true that enlightenment will solve the world's woes. But it is true that a large part of the troubles of life will disappear before a wider knowledge and a broader education. Education will not of itself stop sinning, but it will prevent sin disguising itself as anything but sin. It will be a great advance when we have rightly named all things which cause us trouble and misery in life. A moral classification which was true and universally accepted would help us greatly toward the kingdom of God.

But while there are so many different versions of life and life's purpose, the mission of the educated and the educating is a very patent one. It is to minister to all men's needs in the most charitable and helpful fashion that circumstances render possible. Education is for men, not men for education. The logic of that fact demands that where the man can be reached is the place where the educated man should be found to help and to advance him.

There is imminent danger that an age which lays such enormous stress on knowledge as ours does will fail to give due weight to the moral aspects of education and make needless compromises in surrendering the moral to the intellectual aspects of education. I am not in sympathy with those who talk about the public schools as godless. I do not believe that to be a true statement of fact. But I do wish to say that it is an insane idea of education which leaves out the training of the moral nature and ignores the spiritual movements which are the choicest possessions of the mind.

I affirm as my serious opinion that an atheist is an unfit man to teach anywhere. I believe that a teacher who does not honor the Christian civilization of our day is an unsafe guide to the young. I say without hesitation that a teacher who does not know the Bible familiarly is as incapable of being an instructor in a Christian country as a wild Indian to be the rector of a German university. He may have his own views about religion in its denominational aspect. Personally I do not want any but a Christian man or woman ever to teach my children. But a person in a literary calling who does not know the Bible cannot know the undercurrents of a Christian civilization and is, therefore, *ipso facto* incompetent. Such people may play with mud babies if they want to. They should not be intrusted with the plastic minds of immortal souls.

Let me here take a moment to enforce again a very familiar doctrine. It is of the extreme value of the Bible as a factor in education, and that not merely moral, but intellectual as well. There is no book in this world which has so entered into human thought as the Bible. There is no book which has become so related to all literature as the Bible. Thought and life, therefore, as these have affected civilization and cultural progress, cannot be understood apart from the Bible. It has educated more men than all the universities in Christendom put together. It has inspired more poetry, has made more history, and given rise to greater and more far-reaching revolutions than all other books put together. No man can claim to be educated who does not know the Bible. And many a man is educated who knows little else.

Christian people should make a stronger stand than they are making for the moral education of the young. They need to begin it by making themselves more fit to carry on the work in the Christian homes of the land. Let us not surrender to the doctrine that non-sectarian education is non-religious education. Let us not assent to the stupid notion that to insist upon the culture of the moral and spiritual nature is to invade the rights of the sectarian bigot.

But the place for such education is primarily in the home and by the parents. The most that can justly be required of the school is that it shall cooperate with the home in enforcing what has there been taught and exemplified. At its best the school can but mold the material which comes to it. Its quality is determined by other and deeper influences. But we have the right to demand that no irreligious command-

ment-breaking, half-trained instructor with an atrophied moral
sense shall be given charge of the work even of cooperating
with us.   People do not have their watches repaired with
sledge-hammers.   Neither do we want moral neutrals med-
dling with our children.

The text — which, by the way, is the one which in its Latin
form is inscribed on the tympanum of Sanders Theatre at
Harvard University — closes by linking the teachers which
shine above the brightness of the firmament with those that
turn many to righteousness as if the latter were merely descriptive of the former.   Be that as it may, the true teacher
is he that turns many to righteousness and make righteousness the corner-stone of his instruction.   Of him as of the
Great Teacher it should be said, even if in a lesser degree
than of his great Example, " We know that thou art a teacher
come from God."

The function of a genuine education is to make a man all
that it is possible to make out of him.   It is not to take a
commonplace mind and endow it with the qualities of a
genius.   It is not to produce people who can startle us with
the vastness of their learning or the greatness of their skill.
It is to make men more manly and women more womanly,
and to so develop all the resources of the mind as to make it
happiness for both to serve the generation with gladness and
unselfishness.   And the education which does not make a
man truer and more faithful in the great moral duties of life
is essentially a false one.

There has never been an appreciable lack in the world of
bright men and women.   There always has been a feeling
that we could with profit increase the number of good men.
Goodness wrought out in godly character acceptable to God
and helpful to fellow men is the great end toward which all
efforts of men should tend.   Education has been one of the
best allies the moral forces of the world have had in times
past.   The great powers of darkness have always been
confederate with the hosts of ignorance.   Righteousness
and knowledge have ever been companions in human development.

There are men among us who can still remember the crude processes of the photography of fifty years ago. Many a home has its old daguerreotype, that elementary reproductive process. From these pictures on tin to the instantaneous flashlight picture of to-day is a long advance. But the purpose has been the same throughout. It was to make a faithful picture and an exact reproduction. So in the same measure all the efforts at self-realization on the part of man have been but for the purpose of bringing out into finer outline the image of God in man. We have made great advances in the processes. Let us not lose sight of the aim and fancy that we are merely to make pictures of men. Our business is to reproduce the image of God. With whatever experience, whatever of knowledge God has given, let us bring out the image with greater beauty and distinctness.

Let us not be fragmentary men. Let us not magnify parts of life to the obscuring of others. But rather let us make life what it was designed to be, a complete thing in perfect harmony of form throughout. Let us not make the mistake of believing that when we have fitted the mind for new and larger tasks of civilization and science we have completed the work of education. Let us not be complacent and arrogant in partial development.

On the contrary, as the work of specializing goes on more and more, while the botanist knows little of the work of the geologist, and the psychologist cares nothing for the astronomer's pursuit of the stars, and while the mechanic bent on speed and the reduction of waste thinks the poet a dreamer or a fool, let us hold to them all and gather from each his message, and not lose the well-rounded type of the human man with a mind open to all in freedom and tolerance and giving to all the moral beauty and the moral dignity of the transforming power of Jesus Christ. The botanist must still be a man. The geologist must live with men. Neither mechanic nor poet can do without each other. Let us remain men while our callings are different. Let us not lose the man in the vocation.

Remaining men, we shall see that as we keep to the great

human passions and feel the great human emotions and
follow out the great human aspirations we shall fulfill best
what God has prepared us for.   And we shall continue to
unite, as all men in the past who have kept alive in the
sympathies and yearnings of our race have united, under
the standard of that universal man, the man Christ Jesus.

THE HOLINESS OF TRUTH

Ephesians iv. 24.

It is one of the favorite religious fads of our day to deplore the spectacle of what is called a " divided Christendom." It is pointed out with much truth, but also with much falsehood, that the Christian forces of the world are so divided among themselves that their power is greatly reduced, and the Christian conquest of the world thereby greatly delayed. Against a genuine union of Christendom no Christian can have a single word to offer. That sectarian struggles have done the world great injury is an unquestionable fact. That they have done the world a great deal of good is also beyond question. It is a part of the nature of Christianity to inspire personal and independent thought. The moment, therefore, that such independent original thought comes into existence there is room for wide divergences of opinion and activity. When men differ as to what is most important in thought and what should have precedence in action, the time for the organization of a new sect has arrived. Even if they continue under the same denominational name they are in fact a sect. Names do not constitute real union. Mere symbols do not determine fellowship. Union and fellowship are not things that can be made to order and fitted to the moment. They are the results of growth and experience and spiritual oneness which come not by seeking for them, but because they are grounded in the natures that are thus joined together. What God thus joins together no man can ever hope to put apart by symbols and signs.

This passion for union is probably an outgrowth from the universal prevalence of the doctrine of evolution. The universe developed in all its variety and beauty from a single

185

germ, all philosophy of life and things expanded according
to a single principle, forms the suggestive base of the idea
that all Christendom may be united in a single church or
possibly a single federation.   And, the age being one of
concentration succeeding as it does a period of wonderful expansion, the notion has become a delightful subject of speculation and sentimental hope in many minds.   " If the Church
were only one," they say, " what might we not do for
Christ!"   This same thought probably lies at the base of
the hope of world-wide evangelization " in this generation.''
The student volunteers at their Cleveland convention doubtless meant just what they said and expressed an earnest and
living hope.   But a maturer knowledge of the processes of
Christian growth would have shown at once not merely the
impracticability of " evangelizing " the world in this generation but the uselessness of such evangelization apart from
other and more powerful forces.   There is no merit in merely
proclaiming the gospel.   It is important that it be proclaimed
in demonstration of the Spirit and of power.   The truth itself
can only produce freedom.   It takes some conception of the
nature of spiritual truth to produce Christian character.   And
this is the fundamental lesson to be learned in connection
with the proclamation of the gospel.   It is of infinitely
greater importance that the whole truth shall be proclaimed
than that the whole world should hear only a part of it.
And then we have, have we not, the New Testament warrant
for believing that God has not utterly left himself without
witnesses in any part of his world?

The truth, then, is what we must have about the gospel.
But we must have that truth wrought into the form and
majesty of a mandate from God.   It will be powerless unless
it does so come.   And spiritual truth must have this quality
above all things else.   The truth which we call religious
truth must be holy in its suggestion and influence.   Unless
it has in it the germs of incitement and encouragement to
holiness it avails not.   It may be ever so interesting or beautiful, but that is not the question.   Does it make holy?   This
is the paramount problem of all.   And to bring about this

holiness of truth requires the cooperation of all Christians
and the joint effort of all to bring to the knowledge of each
the experience of all. The message of that form of social
expedient known as cooperation, with the motto, "each for
all and all for each," is precisely descriptive of what must
take place before we can have a holy truth. It was so
among the apostles, as is seen in their manifold discussions
and differences. Indeed, if I may say it reverently, the
temperamental and intellectual characteristics which have
caused the modern sects were potentially present in the very
college of the apostles. Looking over the list of the immediate disciples of Christ it seems to me I can see the types
of the leading modern denominations very distinctly. Only
one I find to be absent, and that is the ignoble religious
bigot who calls himself the "Church" while all others were
something else. So also in the early history of the Church.
Origen in his argument against Celsus writes : "As men not
only from the laboring and serving classes but also many
from the cultured classes of Greece came to see something
honorable in Christianity, sects could not fail to arise, not
simply from the desire for controversy and contradiction, but
because several scholars endeavored to penetrate deeper into
the truth of Christianity. In this way sects arose which
received their names from men who indeed admired Christianity in its essence, but from many different causes had
arrived at different conceptions of it."[1]

To penetrate deeper into the truth of Christianity has been
the inspiring motive of nine-tenths of the differences of
Christendom, and it is not too much to say that without that
inspiration much of what we cherish to-day as among the
choicest intellectual and spiritual possessions of the Church
and of the world would have been lost. A foolish sentimentalism would say that Christ was being divided. A wiser
spirit of God said Christendom was really being united and
the holiness of the truth of Jesus Christ was being revealed
to the world. Every new sect has come into being with woe
and travail, often amid the threats and curses of its elders.

[1] "Contra Celsus," III, 12.

But every human being comes into the world through travail. The birth is not joyous but grievous; nevertheless, afterward we rejoice in the new man who has been created after God in righteousness and the holiness of truth. Such a work cannot be otherwise than glorious in the ultimate purpose of God. It cannot otherwise than glorify Christ. For this is the working out of the principle which St. Paul announced when he said that "some indeed preach Christ of contention, but nevertheless Christ is preached," and this was rejoicing enough.

Now Christian search for the truths of Christ and his gospel, having done so much, should do more. This may be likened to Christ breaking the bread and giving it to his disciples. They in turn must distribute it to the people. We have emphasized our demand for Christian truth as denominations and sects. Let us go one step farther and emphasize it as individuals. Having broken up Christendom into intelligible fragments and found a consciousness for each, let us go still deeper into our penetration of the truth and find the truth which belongs to each of us, for such a truth there assuredly must be for each one of us. For the multitude which Christ fed there was enough and to spare. Of the truth that makes for holiness there is enough and to spare for every man. Just as we have to a great degree found the whole gospel by securing through sects emphasis upon its various constituent parts, so the whole of the Christian life will be found by the appropriate emphasis of individual lives upon the distinctive qualities of holiness in each. Thus each is for all and all are for each, and in the whole Christ is revealed and perfected in the thought and life of every one of us. Thus is outlined to us what is the most important work to be done in the Christian Church at this moment. This is the new spiritual crusade to which every man is invited and in which every man has a vital part.

Augustine Birrell quotes J. S. Mill as saying in his "Autobiography" that this age was one "of weak convictions, paralyzed intellects, and growing laxity of opinions," and then proceeds to a very interesting argument on the probable effect of speculative habits upon conduct, in the course of which he says, "Faith may well be left alone, for she is, to give her her due, our largest manufacturer of good works, and whenever her furnaces are blown out morality suffers." All of which is very interesting, but the kind of truth-hunting which the gospel suggests is not that which waits anxiously for the next verdict on the "Analysis of the Pentateuch" or the next dictum on the "Fourth Gospel," but which looks about anxiously for the next evidence of the presence of the Holy Spirit. Truth-hunting for holiness is a very different thing from the indulgence of speculative habits from the love of discussion. Nor is it true that faith may well be left alone. For faith needs feeding like all things else. Fed upon the products and narratives of credulity and superstition she becomes the mere prison-house of the soul and heart, without truth at all, and really without genuine faith. Fed upon the rational knowledge of the movements of God in the world she grows great with new offspring of love and mighty thought as well as mighty deeds. The faith that stands based only on economic advantage will never be highly cherished by the world. Nor will the fear that morality will suffer be a sufficient reason to most men for making her acquaintance. This is much like those men who think the Church is a "good thing," and will support it, but know nothing about its life and have no place in its sacraments. The "good thing" would perish from the earth if it had to rely upon such men.

No, true faith must be found and loved, just as Andrew Lang says the old Sagas must be loved and found: "You can make no money out of reading Sagas; they have nothing to say about stocks and shares nor about Prime Ministers and politics. . . . The Sagas only tell how brave men — of our own blood very likely — lived and loved and fought and voyaged and died, before there was much reading or writing, when they sailed without steam, traveled without railways, and warred hand to hand, not with hidden dynamite and sunk torpedoes." The motive of interest, personal interest, self-gain, even though it be of a higher intellectual quality, can

never give us the knowledge of a true faith. But the love
of holiness will give it, and the truth sought for holiness will
reveal it. For truth and faith are cousins in the spiritual
life and to know the one is to love the other. There is a
freedom and unconventionality about the atmosphere of genuine spiritual living which is beyond the control of personal
interests and which cannot be tainted by what has self as its
chief end and object. The objective point in the hunt for
truth in holiness is God. The objective point in a genuine
faith is a communion with the God whom the truth has found
for us.

The contemplation of the truth as a holy thing, something
sacred and to be sacredly used, is probably rather new. In
spite of our rather *blasé* devotion to truth — nothing is more
common nowadays than the worship of Truth — the sacredness of the possession of the truth is little appreciated among
us. But a few illustrations will show very simply and clearly
what a vast responsibility comes with the mere recognition of
truth. Suppose a man were passing along the street and saw
a young child that by some means or other had gotten hold
of a stick of dynamite. How full of meaning the glance is
that reveals to him the fact! In that single bit of knowledge,
acquired probably in the most casual way, lies the life not
merely of that child, but of many possibly, and — his own —
for the taking away of that dangerous thing may involve the
loss of his own life. The knowledge of the qualities of dynamite at that moment is not an intellectual asset of a commercial or academic character, but a holy truth, since it at once
suggests the highest and holiest of all duties, namely, sacrifice and service. Merely having that knowledge requires him
to take his own life into his hand. It may involve its loss.
But the knowledge is not one of interest or utility or beauty
or scientific interest, but of duty ; the knowledge of dynamite
has become a holy truth of holy importance to him in an
instant.

There is open to him another course, to be sure. That is,
to run away. But what man among us would not hasten to
brand him a coward and a disgrace to manhood? Now in

the case chosen the importance of the moral use of the truth,
even when the truth itself has no moral character in itself, is
at once seen, because life and destruction are seen to rest
upon the issue. But is the case vitally different when you
see a young man wasting his life in evil habits or debauching
his intellect with vicious ideas, or cultivating associations
which are sure to bring ultimate shame and ruin? In the
one case you hasten to rescue a child from bodily destruction; in the other you relieve yourself from responsibility,
though it may involve eternal destruction not merely of body,
but also of character. If the power to know a stick of dynamite can in one single instant become the whole of the gospel
of Jesus Christ in the self-forgetfulness and self-sacrifice which
it suggests and requires, may not every truth which we have
be a holy possession full of the responsibility and obligation
to find its point of sacredness, and do the act of God at the
point where duty and character are discovered? If a man
knows that a certain place in the road is dangerous and does
not give appropriate warning, is he not held guilty of negli-
gence? If a man knows that certain associations and acts
bring moral ruin and degradation, is not that knowledge holy
truth to him? Is not the mere knowing duty of the most
urgent character? What excuse do we hear oftener than the
one, " I did not know"?

Truth enough there has always been in the world to save
men. But the truth has never been sanctified and made imperative at the point of duty. The world by wisdom knew
not God, the very thing by which it ought to have known
God best. Not many wise are called, though the wise ought
to be the very first to recognize the power and the beauty of
the gospel of Christ. God chose the foolish things of the
world to confound the mighty, but the only possible reason I
can see for his doing so must have been that the wisdom and
knowledge of the world was neither holy wisdom nor holy
knowledge. To know anything is to invest it with a sacredness apart from the mere delight in knowing it or the distinction which the knowledge confers. Knowledge should be holy
knowledge. To know the truth is to be faced with a kind of

responsibility which is like to being the brother's keeper. Failure to use it so is to bring not merely disappointment but the sad, rude awakening that shows the hollowness of greatness apart from the sacred use of the truth committed to us.   It is this that gives such pathetic force to Cardinal Wolsey's lament in " Henry VIII " : —

> Love thyself last : cherish those hearts that hate thee ;
> Corruption wins not more than honesty.
> Still in thy right hand carry gentle peace,
> To silence envious tongues.   Be just and fear not,
> Let all the ends thou aim'st at be thy country's,
> Thy God's and truth's ; then if thou fall'st, O Cromwell,
> Thou fall'st a blessed martyr. . . .
> And my integrity to heaven is all
> I dare now call my own.   O Cromwell, Cromwell,
> Had I but served my God with half the zeal
> I serve my king, he would not in mine age
> Have left me naked to mine enemies !

Moreover truth conceived as holiness is the most if not the only real effective use of the truth as an instrument of righteousness.   The new man to whom Paul here alludes is created after God and not merely in true holiness, as the old version has it, but is a man whose righteousness lies in the fact that the truth is to him a holy thing.   Righteousness may indeed be said to be the ultimate purpose of the gospel.   If men are made righteous, the end for which Christ came into the world may be said to be accomplished.   And Christ announced himself the Way, the Truth and the Life.   Certainly Christ as the Truth is a vision of holiness in life and service, not a mere illustration of character veracity.   It is not Christ truthful, but Christ the Truth.   Christ is entirely conceivable as truthful without being the Truth.   Why does not Paul say, " I am the Truth " ?   It is entirely possible to conceive veracity without righteousness.   A fact in science or even an act in daily life may be without moral interest or character to him who is most concerned in it.   But with his life conceived as truth, as a thing not merely without falsehood but a thing having sacredness, holiness in itself, no such act is possible

at all. It is in this sense the Christ is the Truth. Those
men who imagine Christ to have been mistaken about himself and endeavor to give evasive interpretations to many of
his plainest utterances about himself do not think of impeach-
ing the veracity of Christ. He is perfectly truthful, they say.
But a Christ who is the Truth could not be mistaken in this
way. The language of Christ and the acts of Christ together
are not merely suggestive of one who is acting in good faith,
but whose good faith and veracious character are attributes
of a holy life. In a similar manner Christ is the Life; not
merely an admirable life, but holy life. Holiness is the
interpretative word of the entire New Testament.

There are several very practical suggestions that grow out
of this conception of truth-love and truth-hunting. But these
must be assumed. A man must love the truth first of all for
itself. This love is like all love of man for man and the love
of God for man. It must be all-including and without discrimination. It must not take into consideration whether it
is admirable or disagreeable truth. Then again he must
have the impulse and purpose to find the truth. Matthew
Arnold has called attention to the fact that the text in the
Gospel of John translated, "Grace and truth came by Jesus
Christ," should be translated, "*Happiness* and *reality* came
by Jesus Christ." Whether grace is happiness necessarily or
always is a question which may now be left. It certainly
should be so. But truth must be *reality*. And the search
for reality is one of the first instincts of man at his best.
Contentment with and satisfaction in something other than
reality is the beginning of the final separation between the
heart and God. The new man in Christ loves what is true
because it is true, whether he likes it or does not like it,
whether it helps him or hinders him. Paul certainly illustrated this doctrine over and over again. No man appears
to have had a greater anxiety to be correctly informed. He
rejoices if it is a cause of rejoicing. He girds himself for
new labors if it is otherwise. Paul appears also to have been
a persistent truth-hunter. The progress of doctrine in the
conception of his own life and mission which appears in

Jesus' own mind appears also in Paul's mind. This openness of mind is likewise one of the most endearing things about St. John.

The holiness of the truth involves, among others, the duty of thorough and careful mastery of it. This is best illustrated in the knowledge of the Bible. Most men believe their salvation to be bound up in some way with the truths which are taught in the Bible. They may differ as to details, but it is God's book to the vast majority of the civilized world. Then it is the duty of every man to master it so far as that lies within his power. It is not merely an advantage to him, it is his solemn obligation to himself, to the world, and to God. That truth, whatever it is, that is in the Bible is to him a part of the possible holy character which he hopes to attain. The new man in righteousness after the pattern of God must be thoroughly furnished. He must know himself as a child of God. This is the place to get light upon the subject. He must know God as the Father. This is the book which reveals him. He must find the mission of Christ to his soul. This is the place where that mission is unfolded. And so of the thousand and one spiritual questions which are with us from the cradle to the grave the Bible is the storehouse of information, of instruction, of reproof or warning and of direction. There is no spiritual mood in which the Bible does not meet him. There is no anxiety which it does not allay. There is no burden which it cannot help him in bearing. There is no sin for which it does not show the way of forgiveness. Such truth is holy truth. The getting of such knowledge is the holy search for truth. No man would permit his children to grow up in ignorance of the properties of fire or poison. No more does he permit himself if he be wise to build the fires of sinful living upon the table of his heart or take into his soul the death-dealing draughts of vice and crime. God's word is to him the holy truth that saves his spiritual life as the other is the elementary knowledge that keeps him safe in body.

It is interesting to see the advance, in its various stages among men, of the conception of the value and duty of mastering the truth. To many men truth is valuable because it is profitable. Honesty is the best policy, they say, and truth-fulness is a part of general honesty. This is probably the lowest or the next to the lowest conception possible. The only lower one I can conceive of is that which makes one fearful of the results of something other than the truth; namely, the same instinct that makes a hound cringe under the uplifted lash. But the most prevalent idea about the truth is still that it is profitable. After that comes the idea that the truth is admirable. This may be called the scholastic type of truth-worship. A step higher is that which regards whatever is true as at the same time beautiful, which is a kind of philosophic worship of truth. But only rarely does one see the truth honored and loved and sought because it is holy. This is the highest altitude of truth-love. This is the attitude of Christ. "I am Truth" meant with Jesus Christ all love of God to man, all sacrifice for the salvation of the world, all service and all redemptive burden-bearing that the world might have life and have it abundantly. And because this is the highest truth, Christ himself, the knowledge and obedience of Christ, it should be the first duty of every man to know.

And next to the careful acquaintance with the truth comes the expression and distribution of it. If the former involves a knowledge of the Bible, the latter involves the acceptance of the life of Christ. Christ was the expression of the spirit-ual life in its ultimate and only enduring form. It is this fact which makes Paul exclaim, "For me to live is Christ!" To the man who had made the spiritual life, that is, the life of obedience to conscience and to God, after the model of Jesus Christ, his aim, Christ's life was his life. Living, with Paul, was to be Christlike. Not to be Christlike was to be identi-fied with death. It was decay and lifelessness. This is what he has in mind when he recalls the days of his antagonism to Christ, and says that "what things were gain to me, these have I counted loss for Christ." Yes, he was willing to count all things but loss that he might win Christ. The theolo-gians have in times past laid so much emphasis upon opinions

as the essential part of religion that we have not always realized that Christlikeness is religion, and that alone.   Opinions
never made religion.   Nor did the religious life, the Christian
life, ever derive its strength primarily from opinions.   Christ
did not come to give men opinions.   He came to give them
life.   And the pressing, the imperative, the supreme duty of
the Christian man is to master and express in the terms of
his own capacity and power the life of Christ.   "This," he
must, in effect, be able to say to the world, "is the life of
Christ raised to the power of my own possibility."   "This,"
he must say with clearness and with unmistakable veracity,
"is so much of the incomparable life as it is possible to bring
within the limits of such a sphere as my own."   This is the
expression of the Truth.   This is the expression of truth as
holiness, because it is the expression of the life of Christ
which is the Holy Life.   It is at the same time the most
effective and persistent method of sending the message of
holiness throughout the world.   This is the distribution of
the gospel which never reacts and which never does damage.
It is not merely a true thing ; but it is holy as well as true.
And in the exaltation of the truth into holiness, Christ is
born anew to the world.

SCIENCE AND CHRISTIANITY[1]

1 Peter iii. 15.

CHRISTIANITY is a religion for reasonable men. This does
not involve, however, that Christianity has an answer for
every problem which the reason of man can propound or a
final word on every question of human destiny. It means
that on the great matter of personal religion and redemption
it has the outlines of a solution which is sufficient for every
reasonable man who will reasonably apply it to his own life
and heart. It is a religion of experience and therefore its
fullest evidence is the evidence of experience. It is a religion
of life rather than one of metaphysic or doctrine, hence the
largest verification of its validity will arise from its living
exposition rather than from its rational statement. Indeed,
the degree to which religion is true to life will cause it to
reproduce all the essential characteristics of variety of form,
contradictions in expression and peculiarities of individual
experience which make up the conglomerate life of mankind.
It is manifestly impossible that such a religion can be brought
under the restraint of an intellectual statement which will
appeal to each man with the same emphasis. It is possible,
however, to produce the outline into which every man may
write his own detail. If Christ is sanctified in the heart as
Lord, the rest will follow in due course.

The evidences of Christianity are not studied to-day as
they were twenty years ago. Not that the subject has
declined in interest to the Church or the world, but that the
last twenty years have been so productive intellectually that
in the embarrassment of riches the technical matter of Christian evidences has fallen somewhat into the background,

[1] "Scientific Aspect of Christian Evidences." G. Frederick Wright. Appletons.

while the broader and deeper questions of the seat of authority in religion and the nature of religion itself have come
more conspicuously into the foreground. Discovery, too, has
given special impetus to the documentary and archæological
questions, so that there has been a growing feeling of conservatism in view of the fact that new material was constantly
being brought to view. One cannot dogmatize very long
when each day's discoveries compel a revision of opinion.
Hence the world has settled down to the great practical work
of Christianity and assumed, as it could do so rationally, that
the evidences of the gospel were safe enough, or at least that
while the work was pressing the matter could be left to
experts and academicians. But there is evidence now that
there is a revival of interest in the desire for a statement of
the evidences of Christianity which shall be in accord with
the spirit and vocabulary of the age.

The Lowell lectures a year ago on the " Scientific Aspects
of Christian Evidences" were in the nature of a response to
this demand. This is a fitting place to express the obligation
which Christian people owe, not only to the generous founder
of the Lowell lectures, but also to the wise and far-seeing
man, Mr. B. E. Cotting, who for so many years directed the
trust. Under that careful insight into the needs of popular
thought the whole world has been laid under tribute, and
the best thought from two hemispheres brought to the city of
Boston and its treasures freely offered to all. There is probably nowhere in the whole world a more signal illustration of
wisdom in beneficence and carefulness and conscientiousness
in management than has been afforded in the many years of
Mr. Cotting's administration of the affairs of the Lowell
Institute in Boston. The lectures referred to, now gathered
in a book, are a part of that splendid work.

In the verbiage of modern thought there is no word now
so potent as the word "scientific." With a passion almost
ludicrous we are trying to master everything on scientific
principles, and the pursuit for scientific authority for everything has produced some of the most curious exhalations
of an overheated intellectualism falsely so called. In the

matter of temperance instruction in the public schools, for
example, in the endeavor to give "scientific" knowledge on
the effects of alcohol, the result has been ridiculous in the
minds of real scientists. In the matter of religion even,
science has had to have her sway in the form of a "Christian" science. Charity is no longer a matter of the educated
Christian sensibilities acting under good judgment, but an
affair of scientific regulation. Rearing a family is no longer
the godly attempt to fulfil a duty and enjoy a privilege in
accordance with God's law and with his help, but a matter of
scientific principles which now extends even to the regulation
of the sex of offspring. Sin even has become transformed
into merely a scientific bad smell. Moral corruptness is now
"ignorance" or "disease," and is a matter for the doctor,
not the Holy Spirit.

With all this pseudo-scientific nonsense current it is good
to get into the thought and outlook of a genuine science and
find its opinion on the authority and status of Christianity
according to the demands of modern thought. Few men are
better equipped for this task than Professor Wright. It was
he who, almost if not quite twenty years ago, was one of the
small company in Boston and vicinity who resisted the then
absurd though generally received opinion that was championed by a prominent lecturer that immortality could be sustained by demonstrative proof. The years have proved the
reasonableness of his view taken then as well as his ability to
keep in touch with the scientific movements of the period.
As author, scientist and theologian, Professor Wright has
shown that in each field he has been able to keep in mind its
limitations and peculiar offices. The view of a man so fitted
is therefore worthy of exceptional study, being at once the
opinion of a theologian who, by reason of his eminence in
science, cannot ignore the just claims of scientific thought and
the statement of a scientist who dare not endanger his reputation as a scientist in giving adherence to religious views
which are scientifically untenable or absurd.

The temper of this book is well indicated in the opening
paragraphs of its Introduction. " Among well-founded be-

liefs," it says, "Christianity is not peculiar in being incapable of demonstrative proof and in being open to a variety of objections which are difficult to answer. Of the misleading tendencies in modern thought one of the most serious is that of setting up an unreasonable standard of proof as the necessary basis for active belief. Indeed, in a vast number of instances the insistence upon experimental or demonstrative proof is so unreasonable that it amounts to a species of insanity. . . . In order to serve as a satisfactory basis for religious hope and activity the facts of Christianity must be proved beyond 'reasonable doubt.' The Christian apologist must cheerfully accept the responsibility for adducing such proof." *Such* proof is the proof which Professor Wright brings to the discussion, and it is in precisely this, that this volume differs from the great mass of discussions of Christian evidences. While modern thought has been unreasonable in this matter of proof, it must, however, be admitted that it has not been more unreasonable than many Christian apologists who have insisted that they had precisely what Professor Wright says cannot be produced, namely, demonstrative proof. This has been probably the most fruitful cause of skepticism in our age.

There is a department of Christian thought about the evidences of Christianity which is just coming into being concerning which these lectures give no hint; that is the psychology of conversion and the changes involved in the inception of the religious life. We have only begun to think about the self-consciousness of Jesus himself. Added hereto there is a mass of material in the New Testament which could easily be made the basis for a psychological study of the apostolic church life and religious order and discipline. But here only a beginning has been made, and the elementary work of classification remains yet to be done. Professor Wright confines himself purely to the point of view which modern thought would style scientific, and applies the canons of a sound logical examination to the problem before him. In this examination he reviews successively the "Limits of Scientific Thought," the "Paradoxes of Science," "God and Nature,"

"Darwinism and Design" and "Mediate Miracles," ending the first half of the book with a discussion of the nature of the ground gone over and under the title "Beyond Reasonable Doubt." The last half of the book presents the familiar arguments suggested by the textual, internal and external evidences of the historicity of the gospels embodying some of the newer results of criticism and interpreted with reference to preceding discussions along the same line.

The interest of these lectures is of course chiefly in the part that deals with the relations of science and Christian truth. The New Testament is so secure, and all attempts to invalidate its historical authority have so signally failed, or have been presented in a form so utterly incapable of affecting its spiritual authority, that argument on that point may safely be left at rest for a long time to come. Any attempt to show that Jesus did not know what he was talking about, or that the gospels are a mere collection of legends, has come so squarely athwart the spiritual life and consciousness of the believers in Christ that it has not only failed to result in anything particular but rather deepened the moral and spiritual reliance of men in Christ as a source of spiritual authority and power. On the other point, however, there has been room for many wide divergences of thought.

Take first of all the matter of the limitations of scientific thought. Who would suppose from the attitude of modern thought on the subject of scientific inquiry that scientific thought had any limits? While each day brings more and more astounding revelations of the possibilities of science, the mind becomes bewildered and thinks that nothing can be denied in this marvelous race which the human mind is running. Then again the reports are so vague and so exaggerated that there is a sort of presumption created in favor of any theory or exploitation, however strange and uncanny it may seem. But, as our author shows, scientific thought has limits like all other thought. There are a vast number of things that science cannot know, as there are a great many more that science cannot do. It is infinitely easier to send a fifteen thousand ton ocean liner through a North Atlantic storm than it is to move a stubborn will. It is far simpler to measure the weight of a distant planet than it is to measure the value of a reason that will appeal to a particular mind. What is the value of a reason? It depends entirely on the mind to which it is presented, the mind that presents it, the form in which it is presented, and the subject-matter concerning which it is presented. Yet none of these things can be solved by scientific inquiry.

Now scientific thought is simply thought about matters for which the thinker has special and technical training. The reasons there appeal to him, but that does not make the opinion of the man called "scientist" more valuable than your own on a matter affecting your own personal life and moral need. A man might have the best opinion in the world about a species of South American birds or an Alaskan glacier who would be as helpless as a newborn babe in the presence of sixty children in a schoolroom. "Science says" has come to have pretty much the meaning which goes with the expression "they say." It depends altogether on who *they* are and what they are talking about. Professor Wright shows this in a number of scientific propositions which cannot be reproduced here, though the argument is. The nature of man, the stability and origin of matter and the great vast mass of things which form our material of research and discussion are not matters about which any one can offer a finality as a pope issues a bull. Or if he does, it has exactly the value that a papal bull has. If you like that particular kind of authority, then it is good, otherwise not.

But it is hard to realize the truth of all this when there is such emphasis on "science" and "scientific thought." It is very much like the emphasis which is laid on arithmetic as a study. President Eliot says that there are "four things in which the individual youth should be thoroughly trained if his judgment and reasoning power are to be systematically developed: observing accurately ; recording correctly ; comparing, grouping and inferring justly ; and expressing cogently the results of these mental operations." But he adds later on that "from one-sixth to one-fourth, or even one-third

of the whole time of American children is given to the subject of arithmetic; a subject which does not train a single
one of the four faculties which should be the fundamental
object of education."[1]   There you have the slaughter of one
of the educational trinity of the Three R's to which the great
bulk of mankind clings as to a thing of eternal value and
power.   Tell that to the mass of mankind and they will turn
from you in scorn.   Yet it is the opinion of the foremost educator of the greatest university in America.

In just such a way people think about the claim of things
"scientific."   There is something profound in the name itself, just as there is something to the average mind "practical" about arithmetic.   But if human life is what it is, and
human thought is what in its nature it proves itself to be
daily, then scientific thought is as apt to be mistaken as any
other kind of thought.   And the term itself carries with it
only the presumptions which are contained in the personality
of him who speaks and the question concerning which he
speaks.   It is doubtful whether many thoughtful people
would not shake their heads over President Eliot's observation, knowing it to be his, and knowing his right to speak
with authority on such a matter.   But it is entirely probable
that in this matter he is absolutely right.   At all events my
own experience confirms what he says in every detail.

In a similar way there is great confusion in the popular
mind with reference to the terms "nature," "evolution" and
"miracles."   It would be unjust to say that all the confusion
that prevails about these terms has been brought about by the
scientists and their pseudo-followers.   Some of it has been
produced by poets.   A good deal of it is due to theologians,
and much more due to the careless and thoughtless use of
such terms by teachers and others who have to do with the
diffusion of educational ideas.   There is a sort of mystery
about the term "nature," which is often made the veil for
ignorance or cowardice or both.   It is like the terms "Deity"
and "Beneficent Providence" in public documents, procla-
mations, and the like, used by the cowardly magistrates, be-

---

[1] "American Contributions to Civilization," pp. 220, 221.

cause they are afraid to say frankly and openly what they
really intend the mass of the people to infer, " Almighty
God." To say that Nature does this or that is like that form
of discussion which gives personal and often supernatural
characteristics to things. To say that Law does this or that
is to mean, when anything intelligent is meant, that such and
such an instrumentality is used by human beings to secure
certain ends. No law ever accomplished anything. In a like
manner, Nature never did anything of its own accord. " Natural selection " is God's selection. " Natural law " is God's
law. " Nature's law " is God's law. But the personality of
God is often thus obscured, and the divine activity in the
world made to seem rare and extraordinary when it is, in fact,
constant and undeviating.

Professor Wright justly says that when the term " evolution " is used it needs definition as to just what particular
kind of evolution you mean. There is " theistic " evolution
and " paroxysmal " evolution and a variety of other kinds of
evolution. Some of these assume the existence of God, and
others try to get along without any God. Yet the popular
thought does not make these discriminations. The result is
confusion about the method of God's operations in the world.
And this is even more true when we come to a term like
" miracles." Professor Wright himself defines a miracle as
" simply an interference with the ordinary course of Nature
by the Creator so pronounced as to command public assent
and attention, and so timed as to confirm an important revelation or enforcement of truth." This definition, satisfactory
to the author, has in it nevertheless the material for endless
controversy. It is very certain that many persons devoutly
believing in miracles do not think of them as in any sense
interferences with nature. I certainly do not think of them
in that light. Then again great stress is here laid upon the
element of time in a miracle. And a special office is given
to miracles which might apply to Biblical miracles, and
apparently this was in the author's mind. Then " revelation " has a pretty wide scope and the " enforcement of
truth " may mean a great many things. Professor Wright's

discussion of miracles is very illuminating, but the simple
truth about miracles is that they are wonders, and wonders
only, about which rationalizing can give no satisfactory
answer. The author does show a great many interesting
facts, though the strength of his argument is in showing that
what are often supposed to be miracles are none.

The whole subject lies in just the region about which mention was made, namely, the psychology of religious living.
Our Lord himself said concerning certain unbelievers, "They
have Moses and the prophets; if they will not receive them,
neither will they believe though one rose from the dead."
Miracles may or may not confirm a truth or revelation. It
depends upon the mind that receives the revelation or the
nature of the truth to be confirmed. It is very certain that
modern confidence in the Bible does not rest upon the miracles of the Bible, though that confidence may have sprung
from a belief originally founded on the witness of miracles.
But even so, the matter of miracles has little appeal to the
modern mind even when devout and believing. Whether
a miracle is mediate or of some other kind makes little difference so far as confirming faith is concerned.

The strongest appeal to Christian thought in the whole
book is in the idea wrought out in the chapter entitled "Beyond Reasonable Doubt." It is here that Professor Wright
makes the vital point that even scientific proof is not necessarily demonstrative. It is strange that in the matter of
evidence what has long been the rule of our courts of law
should not have had its rightful influence in adjudging the
evidences of religion. Professor Wright shows with great
clearness and inexorable logic that the vast mass of the facts
of ordinary life are not provable, and in fact proof for them
is never demanded. To demand proof would be to introduce
a schism into life and humanity itself. Man eats his meals,
takes his conveyance to his business, carries on all kinds of
relations upon the slenderest threads of presumption, and to
ask proof for his belief in them would be to overturn the
whole circle of his life and actions. The fact is simply that
belief follows on after experience in a way which throws the

burden of proof on the doubter. And just as the court of law requires that a case shall be made out, not mathematically or demonstratively, but "beyond reasonable doubt," so that is all that can be required of the Christian in giving a reason for the hope that is in him. Is it beyond reasonable doubt that Christ is the Saviour of mankind? Is it beyond reasonable doubt that the Bible is the Book of God? Is it beyond reasonable doubt that faith in that Christ and the instruction of that Book make for happiness, moral uprightness, peace of soul and purity of life? Then the cause of Christianity is established in accordance with the demands of the best scientific thought.

The great intellectual danger of the world is not from ignorance and superstition, it is rather from knowledge, falsely so called. To set up mathematical standards for the gospel and to compel the arguing of Christian truth on a basis which could not for a moment stand in a court of law seems a curious way to find out the relations between science and such truth. But as a matter of fact a large part of what has been called scientific thinking about Christian truth has set up just such standards. Of course the result has been to the damage of Christian truth. It could not be otherwise. But luckily Christian truth does not rest upon such reasoning, and the net effects of all such attempts to invalidate the gospel have only resulted in a profounder trust in Him who was the Light, the Truth and the Way. Without understanding the reason why, Christian men have often felt the fallacies of such reasoning, and been governed accordingly. The appeal to reason is not the only appeal in the human mind. And the appeal to false reasoning carries its own destruction with it.

It was a happy stroke of the author's literary insight, as well as genius, to present, as showing the form of his argument on the subject of reasonable doubt, the charge of an Ohio judge that had been approved and adopted by the Ohio Supreme Court, and printed entire as showing the form of the doctrine as held by the courts. I commend that chapter and that charge in particular to any one who has fears of his

capability of giving the answer which Peter suggests in our
text as suitable for the believer. A mass of petty objections
to Christianity and all sorts of pettifogging will crumble to
the dust in the mere reading of Judge Nye's charge. Especially interesting is the sentence which charges the jury to
distinguish between "mere captious doubt, a mere possible
doubt, a mere arbitrary and speculative doubt." Such distinguishing, in the minds of men troubled with religious
doubts about the gospel, would bring a great deal of light.

But the commanding fact about Christianity is, not that it
commends itself rationally to man, but that it meets the
moral necessities of man, and answers his spiritual wants
with exactness and satisfaction. When Jesus identified the
Truth with himself he did at once the rational, logical and
practical thing. Christianity's strongest argument is in the
character of the beings who are ostensibly under its influence.
The personality of Christ has answered more objections to
Christianity than were ever answered by the apologists,
ancient or modern. There is the Christ. "Behold the
Lamb of God," said John when he saw Christ coming. So
we say when the validity of our faith is called into question,
"Behold the works of God." In the name of Christ we have
builded these vast monuments of love, benevolence and
human helpfulness which without dissent mankind have pronounced good. A fact is still worth a thousand arguments.
But it is well to know that, even in the crucible of intellectual
criticism and inquiry, Christianity can and has vindicated
itself.

It is high time that the Christian man with twenty centuries
of Christianity in the world behind him shall take the field for
aggressive rather than apologetic proclamation of the gospel.
In an age which delights in vagueness, and which has little
disposition for the positiveness in tone or the decisiveness in
life which were the primary features of apostolic Christianity,
the Christian man can do no better for himself or his cause
than to announce with determination and clearness that the
foundations of God stand secure. Let us not preach Christ
as a vague idealistic notion, but as a personal Redeemer and

Lord.   Let us not preach a Bible which is merely a congeries
of delightful anticipations, but a moral and spiritual mentor
which aligns itself with the heart and the conscience of man.
Let us not invite men into an assembly of timid children
scared by every wind of doctrine and called by courtesy the
Church, but into the fellowship of just men endeavoring to
become perfect under the power of the Holy Spirit, and living in the shadow of the things to come as well as the things
that now are.

LITERARY AND ROMANTIC

THE CHRISTIAN IN NOVELS AND NEW TESTAMENT

ACTS xi. 26.

IT may be counted one of the fortunate things in the history of Christianity, that the title by which it is known to the world incorporates in it the name of the Founder. Christianity is inseparably linked with the person and work of Christ in any event. But the name of our religion must suggest, whenever it is uttered, the Central Person in it. And what is thus true of the name of our religion is also true of those who espouse its cause. Followers of Jesus Christ are called Christians. The church which Jesus established is called the Christian Church. In all these titles the Lord stands out as the determinative constituent power of the faith we profess.

It is not less interesting that the names which thus form the suggestive group of titles for the various elements of our faith are based upon the Messianic title of our Lord. Humanly speaking, the Lord's name was Jesus. And this name, not uncommon among the Jews, has acquired its significance in the world only through its association with the Christ. The mere use of the name Jesus, if persisted in to the exclusion of the title Christ, would soon obscure the most powerful truth in the history of our Lord's life. Doubtless some would rejoice to see the Messianic nature of Christ thus obliterated. But in the providence of God that has been made forever impossible, partly through the group of titles which has been chosen for the religion, the Church and the disciples of the Christ. To be his disciples they have to be Christians, and they have to show forth in the very title the historic hope and the Messianic character of his mission and sacrifice. We would honor the human Jesus wherever he might be found. We can rest our faith only upon the eternal and the redeeming Christ.

This is appropriately the case, also, from the fact that Jesus' claim to attention is as the Christ. If at one stroke we could separate him from his connection with the hope of the Jews and could blot out the striking resemblance between the foreshadowed Messiah and the historic Christ, much of our interest in Christ would vanish at once. The events of his arrest, trial and crucifixion, which have always had such an impressive interest for men, would take on a very different character. It was his Messianic claim which brought about these things. Jesus as a new Rabbi would have aroused no such sentiments among the Jews as he did arouse. The Jews were exceedingly broad and liberal in their tolerance of schools of thought. It was the fact that Jesus claimed to be the Messiah which invoked their murderous hatred. Jesus' hope of persistence as the central figure in the history of the world lies in the security of his claim that he was the Christ.

The term Christian is now so wide in its application that it includes a great variety of thought and sentiment. Innumerable philosophic distinctions separate various sects and creeds of Christians, but they all agree on the personality of the Lord himself. Even concerning him the Christian world has more than once been rent in twain, but all held themselves to be under the standard of the Son of God and the Messiah of the Jews. But while all these differences of thought and interpretation have been abroad on other matters, about the Christian life there has been substantially little difference. All have agreed that a Christian in life is one who approximates to the life of Christ to the degree of his ability and opportunity. A Christian is one who in his life and service suggests Him whose name he bears. Failing that, no matter what else he may be, he is in no proper sense a Christian. For Christianity is first life and then doctrines about life. And the theories of Christian living have sprung out of the endeavor of godly men to live the Christ life.

It has been a favorite theme with writers, particularly novelists, to portray what they conceived to be the Christian life, under the forms of literary art, with dramatic and fictional surroundings. Such novels, having ostensibly the Christian motive at their base, have usually attracted extraordinary attention, from the great human interest in the underlying motive. Redemption is the one motive which never grows stale. The sins of mankind are ever here to be forgiven, and the vicarious life, in whatever form it presents itself, has always the singular and unique charm that attaches to Him from whom it is primarily derived. Often the mere suggestion of such a life has been strong enough to give vitality to materials whose literary value, under any other conditions, would never have secured for them the slightest recognition. So powerful is Christ, even when remotely viewed. Lately there seems to be a special revival of the attempt to reveal the Christian life in literature.

The most striking effort in this direction has been a novel which bears the impressive title, "The Christian." The author expressly informed his readers that he sought to exhibit types of mind and character, of social ideal and religion, which he saw in the life of England and America. Out of these prevailing ideas he proposed to draw his materials, and then portray the Christian in the midst of them, working out the Christian ideal and purpose. This surely was a most praiseworthy undertaking. The great need in any age is the ability to discern the method of applying the teachings of Christ to the most pressing needs of the time. Whatever can help us to do this is a most welcome addition to our knowledge and efficiency. In other words, the Christian, as a redeemer after the pattern of Christ, was to be a Christ to his own generation. The purpose seemed to be to show us this redeemer in the modern world.

With this announced problem before him Mr. Caine sets to work. His observations in England and America lead him to conclude that the one sin most strikingly in evidence in the world is the sin of lust. That the most characteristic thing about our social life is unbridled passion, and, with this as the central evil to be aimed at, the whole plot is made to turn upon the battle in that particular direction. His hero

is one John Storm, who is to show us the modern Christian
displaying the redeeming function of the vicarious life, in
various surroundings.   Side by side with this hero there is a
heroine, if she may be styled so, who is also to show in some
measure, by contrast and otherwise, the excellence of the
Christian in his struggle with the sins of the modern life.

Sketching briefly the characteristics of this novel-made
Christian, we are at once impressed with the contrast between
him and the Christian as he is shown to us in the New Testament.   John Storm may be a Christian truly enough, and
there is no doubt that there are such unreasoning and thoroughly irrational creatures in the world ; but if he is a Christian, he is in the most elementary stages of the Christian life.
It is conceivable that a man of education, of excellent birth,
and with some ability to discover the injustice which lies in
the social structure of to-day, might, on the ground of these
observations, determine to become a Christian, and give his
life to Christian service.   But just here appears the first fundamental distinction between the Christian of the novel and
the Christian of the New Testament.

There is not a single illustration in the whole New Testament of a man who primarily undertakes the service of Christ
for the purpose of saving the world.   The New Testament
Christians are first of all impressed with their own sins, and
only with those of the world after they have become themselves reconciled to God.   This strikes one as rational and
true to human nature under the guidance of the Spirit of
God.   But John Storm, true to his name, begins his alleged
Christian life in a mad and thoroughly insane notion that his
main concern is about the world.   The whole course of his
life, as Mr. Caine depicts it, shows with perfect clearness
that while he was wondering about the world's future and
morality he was showing in himself the most grotesque combination of irrationality and senselessness one can imagine.
His treatment of the heroine Glory Quayle, for example, is
such as no woman of strong mind and heart could or would
endure.   And it is such that no woman ought to endure.   The
mere fact that a man has what is in itself an excellent ambi-

tion is no reason for approving him. Philanthropic madness is madness none the less for its philanthropy.

This works itself out further in this curious Christian, in his utterly throwing off the usual restraints of personal accountability for his deeds. Few men would care to attribute their actions so recklessly to God as does this novel-made Christian. Most Christians in daily life humbly ask God for guidance, and then trust that they may so interpret the divine will as to do reasonably well. This insane person takes God and Satan into his life and actions as freely as though they were puppets whom he could pose or dispose at any moment he saw fit. Surely this is not the Christian life as we have it in Christ or any of his immediate followers, as we know them in the New Testament.

The Christian life is rationality if it is anything. All the human passions and interests which move to self-sacrifice are under the control and the direction of the reasoning powers. A man does not start off to Asia or Africa or anywhere else on a mission to Christianize the heathen without thinking these things carefully through as to cost and method. He does not recklessly demand of every one with whom he has any relations that they shall blindly accept his standard of action whether or not it commends itself to their judgment. On the contrary, the reasonableness of Christianity lies in just this respect for individual judgment and personal responsibility to the whole problem. But Hall Caine's Christian knows none of these things. He is simply a selfish enthusiast who has become enamored of an idea which, without rhyme or reason, he tries to cram down every one's throat.

The sins of the modern society are grievous enough; of that there is no doubt. But granting that we were able to fix responsibility with absolute certainty, which we are not, even then the average Christian might well ponder over any such reckless attempt at wholesale reformation as this young man undertakes. And, most of all, if he were wise he would not try it in such a theatrical way as the Christian of this novel does the experiment of world-reforming. In fact, the real Christian needs to master first of all his own life and its weak-

nesses and this takes pretty much all the strength that he has.
Not that he has no concern for the world, but that the most
powerful reforming agency in this world is a vigorous Christian life itself without bluster and without storm.

Sin is not the sentimental thing that Mr. Hall Caine
depicts in his novel. And the sin of lust is not the only sin
in the world, nor is that particular sin one-sided in its guilt.
In no one thing does the New Testament display its moral
attitude more than in its portrayal of the sins of the world.
Always just and always in the full recognition of human weakness and frailty, there is never a note of sentimental foolishness such as runs through this entire book. Sin in the Bible
is located in the human will. It is deliberate and is recognized as an enormity because of the moral dignity which
belongs to man. But sin in Mr. Caine's novel is simply a
hysterical condition resulting from confused social and moral
distinctions, and he gives us nothing in the view of redemption
which he presents to which a strong man can feel the slightest attraction.

Moreover, the taking up of the gauntlet against sin is not
a holiday matter that is so easily handled as John Storm dis-
poses of it. If the social estimates of sin are wrong, merely
hallooing against them will not bring about a remedy. The
people must be shown why their estimates of sin are wrong
and why it is unjust to visit severe punishment upon one
class of offenders and to deal lightly with another. That is
a matter for patient instruction and not for mass-meeting
resolutions.

And here again the sanity of the New Testament appears
in marked contrast to the novel-made sins and sinners. The
world's ideas of righteousness have not been acquired by any
hocus-pocus process, but by patient and hard experience.
One social ideal is abandoned and another taken up only
because the world has tried the former and found it wanting. The same is true of ideas of righteousness and sin.
Absolute holiness in this world is not to be hoped for, immediately at least. The New Testament and Christ distinctly
recognize this. Christ himself tells his disciples that there

are many things that he cannot tell them now, because they are not ready for them. What is that but the recognition of the fact that ideals of righteousness are acquired in service, by patience, earnest and laborious waiting and education in the method of Christian living? Our generation has been thoroughly saturated with the hocus-pocus idea of social transformation. One seldom hears of making the world better by simply day by day being better, and behaving decently and properly. No, indeed; every man has a "plan" and while his "plan" is maturing he simply runs riot through all the homely virtues of Christianity.

But by far the greatest weakness of this literary and dramatic Christianity is perceived when we compare John Storm to Christ himself as we may reasonably think of Christ approaching the modern world. Christ is attractive, moderate and appealing; he comes not to plunge one day into ecstasies over a possible mission to lepers and the next day to bury himself in a monastery, but to show by the calm, even and matured moral poise of his life the rational sweetness and simplicity of godliness. But John Storm is forever keeping us wondering what he will do next. We feel that a world of such Christians would be a veritable bedlam. We would not be able to sleep nights or have a minute's rest in our religion, if such ideas of Christianity were ever to become widespread in the Church. We might reject Christ because he was too great for us. It is the fate of great natures to be misinterpreted and often abused on that account. Some would say, as they did in Christ's own time, "He is a good man." Others might say, as they did in Christ's own time, "He hath a devil." But in any case it would be because he was too great for us. But John Storm is not too great for us and we reject him at once because he is such a disgusting exhibition of prejudices and whims utterly irreconcilable and never once genuinely human and inspiring for love and courageous manly fortitude.

The New Testament Christians, on the other hand, with all their blemishes show the elements of genuine Christian feeling. St. Paul, missionary as he was, and sufferer for the gospel's sake, never once lost sight of his own great need. " Faithful is the saying, and worthy of all acceptation, that Christ Jesus came into the world to save sinners ; *of whom I am chief.*" That was the way St. Paul felt. But John Storm feels that the great sinners of the world are other beings, not himself. Even then they are people who are guilty of particular sins. It seems to be a species of social offense that is repugnant to him, not the moral delinquency itself. Therein lies the difference again between the novelists and the New Testament. One deals with generic morality and the other with particular offenses. One is theatrical and melodramatic ; the other is human and universal.

The Christians of the New Testament are men whom the consciousness of great responsibility has made thoughtful, sober and self-forgetful. Their duty is first entirely independent of their emotions. When they are weak, as they often are, it is a sheer drop from a severe standard of duty. But they are never weathercocks of whom nothing can be predicted. When they argue about doctrines, they battle just like other men and have intense feelings and express themselves with vigor and plainness. But they hold to their positions. They can be identified always. Paul and Peter show at the end of their Christian lives the same mental traits that distinguished them at the beginning. Matured, to be sure, but still clearly differentiated, they are the same people.

Now the particular effect for which the possession of a deep sense of responsibility is distinguished is a wise and healthful conservatism. The man who has much at stake is careful about jeopardizing it. It is the man who has little or nothing at stake who is ready to follow every *ignis fatuus* which presents itself to his vision. A man's personality consists very considerably of the things with which he is identified. And concern for these often, when he has no thought for himself, makes him think carefully before committing himself to enterprises which ask his aid. But Hall Caine's Christian has no such sense. His feeling of responsibility is simply sentimental rhapsodizing about fallen women. In the course of the book no less than twenty differing life ideals are adopted and rejected by the Christian who is to be a redeemer to his generation. Responsibility produces no such result as this. On the contrary, it plants the man in his rationally conceived task and develops him in it. This is also the New Testament presentation of the Christian at work.

The novel-made Christian is simply therefore not a Christian at all. He is merely a modern sentimentalist who talks about the wrongs of the world without having any very definite ideas as to where the seat of the trouble lies; who diffuses his energies in space when he ought to be engaged in prayer; who bewails a lost world when he ought to be practicing kindness and charity; who is distressed about social conditions while he is himself in a state of moral delirium; ever worrying about and never practicing the simplest precepts which lie at the root of Christian living. If these are the only ideals which Mr. Caine could see in England and America to any considerable extent, then we may well give ourselves up to lamentations and prayers, for we are all but lost.

But the truth of the whole matter is that we have here what we have so often had before, — a theatrical Christianity for book-making purposes. It is not the gospel Christian and never can be. The Christian life is not a sensational thing at all. It consists in a very few precepts and a great deal of prayer to God. It is by no means a thing for dramatics, whether in books or on the stage. The novelist was thinking of startling effects, not of the Christian virtues. He was thinking of shifting scenes and colored lights and the *gaudium theatri*, not of the joy of the Christian soul growing in grace. It is not strange that the result should show what the real motive was, whatever may be put forth as the ostensible motive.

Men and women are not helped to a better life by highly seasoned accounts of the aberrations of excited minds, even when these have their aberrations grow out of themes which are in themselves admirable. A man may become crazed on the subject of philanthropy or religion just as he may become crazed about anything else. In either case, he must be treated as an insane being. If Christianity offered as its usual product such beings as John Storm, then the world would be perfectly justified in throwing it out-of-doors. But Christianity produces no such men. What it does produce is men who, thoughtfully facing the world's sin and woe, apply themselves with energy and reason to the amelioration of both, with the best appliances at hand and with patience and good sense. It helps them to realize that in this world the wheat and the tares will grow together for a long time yet. It does not make men who become hysterical and excited when they fail once, but men who resolutely go to work to succeed better the next time.

That this novelist should have had the courage to offer such a picture of a Christian to the world shows to what an extent we are still in the bonds of spectacular religious ideals. Ordinary faithful service is still something too humdrum and tame to be admired. The great homely truths by which the world must live, if it is to live at all, must be dressed out in feathers and ribbons and have a brass band go before. The mere fact of rightness and wisdom and honor makes the life of sobriety too inert. It must have the sensational accompaniments and must finally die a violent and picturesque death before we take full account of its truth.

But the real Christian life is nothing like all this. The great battles of righteousness are not fought in the sight of men. The great heroes of Christianity were men who had to be dragged into publicity, not men who were constantly parading themselves before the footlights and every little while looking up to the boxes, waiting for applause. They were more akin to the soldier in his bivouac thinking about the great contest at arms to-morrow and sleeping with his musket beside him ready for service, than to a semi-educated dilettante who is all aglow about saving the world while he cannot behave himself with decency.

Precept upon precept, line upon line, here a little there a little, is far more descriptive of the true Christian life. It shrinks from the blare of trumpets and the analysis of the novelist. It just lives on in patience, hope and prayer. When a man gets interested in the world in these days, if he is a true Christian he begins by becoming gentle and kind in his home, by supplying more comforts for his family, by giving better education to his children and by spending less money in pure foolishness. He goes to church on Sundays and is found in the caucus and the election booth. He tries to pay his debts and rear his family properly. He tries to be charitable and just. He tries to be open-handed and fair-minded. He hates liars and hypocrites, and he thinks more about making one less flagrant sinner in the world in his own person, than of reorganizing the social law. According to Hall Caine's type he would pollute the minds of his children, if he ever lived in one place long enough to marry and rear a family, with all kinds of nauseating recitals of crime. Instead of the Bible they would feed on the Sunday newspaper, and instead of a quiet, wholesome and uplifting life he would rend his household with sensation and claptrap. Nobody but a novelist would ever think of calling such a man a Christian.

Literary and dramatic Christianity will never be truly descriptive of the actual Christian life, because there is so much of it that lies beyond the power of human portraiture. The human elements may be given with reasonable accuracy, but what makes the Christian life Christian is the infusion of the divine, and that is beyond the power of man to reveal except by suggestion. The Christian life is an experience in which the human and the divine are united in a common purpose, and it is for that reason essentially a secret which can only be guessed by experience and obedience. The human rule is, By their fruits shall ye know them. But there is a vast fund of spiritual feeling and knowledge which cannot be translated into works, of which only the Eternal Father, who knows the hearts of men, can be aware. And the Christian life with its varying chords of hope and fear, of joy and pain, of exultant triumph and of despair and discouragement will be fully revealed in the day when the hearts of all men are laid bare. Then, and then only, shall we infallibly know what and who is a Christian. Until that time we can only contemplate with patience and loyalty the divine Model, and strive to be like him.

THE FORERUNNER OF GOD

LUKE vii. 28.

THIS is unique testimony. It is remarkable not merely for its unqualified character, but not less so for the source from which it comes and the subject of which it is uttered. The praise of Jesus Christ, even in the slightest degree, would be a possession which might well satisfy any man. The unqualified praise of Jesus Christ is one of those astounding things which none can hope for other than a man utterly lost in devotion to the cause of God. It is this fact which renders the praise of Jesus for John so interesting and unusual. John was a man, and a very fallible man. He was a preacher whose doctrine and method furnish occasion for wide diversity of opinion. His was one of those volcanic natures that apprehend the truth, but yet give expression to it in forms which only a few may understand, and which many must misunderstand. We have only to imagine a John the Baptist of our time endeavoring to bring to us the message which was given to John to proclaim, to understand how greatly the Baptist's temperament and mode of approach to spiritual truth differ from our own. Indeed, we should almost be tempted to doubt the validity of a spiritual message which began with the fierce imprecations and violent epithets which were apparently the main body of John's preaching. We should not deny the facts. We should deny his authority to utter them in this form. We are not offended when Jesus calls us Pharisees and hypocrites. We are rebellious when one less than the Christ uses these expressions.

What gives a greater air of mystery to the unqualified praise of Jesus for John is the suspicion which is always clinging to us that perhaps John exceeded the terms of his mission. Was the preaching of John the Baptist spiritual preaching? Was it a genuine spiritual message which he brought? Are we conscious to-day, as we read through those fiery denunciations, that they have a spiritual quality and tone which give them eternal significance and power? Is there not an atmosphere of temporalness and practical reform about John's manner and language which speaks of the practical reformer rather than the bearer of spiritual tidings? Can the fierce denouncer of wrongs and the instructor in practical righteousness and the man of the monastic mind and temperament be the vehicle of profound and abiding spiritual truth? These are the doubts which force themselves into our minds as we read through the remains of John's ministry as we find them in the New Testament. It was a stormy and fretful life. It involved not merely a striking religious reformation and an earnest national expectation, but also a personal problem of supreme and almost surpassing interest. What did John think? What was in John's mind concerning the mysterious One That Cometh After Me, and how did he reconcile in his mind his own acts with the character of that majestic Being of whose power he was so sincerely convinced, and the thought of whom alone could make him conscious of humility? For observe that John is never at a loss for action and speech except when the thought of Jesus comes into his mind, and this thought alone makes him self-forgetful. Turbulent, vigorous, determined and resourceful always, he sinks into nothingness when he thinks of the Coming One.

That in itself would furnish a problem of great interest, and would challenge all our abilities to fathom its depth. With the message of repentance as his chief doctrine, John was eminently a man of practical reach. He might almost be called a politician. Certainly his utterances had political significance, and his execution was unquestionably in part a political act. John's preaching to the soldiers undoubtedly had the effect of a political disturbance. It was possibly regarded by those in authority as designed for political ends. At the same time it could hardly have been a court sermon in which he so drastically proclaimed the sin of Herod, which ultimately cost him his head. And if it was preached to a mob, that surely would have a political significance in a country and in an atmosphere where almost every act in which the ruler is at all mentioned is supposed to be fraught with great results. Add to this John's intense nationalism, and the circumstantial evidence for the political character of John's preaching is very strong, well-nigh irresistible. Yet John was the messenger of God. He was the forerunner of Christ. He surrendered all pretension and all authority, yes, even became silent before the Coming One, whether in thought or actual presence. What did John think of Christ? Did he really know him? Did he really recognize him? To the very last we are left in doubt on this point, apparently the most vital one to the understanding of John and his work. From the prison he sends to ask the question, "Art thou he that cometh, or look we for another?" What did that mean from a man whose whole public career had been spent in announcing the Coming One, and who had publicly baptized him? Thus, to the very end, John is to us a profound mystery.

Attempts to understand John and interpret him to the world have been made without number. We should be glad to have any one who was able to penetrate into the mystery of that strong nature and its conflicts tell us all about it, and many have tried it. Preacher and poet, historian and seer, have sought to give us pictures of that career which should explain to us the fragments of his mind and life which we still have. Like those of the extinct monsters of other ages, we know that he of whom they were a part was a giant. But who can from the fragments give us the whole man? The latest to attempt this is a great modern German dramatist, Sudermann, whose tragedy, "Johannes," has lately been published. For originality in treatment, and power in delineating motive and dramatic strength, and mastery of Biblical material, this must probably be ranked as one of the great dramas on Biblical subjects. There are in this tragedy a dignity and spiritual understanding which will always make it worth while for the student of Biblical character and thought to read it as a part of the necessary literature of the subject of the character of John. To be sure, the result is what might have been expected. What the Bible does not reveal to us, the historical and spiritual imagination of a modern dramatist is not likely to bring into clearer vision. But the attempt is excellent and, on the whole, illuminating and intensely interesting.

It is well in this connection to pause a moment to consider a point or two on the general subject of Biblical drama. The Bible, as is well known, is not a treatise on theology, but a portrayal of life. It is the record of the religious aspirations and spiritual expansion of a single nation, from the first personal and tribal intimations of religious service and sacrifice to the final culmination in Christianity, the world religion. It is impossible that such a development should not have contained in it numberless episodes which are of the highest dramatic interest apart from their religious significance. Indeed, there must be something of an alliance between the very drama of religion and the religion itself. For our first aspirations come in connection with the movement and symbols of religion, which have been handed down by tradition, and this of itself constitutes a kind of drama, a kind of religious story, which is all that the drama properly considered is. To tell a story by visible forms is to dramatize it. To bring to that presentation the vestments of local coloring and the temporal surroundings as an aid to the imagination and an inspiration to the feelings, is merely to expand what was essentially a drama in the beginning. The very rites of the Church are of this nature. When we practice the symbol of baptism, we really enact a part of a drama of redemption, which is for us symbolically completed when we continue it in the equally dramatic symbols of the Lord's passion. The Bible is full of moments, occasions, national movements and personal experiences, which require just this dramatization for their highest understanding; and the Bible in many cases does just this thing. There can be no doubt whatever that many of the incidents in Judges, in the Books of Kings and Chronicles, are really the dramatized versions of these events. Certainly, if one will read the triumph songs of Deborah and Miriam he will find the most highly wrought drama that can be found in the history of literature.

The sacredness of the theme, and a false conception of what loyalty and reverence to the Bible involve, have kept us from understanding these things. It has given to the utterly faithless, and one might almost say godless, men the only freedom that there was to fully enter into the beauty and power of the Bible. Churchmen and scholars have reverently covered their eyes, in the vain belief that by hiding the beauty of the Bible they magnified its ethical power and interest. It is doubtful if this result was secured, though there is no doubt that an exaggerated interest in the mere injunctions of the Scriptures was obtained. But the Bible is not all precept. Much of it is example. And example, and the history of example, are drama. And the telling of the story of an illustrious example, whether it be of a king or a prophet, is essentially drama; spiritual drama, of course, in which the motive is a celestial rather than a terrestrial one. But as with the Book of Job, there is often prologue and epilogue and *mise en scène*, which are all a part of the literary structure of the incomparable Book of books. They are in the Book because they are in life. They are in life because they are a part of the redemptive activity of God, in which man is the object of the Father's solicitude and care. Every parable of Christ, every sermon of the Lord, abounds in these characteristics. Even his end, that mysterious death in which he was offered up for all men, is to this day called, and properly called, the great World Tragedy. Shakespeare was right, the world is a stage, and men are the players.

In Sudermann's "Johannes" the power and originality of the author center about three points, the first being the battle in John's mind between the gospel of rage and the gospel of love, the second in John's skepticism about himself and his task, and the third the revelation of Christ by contrast. In each of these there is a distinct advance on the traditional understanding of the character of John the Baptist, and one that is religiously instructive and useful as well as it must be dramatically effective and touching. The fragments of John's preaching which remain to us in the New Testament show us very clearly that it was strong in the sanctions of wrath. John's gaze was steadily fixed on the sins of his generation. In his vision he saw the ax laid at the root of the trees. He saw the evil men and women of his time receiving their proper reward in the fearful penalties which his imagination pictured for them. In this John greatly resembles Mohammed, whose main appeal was like John's, the exhortation to flee the wrath to come. John urged repentance. But the repentant man, whosoever he be, must pass under the fierce lash of corrective denunciation and scourging. John is never at a loss for answer to those who, driven by the torturing fears which a vivid Oriental imagination creates, came to him to know what they must do. In this we have a very fine opportunity for contrast between John's gospel of rage and the genuine gospel of love. When the people come to John, note the intensely practical, mundane character of the replies which John makes. He wants the visible fruits of repentance. He that hath two coats, let him impart to him that hath none. To the publican he says, "Extort no more than that which is appointed you." To the soldiers, "Do violence to no man, neither exact wrongfully." All, you observe, practical, and one' may almost add, statesmanlike directions. Not a word about the heart and the spirit. This is not the message of a man dealing with spiritual beings. It is the language of a political ruler endeavoring to keep order, and to protect property rights and to maintain political security.

Now notice, by contrast, the language of another preacher. I choose the case of Paul that the contrast may be a perfectly fair one. It is too obvious at the outset that this is not the gospel of Christ. But take the plea of St. Paul at Athens, and then contrast the tolerance and argumentative dignity of that discourse with this violent speech of John's. Take especially Paul's fine quotation in his sentence, "As certain even of your own poets have said, For we are also his offspring," and the fine appeal based upon it, and then remember that John's sermon was usually introduced by the salutation, " Ye offspring of vipers, who warned you to flee from the wrath to come?" To Paul men are the offspring of God, to John they are the offspring of vipers; and just there lies the difference in their conception. But John was not entirely unconscious of the fact that he was thus not entirely representative of the Coming One. For when the people try to take him for the Christ, he knows at once that Christ is not such an one as he. This he afterward recalls to the minds of the people in self-justification when he tells them that he told them plainly that he was not the Christ. John knew in his heart that the Christ of God was the offspring of love. God did not give his Son for vipers. God loved the world, and the baptism of the Holy Ghost was greater even than cleansing with water. John knew all this. This battle in John's soul is visible, even in the New Testament. Sudermann has brought it out with vivid and almost terrific distinctness in his tragedy. When the messengers have brought back to John Christ's reply to his inquiry about himself, John thinks not of the reality of Christ, a skepticism which was strong upon him when the messengers left, but of the battle in his own soul about the relative truthfulness with which he has fulfilled his mission. John may have expected Jesus to do violent things. Now he sees that the master method is the attractiveness of love itself. It is here that the dramatist makes John say : —

" I understand it full well, I to whom he spake. I have offended him for *I knew him not*. And *my offence* fills all the world *for that I knew him not*. Ye yourselves bear me witness that I said I am not Christ, but I am sent before him. But a man can receive nothing except it be given him from heaven. And unto me nothing was given. *The keys of death — I did not receive them ; the scales of guilt — they were not confided to me.* For out of no man's mouth may the word 'guilt' be sounded save out of his that loveth. But I came to scourge you with rods of iron. *Wherefore is my kingdom turned to shame and my voice is sealed.*"

Notice the strength and insight of the italicized words. John appears to think that the supreme mistake of his life, even now, is in not being worthy of the custody of the sanctions of God. *The keys of death* — his lament is that he did not receive them. *The scales of guilt* — he is sorry that they were not confided to him. This is the echo in the soul of the man of the gospel of rage, of wrath. But the lesson has been learned, especially in that he sees himself superseded rather than expanded upon. Christ does not fulfill his gospel, he supersedes it. This is the strong original point in Sudermann's conception of John. It is that he is simply overborne, left out, that furnishes the crowning lament in the soul of the Baptist. And truly so it was. With the unqualified encomium of John before us, Christ must needs add, "yet he that is but little in the kingdom of heaven is greater than he." This is a most wonderful and powerful contrast. We see the impotency of rage. We see the superlative beauty of love, as even John saw it before his death. For he adds : " A throne has descended from heaven with pillars of fire. The Prince of Peace, clothed in white robes, is seated upon it. And his sword is Love, and Mercy is his war-cry." Thus is the Baptist overcome in the final revelation of the power of divine love and the majesty of the mercy of God. John still lingers on the border of the wrath gospel, but he has heard the good news. The gospel is life and peace, not death and shame. Christ is a Saviour, not an Avenger.

Then, again, the element of skepticism in John's nature comes out with a power and interest that are very suggestive and at the same time very true to the New Testament presentation of the prophet. Indeed, there reappears here in John the Baptist the problem which has appeared in all great skeptics, using that term now in its proper sense. The doubt and distrust of Job are here again delineated, but with a new dress. It is the eternal problem of Prometheus, of Faust and of Hamlet. In John it takes a form which is not so deep-seated intellectually, but it is in many respects emotionally stronger than that of Hamlet or of Faust. Meeting the Galilæan pilgrims and proclaiming his Messiah the Man of Rage and

of Wrath, our author gives the key to John's real attitude of
mind in the colloquy that follows in which the pilgrim reveals
the Messiah she is seeking, as a helper of the poor. She
says to John : —

"Not him do I want. So many have come ere now clothed
in golden mail and have lifted their swords on high, till Israel
is bleeding like a beast of sacrifice. And he must be no king.
When kings come they come to kings. To us poor none
hath yet come. . . . Go, stranger, thou robbest me of my
remnant of hope. . . . Go, thou art *a false prophet;*"
whereupon John recoils with horror at the thought of his
heart thus boldly put into words, — "A false prophet." What
if it be the truth ! and John is for the moment utterly beside
himself in the expression that has been given to the lurking
unbelief of his soul, in his cause and in himself. Upon this
he asks further information. He is told that Christ is teaching "all kinds of silly things," that we must "love our enemies," and "bless those who curse us," and "pray for those
who persecute us." This is too much for the preacher of
wrath. His confusion is now complete, and we hear in all
his words the sighs of the man of doubts and of fearful looking-for of the judgment he passed upon others. John does
not know what to think. Who ever heard of loving *enemies?*
Who blesses the *cursing?* John cannot understand it.

Of course this is false historically. No devout pilgrim
would have been satisfied with other than a thoroughly
national Messiah. This was proved in the event. Strong
as Jesus was in his national feeling and enthusiasm, he could
not satisfy the desires of those who wished him to assume
temporal dominion and hurl the hated Roman from his
throne. But it is dramatically justifiable to reveal what a
tumult there was in John's soul, as indeed there must have
been. The mystery of love is too deep for John, just as
the mystery of life is too great for Hamlet. He cannot
bring himself to understand how he has been chosen the
messenger of Christ if this is to be Christ's gospel. If the
enemies are not to be slaughtered in great masses, and if
there is not to be the overturn of the sinful and the joyful

delight of the righteous in the humiliation and punishment of the "offspring of vipers," there is no joy left to the Baptist. He cannot understand it. We almost feel here the movement that makes the Book of Jonah so effective when that desponding prophet, seeing he cannot call the divine wrath down upon sinning but repentant Nineveh, exclaims : —

"O Lord, was not this my saying, when I was yet in my country ? Therefore I hasted to flee unto Tarshish : for I knew that thou art a gracious God, and full of compassion, slow to anger, and plenteous in mercy, and repentest thee of the evil. Therefore now, O Lord, take, I beseech thee, my life from me ; for it is better for me to die than to live."

This is how John felt. Love is simply weakness. Is the trump of God nothing but a call to caresses ? What shall become of the prophet then ? Herr Sudermann works this out in a very powerful scene where John as the leader of a mob essays to throw a stone at Herod, but doubt has overcome the preacher of wrath to come, and when the "chief viper," the adulterous Herod, comes to view, he cannot throw it. The idea of love even has been too strong, and the helpless hand falls to his side and the crowd spurns him whom it once followed with fear and trembling. The spell is broken. The thought of love has rendered wrath harmless.

The total result of all this is to bring into greater clearness the real mission and purpose of Christ. If the depth of a shadow reveals the strength of the light that causes it, then we have here a most powerful presentation of the real Christ by the portrayal of that which Christ is not. It was not to be expected that any writer could give us what the New Testament has not given us, and so there are many unsatisfactory things about this presentation of John. There are tender elements in the nature of John which the New Testament reveals dimly but unmistakably. There is the feeling of power and sweetness in that majestic saying of John's, one of the finest in the New Testament, when he sees Jesus coming to him and says out of his full soul, "Behold, the Lamb of God !" John was not so utterly devoid of all the finer and truer elements of Christ's gospel as Herr Sudermann would

lead us to think. But he is true in this, that John, unlike
the other prophets who preceded Christ, did not see his message fulfilled in the sense in which Isaiah's was or others
were. Indeed, John says the truest thing that has been said
about himself when he says, "He must increase, but I must
decrease," which must mean that John was utterly to be
effaced when the true gospel came to light. But he could
hardly have known or felt how completely he must be
effaced. Wrath as a motive must ultimately disappear from
the world. Even in a world which is continually filled with
wars and rumors of wars, wrath must depart. Man is not
made for wrath. It is not the will of God that any should
be lost; and the sovereign motive of all life, divine life as well
as human life, must ever be love. This is the great fact which
the German author brings out with great beauty and power.
We can forgive a fragmentary John the Baptist if he reveals
to us a greater Christ. We can overlook a note of historical
weakness if out of it comes a spiritual inspiration; and the
dramatist has really done this and made the Christ of God
more glorious in his presentation of the forerunner of God.

The true prophetic vision of the triumph of the Son of God
is always a vision of peace. So from his heights Isaiah saw
the New Jerusalem, and the vision was one of beauty and
sweetness, not of smoke and of war. His sword is ever the
sword of Love, and Mercy must be his war-cry, as Sudermann
makes John truly say. It is difficult enough in a world of
strife to realize the power of love. There has ever been an
attractiveness about the shield and the spear which have been
fatal to man. But destruction is never redemptive. Nothing
is ever gained by destroying other things. Nor is man saved
by the destruction of man. Man is most moved when he is
most loved. He is most quickly saved where there is the
largest movement of salvation actually in progress. This is
because, as the offspring of God, as the Greek poet from whom
Paul quoted said, he must live forever. He cannot be destroyed, and because he must live he must love and be loved.
The essence of Eternal Life is Eternal Love. Men have
never known it or realized it. But the Son of God has

known it and demonstrated for us the power of living love.
Therefore it is in the life of Christ and the intercession of the
living Christ that mankind draws its supreme inspiration to-
day. We are moved by the majesty and impressiveness of
his death. We are lifted and encouraged by the helpfulness
of his life. It was more than a mere poet's fancy that wrote
in our well-known hymn : —

> Here I would forever stay,
> Weep and gaze my soul away.

But the duty of mankind is not to weep and certainly not to
gaze the soul away. Life is power and ministry, not weeping. It is the strength of service, not the despair of tears.
It is the majesty of heroic toil, not the lament of plaintive
listlessness. Better a wrong-headed John in the turmoil of
skepticism and fear, than a cowardly Joseph who is a secret
disciple. John's misunderstood Christ is yet a living Coming
One. Joseph of Arimathœa has only spices for a Christ in
the tomb.

Mighty forerunner of God! Thy Christ was not the Christ
of God. But in thy vision of a Coming One thou sawest from
the towers of thy soul the human passion of life. Thou didst
prevail, for a greater than thou was never born of woman. But
thine was not the life of the kingdom of heaven. There all
are as children in love and faith, not as warriors in the grime
of strife and blotched with the blood of men. Thou didst
learn it in the prison. May we, too, out of the strife of the
world and the prison-house of torment find the Christ of love,
and see the descending throne with the Prince of Peace upon
it. His sword is Love, and Mercy is his war-cry. "God so
loved the world, that he gave his only begotten Son, that whosoever believeth on him should not perish, but have eternal
life."

A MEMORIAL OF LOVE

MARK xiv. 9.

THE devotion which Jesus Christ inspired among those who had immediate contact with him through his earthly ministry has furnished us with some of the choicest examples of tenderness and attachment which can be found in the history of mankind. This is not to be wondered at, considering what sublime motives induced that affection, or remembering the natural graces of manhood and moral beauty which must have shone in every movement of the Saviour's earthly career. But the love and the chivalric loyalty of those who truly caught the spirit of Christ's service is nevertheless an inspiring chapter of the ministry of our Lord, and one that has always had great attraction for men in their study of the New Testament.

Among the figures that thus charm us with the singleness and power of their love to Christ is Mary of Bethany, the woman who anointed him, as he himself said, to prepare him for his burial. That scene is one of those exquisite gospel cameos wherein all the power and sweetness of human love, linked to a divine and soul-compelling ideal, are brought out into the clearest outlines. It gives a grace to Christ which is peculiarly human and tender. It reveals at the same time, not less clearly and not less human, the grasping avarice of the traitor who carries the bag. It shows us the depth and the overflowing fullness of a woman's love. And all this in the brief compass of seven verses.

Jesus is in Bethany, having come to Judæa for the last time in his life. He is at the house of Simon the leper, with his disciples, and the conversation is doubtless turning upon the tragic events of the Passion Week into which they are coming, and the Master is without doubt trying, in the few days left to him, to impress upon the disciples the most important lessons of his ministry, that they might be remembered when he was taken from them. It was important that this should be done. The crucifixion, when it came, would have a scattering effect. Many would be frightened from his cause, which was, in fact, the case. Many more would return to their homes disheartened, and think that, though a beautiful dream, yet, after all, it was but a dream. Some must stand firm. And, foreseeing the end, he was endeavoring to make the things that were most important clear in the minds of those upon whom the burden of sustaining his work should fall.

In the midst of this conversation there comes in a woman. Perhaps she has already been present though not conspicuously. Martha, her sister, has been serving, and Lazarus was present, the same whom Jesus had called forth from the tomb. We learn these facts from the account of the scene which St. John gives. The supper over, or partially over, the Master is in the act of instructing his followers, when the woman, observing her opportunity, comes into the midst of the assembly and pours over his head the ointment. A "very costly" ointment, as Mark puts it. But not only his head, for, as St. John adds, her love could not stop there, but proceeded to anoint his feet also and to wipe them with her hair. "And the house was filled with the odour of the ointment."

What now occurred was just what might naturally have been expected, and what occurs almost every day of our lives. Seeing the contents of the alabaster cruse given so lavishly, and apparently so unthinkingly, there arose at once a murmuring among the disciples. It was Judas Iscariot who said it might have been sold for the benefit of the poor. But there was probably not less indignation among the rest, because the nature of that love token was not understood, in all probability, by any man of the whole apostolic company present. They saw only the alabaster cruse and the costly contents, which to their minds were wasted. As usual, the money value was to them the most impressive thing. Not one of them thought of the woman's heart which prompted that offering. But Christ saw at once that the real sacrifice there was not in the costly ointment nor even in the passionate love that wiped his feet with the hairs of her head, but in the heart within that was burning to reveal the great devotion with which it was overcharged, and to express which nothing could have been too great. It was this that made him utter these impressive words, which have linked this memorial love forever with the gospel of redemption, "Wheresoever the gospel shall be preached throughout the whole world, that also which this woman hath done shall be spoken of for a memorial of her."

Now, as to the indignation of the disciples, it would be a great mistake for us to be indignant with them. We may except Judas, perhaps, because subsequent events show that John was right when he said that his words were uttered, not because he cared for the poor, but because he was a thief. But it was natural that the disciples should recoil from this lavish apparent waste of a thing, relatively of great value. They were men most of whom had been reared under conditions of great hardship and penury. None of them could possibly have been used to any mode of life that made such a thing natural. Hard-working men themselves, they were naturally frugal, and had contracted ideas of generosity in the matter of personal expressions of love. They loved Christ, too. But a man's love takes the form of loyalty ; a woman's usually takes the form of sacrifice. That cruse of ointment represented Mary's heart far more than it did three hundred pence. It was a product of sacrifice, every drop of which came from the heart. It was not strange that the fishermen who toiled all day and night, and lived the rough, crude life of such laborers, did not understand the delicate feelings that were at work here.

A similar blunder is made by charity workers to-day. Philanthropic people keep wondering why the very poor will spend so much of their hard-earned money for toys and playthings for their children, and why many a workingman

will take his wages and give it all up for some trinket for
his loved ones at home, when it might far more wisely be
spent for the simple necessities of life. The reason, however,
is neither deeply hidden nor mysterious. It is simply that
when that mood of love comes over men, it makes no difference whether they are poor or rich, it acts in just the same
way, the value of things is lost sight of entirely. What does
he care that he toiled five days in the broiling sun to get
that money? It is a trinket of love to probably the only
being in the world with whom he has any fellowship whatever. The hot sun and the dreary work are all forgotten in
the exuberant joy of the visible token of love.

In a not less impressive way it is seen again and again
how some abused and wretched woman will cling to the
object of her love, notwithstanding his kicks and cuffs. At
some time he has made some such an expression of his love
to her, and the remembrance of it keeps her loyal almost to
death. The sight of some trivial thing which he brought,
with delight and evident happiness in its bestowal, makes
her forget all her wrongs, and cling to him, brute and tyrant
though he is. In vain philanthropy urges the relief of the
courts and the jail. She clings to the dream of her youth,
and remembers the joys of the early and unstained love.
That is why the so-called "scientific" charity is so often
frustrated in its well-meaning but utterly inhuman efforts at
helpfulness. The affections of the heart are not a matter of
scientific regulation. A wife, scientifically, ought to hate a
brute of a husband who neglects and bruises her. But a
single kind word from that very man, when sober and in his
right mind, will play havoc with all the well-meant efforts
of those who match science against love. A hundred beggars might have been clamoring outside, but that alabaster
cruse would have been broken nevertheless.

Rationally such sacrifices are undoubtedly unjustifiable,
and economically considered they are more than wasteful.
But it is the facts with which we are dealing, and with which
most of the scientific world is not yet prepared properly to
deal. An economist of to-day would have said, apart from

the persons involved and the doctrines with which it is connected, that Judas' comment was scientifically the correct
one. Taken by itself, it does seem a foolish proceeding to
make a present of three hundred pence as a personal tribute,
when there are so many poor who are in need of the bare
necessities of life. But that is not the whole story, and life,
though rational, is not exclusively a matter of the reason.
No man thinks about disease germs and the possible dangers
of epidemic when he comes home from a long journey and
kisses his children. Perhaps if he were truly scientific he
would, but it is not likely that such a high state of scientific
living will ever be secured in this world. The scientist and
the economist are important personages, no doubt. But they
are far from being the most important individuals even in
this money-loving and money-getting age.

This woman's offering was a memorial of love. And love
is the strongest thing in this wide world. It can endure more
things and undertake more things than the scientist and the
economist ever dreamed of, notwithstanding all the modern
marvels of science. And though the worldly-wise may sneer
and the learned add their jeers, the mass of mankind will be
more influenced by love than by any other motive that can
possibly be brought to bear on the mind. The heroism of
the world is the story of the world's loves. The sacrifice,
the patience and the suffering of the world are all a part of
the story of its love. It is the perpetual romance of the human
race that it loves and is loved. Mistaken a thousand times, it
loves on just the same, and believes, with Tennyson, that a
heart untouched by love's sacred fire, however free and unhin-
dered in its own pursuit and desire, is not to be envied : —

> Nor, what may count itself as blest,
>   The heart that never plighted troth,
>   But stagnates in the weeds of sloth ;
> Nor any want-begotten rest.
>
> I hold it true, whate'er befall;
>   I feel it when I sorrow most;
>   'Tis better to have loved and lost
> Than never to have loved at all.

And truly the words of Christ have been fulfilled in the world-wide renown of this token. Womanhood has never been so lovely as when it has shown forth the same beautiful devotion that was shown here. Never has it so thoroughly commanded the homage and the tenderness of all ages as when in the outburst of its great passion it has been able to reveal what is the dearest thing to the heart of man, an utterly unselfish soul. Men sometimes do these things. But we have always associated it with womanhood as a trait of the sex, a natural spiritual loveliness that is expressed and completed in a beautiful outward form and presence. And well may the womanhood of the world rejoice in such sacrifices for the glory of Christ. For wherever the gospel has carried the good news, the first result of its sway has been the elevation of woman to her rightful position in the home and in society. To Christianity the womanhood of to-day owes its exalted place. Its education, its culture, its refinement and its security in the social body, so far as these have been secured, are the direct and immediate fruits of Christ's message of redemption to the world. To no class has the gospel been the good tidings of great joy vitalized with meaning and emancipation more than to the women of the world.

The honor which our Saviour conferred upon this anointing by Mary was so signal and exceptional in its nature, that it is worth inquiring why the Lord was so impressed with it that he proclaimed that this memorial should be made known as far as the gospel carried the good news of man's salvation. There were here, surely, elements of service which must have made a peculiarly strong impression upon the Saviour's mind. Striving as we do ourselves for the approval of Christ of our own lives, perhaps this episode may furnish light and suggestion for similar service in our own endeavors to be acceptable to him.

It was a token of exceptional and conspicuous devotion to Christ's person. But Christ honors devotion to the spirit which he presents to the world more than any devotion to his person. We cannot imagine Christ having any great satisfaction in the great crusades undertaken solely for the purpose of possessing his grave. Almost the last thing that could symbolize or suggest anything in relation to the gospel is a sepulcher, even though it be a Holy Sepulcher, because, for the Christian, the chief concern is that it is *empty*. We think reverently enough of the graves of our ancestors. But Christ rose out of the grave, and the fact that crowns and commends the gospel to-day is just that very truth that his grave *was* left open and empty.

But, after all this has been said, it yet remains that Jesus was a man and was in all respects susceptible to all the feelings of personal satisfaction and enjoyment which we are prone to delight in ourselves. As his career was about to close and in his mind the shadows were lengthening out into the gloom of his great trial, completing with fitting somberness and darkness the life of a man who was despised and rejected of men, and of one who had not where to lay his head, what a ray of light and comfort the token of *personal* devotion of this noble woman was! In an instant he thinks of the tender way in which loving hands anoint their dead, and immediately follows the thought, "This is love's anointing for my burial." If ever the Master felt deep, strong and peculiarly personal gratitude, it was at this time. This was not the homage of a man who wanted a high place, or the right hand or the left hand or something else, when he came to his kingdom. It was not the warrior's reckless following with hopes of spoils of war. It was not the fierce attachment of a nationalist chafing under Roman rule and looking only to the slaughter of the oppressor. He had seen all these. Nay, it was not even the grateful tribute of one whose helper and breadwinner had been rescued from the dead and thus saved from want or servitude or worse. It was just the outflowing of a woman's love toward him because he was to her the loveliest and holiest embodiment of all that her spiritual nature could desire. It was not his power or his kingdom or his glory that she rejoiced in. She just loved Christ himself as she knew him.

What a balm that must have been to the weary and heart-burdened Lord! There sat the disciples — loyal fellows,

every one of them, but the traitor. He could forget the
traitor. But how much those strong fishermen had to learn
about the Lamb of God that was to take away the world's
sin! How crude and thoughtless they were! How busied
about the temporal kingdom which was always uppermost
in their minds! They little knew and not even suspected
through what they must pass before they were to receive
their crowns of rejoicing. But an observing, silent woman,
knowing no more than they about all these things, cared for
none of them and busied her thought about Christ himself.
And so forth comes the alabaster cruse and the costly oil, and
the tribute is bestowed, not for anything in particular, but
just because it was the best possible expression of a faithful
and all-absorbing love that was at hand. Do we not all of
us know something about that? Have we not done in our
own lives things just like this? Did we not give our gifts
and make our sacrifices, not *for* anything, but simply because
we *loved* to?

The ministry of Jesus was so inseparably linked with his
Messianic office that purely personal tributes of this character were exceedingly rare in his life. And in this respect
his experience was not different from that which is common
to man. Who would think from what we know of the magnificent aims and the splendid history of the Red Cross
Society, with our knowledge of the thousands of sick and
wounded men who have been helped and saved, and of the
spirit of humanity which has penetrated into the midst of the
bloodiest battles of modern times, that the founder of that
society should be spending his last days in a workhouse in
Switzerland! When the International Medical Congress met
at Moscow recently to bestow its prize to "the man who has
done the greatest service to humanity and medicine in the
present age" Henry Dunnant, though the fame of his service
had travelled around the whole earth, *personally* was so forgotten that he had been suffered to lose his mind and become
incarcerated in a workhouse. It was very much so with
Christ. People thought of being healed or of escaping danger or of coming into power and glory, and thought little or

nothing about the Lord himself. Hence his grateful recognition of this Mary's loving thought for *himself* without thought of recompense or reward.

Again here was a tribute of love which was not a veneer of the principle of utility. While it is true that most of Christ's own mighty works were of a type that might very truthfully be described as needful and useful or at least as embodying the principle of utility, it is not true that utility is the root of the highest or even a genuine love. An intelligent affection may seek what is useful rather than what will please, but if it does, it will do so for other reasons than the mere fact of usefulness. Genuine love does not ask whether such love is useful or not. It acts rather upon the principle of the New Testament expressed in the verse, We love him because he first loved us. Where the treasure is there will the heart be also. The object may often be unworthy, but the heart does not stop to ask of what use such love is or for what gain it is bestowed. It is perfectly plain that this alabaster cruse and its contents might have been worth five hundred or five thousand pence so far as Mary was concerned. She was not thinking about the money. She was not thinking even about the ointment itself. She was thinking of the object of her love and all that occupied her mind was to make Christ realize the greatness of the gratitude and affection of her soul. Christ would have understood it just as well if it had been valued only at thirty pence. It was the quality of the love, not the value of the thing that expressed it, which made the impression on Christ's mind. It was an offering that was unqualified and untainted by worldly feelings or ideas of cost or trouble.

Is there not a great need of just this kind of loving at this time? Might we not with great profit learn the spirit of this woman whose act was so memorable that Jesus was willing to have it go the whole earth over as fit to be linked with the eternal gospel of salvation from sin? Is there not even in our holiest things too much admixture of ideas of gain or good will or profit of one kind and another? We sometimes hear a young woman spoken of as having married well. Do

we mean by this that she has won a true heart and loyal
lover, or do we mean that she has gained plenty to eat and
wear and the reasonable prospect of a comfortable living?
And if we do mean this, is it not a reproach to us that we
should think that marrying well should mean these things
and nothing more? Men ally themselves with the cause of
Christ because it is right and admirable and just that they
should. And against these motives there is nothing to be
said. But would there not be something warming to our
hearts in the knowledge of some that had taken the service
of Christ just because they loved Christ with the warm earnest devotion simply because he is lovely and lovable? If
ever there was need of such a revival of love it is now.

Christ rejoiced and we should rejoice when men do well
even with mixed or only partially worthy motives. But how
much the enjoyment of Christian service would be increased
by doing the will of God from the highest motive and with
absolute singleness of aim! It is probably too much to
expect in this world that men should do everything from
absolutely unselfish devotion to what is lovely and lovable.
But it is not too much to expect that we shall do some things,
yes, a good many things, from this motive. That is an ideal
which is not so far from attainment as much of the current
history would lead us to suppose. There are other things in
this world beside money and gain and social standing and
fame and honor among men. We have recently seen how
the idea of liberty applied to the concerns of a great munici-
pality can rouse the sluggish conscience of a great city.
That was worth something even if the aim was not secured.
To attempt holy things is itself a kind of holiness and not a
despicable kind either.

Let us not in the clamor about the poor, or any other appeal
that calls for charity or philanthropic effort, forget that the
seat of holiness is not in the hands, but in the heart. You
hear it often said that if a man's money is converted he may
be said to be fully converted, but I do not believe that doctrine. Many a man would be glad to give his money if he
could purify his heart. Many a soul has tried, and tried in

vain, to buy the commendation of God with money. The outward expression is important, and every one in our day has seen enough to know the value of money to the kingdom. But what God wants is the heart. Then he will have the money, too. But our tribute should be as Mary's was without thought of the value of the things, but only of the Christ upon whom we gladly bestow them. It is the Judas argument which keeps men in the bondage of many low ideals. How often we hear that same thin argument applied to the house of God! We can worship just as well in a plain house with dirty and dusty surroundings as in a most beautiful cathedral; why put our money into stone and beautiful columns, when we have the poor with us? That sounds to me just like Judas. It is the mockery of the three hundred pence. We build stately cathedrals for the glory of Christ. We enrich our worship that we may give ourselves all the help possible to approach the ideal worship of God. We seek out every addition to service that we may the more effectually reveal to the Son of God and to ourselves our gratitude and homage for his unspeakable love to us. Unselfish love, this is our great need. Untainted devotion, this is our ideal. Let worldly men and imperfect and unthinking disciples be indignant if they will. Let Judas figure out what it costs. But let us bring our hearts to God's service, and our souls to Christ without thought for these things.

And did not the odor fill the whole house? Has not history been made sweeter by that graceful and beautiful token of woman's love and woman's sacrifice? And shall not our own houses be made sweet with the odor of many such deeds, and our community finally receive the overflow of such sweet devotion? May we not have pouring out of every door the rejoicings of Christ's commending word, that the social and civic life, too, may be purified by the power and attractiveness of holy and unselfish living? Make your own life sweet by seeking the highest love. Give Christ the throne and rejoice that he is there. The kingdom will come by and by. Only in thinking of the kingdom let us not forget the King.

THE REDEMPTION IDYL

LUKE ii. 12.

THAT was a strange message which broke the stillness of the Judæan night, when the angels announced to the watching shepherds the birth of Jesus Christ. It had not merely the joyful promise of peace and good will on earth, but it had a sign to humanity which has made the most lasting impression on the mind of Christendom that any sign in the religious history of the world has made. It was so unlike human expectation, and so apart from mere human method, that it revealed humanity to itself for the first time. It overturned in one single night a whole worldful of false traditions and a whole worldful of false ideas of power and authority. It would have been an epoch-making event apart from many of the sublimest remembrances which Christ left on the earth. It was an idyllic presentation of the redemption of man wrought into a form so exquisite and tender that, for the first time in history, humanity understood its own birth-right and divine heritage.

Signs and wonders have played a great part in the history of religion, and do still. If, instead of its miracles, we look to a more commonplace operation of the laws of God, we nevertheless still watch for the omens of favor and wisdom. We are pleased when a favoring condition of circumstances seems to encourage and indorse us as we undertake great tasks. We are depressed when the conditions point to disaster and defeat. And yet why should we be concerned what the result is, if the act has been done and the duty weighed in the light of conscience and of God? But it is true, nevertheless, that we rejoice in signs, and probably the desire for a "token" is one of those spiritual needs which

God has planted in the human soul that he might satisfy it in his own time and way. We still love the sign, and are still impressed with the wonder.

It is not strange, then, that to the wondering shepherds at Bethlehem there was given a sign. Moses was called to his great national duty to Israel by the sign of the burning bush. Samson and Gideon and others were similarly called. David and Saul, Micah and Isaiah, the kings and the prophets of God, waited for the manifestation of the will of Jehovah, and looked to the signs by which that will was to be indicated. Much more would the simple-minded men, sitting under the starlight in the night, living their plain and unmarred life amid their flocks and herds, need and require a token to confirm the strange tidings which the angels had brought. And the sign was given them, and this was the sight that met their eyes to certify the sublime message to which they had listened from the hosts of God: " A babe wrapped in swaddling clothes, and lying in a manger."

If the shepherds were astounded when they saw the whole heavens alive with glorious beings singing the praises of the Son of David, they must have been even more astounded when they saw the simple cause of all the rejoicing of which they had been witnesses. History has glorified that manger at Bethlehem, and it is hard at this distance to conceive what it was actually like. The clouds of incense which have been ascending to that Babe of Bethlehem have almost made us forget the more than simple severity of the scenes through which he came to the earth. And yet they were severe and simple to a degree that might well encourage the humblest of men. There were no halos of glory around the Holy Mother and the Divine Child that night. There was no rapt adoration ready to give glad acclaim to the new-born King. Even the earthly comforts and benefits were not all there. For, mark you, when the Holy Family arrived, there was no disposition to give place to them by the inmates of the already crowded inn. They must take their lot as the rest. The travailing mother of the Son of God was not surrounded by loving and anxious attendants in the pains of that birth.

Do you think the womanhood of our day can appreciate the situation and thoughts of Mary that night? Does any mother among you recall the anxious days and nights when she awaited the coming of some beloved child? Does she remember how she craved the presence of her *own* mother and her kindred in the household? How she sought to be encouraged and comforted through the hours of expectation? Think, then, of the young virgin on that Christmas eve, alone and travel-stained, coming to a khan of the Orient, a simple thing at the very best, and finding it already filled. And, unable to seek farther, they accept the host's offer, doubtless prompted by kindness, seeing the pale countenance of the beautiful young Jewess about to become a mother. There is room in the stable. A bed of straw and the honest pastoral companionship of the herd that must supply to-morrow's needs to the guests. If ever a young, expectant mother was placed in a situation of peculiar trial and hardship, it was the young virgin Mary on that first Christmas eve.

But Mary had more than even hard physical conditions to deal with. She knew that she was to bring forth Israel's Messiah and King. She knew that the long-deferred expectation of her nation was now about to be fulfilled. But she could not, and probably did not, have any idea that the King of Israel was to come under such lowly conditions as these. We can feel the doubt and anxiety in that loving heart, knowing that this child was to be the great Leader and Commander in Israel, when she finds herself compelled, like any other late guest, to take the exceptional and inferior accommodations at the inn. Is the Messiah then, after all, to have none of the glory and exaltation of life? Does to be the mother of the Lord's chosen mean that one must suffer unusual trials and pains? And then perhaps she already felt that a sword must pierce her own heart, and she wondered why it must come so very soon.

And then there was Joseph — righteous Joseph and a loyal son of Abraham. His thoughts, too, what must they have been when he saw the young bride in her throes of pain, and knew the deep course in which her thoughts were

moving! Perhaps the old Davidic blood was stirring, and
they felt that prophetic strength and endurance which can
calmly face a scene of agony and distress! But to be so
helpless! To stand by and not be able to divide the pain
with the young mother in her throes of travail! That was
hard. That was a cross for a noble man of feeling and compassion, and Joseph had both.

But God's hour is come and the Wonderful is born. And
soon there is heard the clatter of approaching steps. A
crowd of rude shepherds, wet with the night dew, come to
inquire if a child has been born. They press in with true
rural curiosity and helpfulness. Perhaps quick and kindly
hands bring comforts and conveniences from the inn. Lights
are brought, and the inn is aroused. Perhaps in that very
inn were the wise men who came journeying from the East.
Perhaps it was they who had Mary and the Child removed
to the house where, it is said, they opened their treasures,
and laid them at the feet of the new-born King. The guests
come forth quickly, and there is a genuine Oriental rejoicing
over the birth of a man-child. And then the shepherds tell
their story, and the wondering guests hear of the angels'
song. And, finally, the first burst of curiosity over, the
crowd slowly disperses. The shepherds go back to their
flocks. The guests retire to rest again. The last light is
out, only one here and there, gleaming on the distant hillside, where the shepherds talk over through the night the
strange things which have happened to them, and try to
apprehend their meaning. Christ is born. The first Christmas morning is stealing over the landscape. In an hour the
sun will peep over the horizon. The work of redemption
has begun. The first danger in human life has been passed.
The Saviour of the world is born.

There is a power and an inspiration in this idyl of our
Lord's birth which has filled the whole earth with sweetness
and light. It has sanctified and ennobled womanhood and
motherhood. It has so lifted into an atmosphere of sacredness the domestic relations of men, that from that hour a
new conception of life and home was also born. It empha-

sized with such impressiveness the utter lack of necessary
coherence between earthly conditions and moral and spiritual
rank, that aristocracy and caste rule date their decline from
that very hour. It points out the contrast between the
divine humility and earthly bluster and insolence with such
unerring exactness that it has been the instructive symbol
of real greatness ever since. It stands so squarely opposed
to every natural instinct and thought of man as to the proper
conception of position, authority and power, that it has been
the fruitful seed of spiritual revolutions in every generation
of Christian history. It is so intimately connected with the
religious hope and the spiritual desires of men, that it has
been their consolation and their pleasure above all the incidents of the Saviour's life.

Its universal touch was so perfect and delicate that it is
one of the two dramatic incidents of Christ's life upon which
the Christian world has universally agreed especial emphasis
should be laid. These were the Epiphany and the Resurrection. The birth of Christ and his re-birth after his crucifixion have been the two great facts around which the thought
of Christendom has settled. No one has cared, or dared, to
challenge the Christian consciousness in this respect. The
one filled the earth with rejoicing in the beginning of the
human career of Jesus Christ. The other filled it with joy
in the knowledge that that human career was to be carried
on in the larger relations of immortality. Humanity and
immortality are the centers of Christian comfort and hope
in Jesus Christ. Both are the symbols and the interpreters
of life. Christmas celebrates the one, Easter keeps alive
the other.

It is fitting, as we celebrate the birth of Christ, again to
bring to the mind the enormous changes in the life and history of the world which that event has brought about. Men
are often discouraged at what seems to them the degeneracy
of the world. And there are many depressing indications in
the moral and social order of our time. But when we take the
sweep of the ages of Christianity's progress, and consider
the conquests which have been wrought, the case takes on a

somewhat different aspect. It is right and wise to contemplate these changes, especially as they harmonize with the incidents of the Saviour's own birth and historic career. They encourage the Christian Church in its loyalty to Christ and his cause in the world. They serve to awaken the consciences of non-Christians, and make them conscious how far removed a life untouched by the power of Jesus Christ is from the real life currents of history. They are a source of inspiration to the young, and demonstrate, better than any exhortation could, how great is the privilege of fellowship with Christ in the work of the world's salvation.

Take, first of all, the growth of the principle of equality among men. If the lowly birth of Jesus has taught the world any one thing, it has been the lesson of the absolute divorce between what is about a man and what a man is. It reveals the amazing spectacle of the Name upon which the whole earth relies for salvation borne by a helpless child, to whom, nevertheless, the Magian princes and the shepherds alike, the extremes of culture and life, bring their tributes of willing adoration and praise. Those wise men represented what was in their time as exclusive a cult of scholars as could be found in the earth. It was not merely an aristocracy, but an aristocracy of high character and of great intellectual elevation. The shepherds, on the contrary, represented not merely simplicity, but simplicity as far removed from the centers of mental life and conflict as could be imagined. Thus both extremes of society met at that cradle, and both came with the spirit of obedience and worship. Here was a manifestation of an intellectual union which has been typical of Christianity ever since. Philosophers and scientists have rejoiced in Jesus Christ. The poor and ignorant have rejoiced in him not less than the others. Separated by nature and training and outlook in all else, they are one in their view and feeling when they look toward Jesus Christ.

But the equality thus typified was even more powerfully accentuated in Christ himself. It was not merely afterward, in consequence of his bold and truthful preaching of his gospel, that he became a man acquainted with grief, and

one who had not where to lay his head. Scarcely is he in
the world than this experience is his. Nay, it is his mother's
before he is born. She comes to the inn. But there is no
room. How many times that was the experience of Jesus Christ
in the years of his own ministry! " He came unto his own, and
they that were his own received him not," is the pitiful comment that St. John makes in the prologue of his Gospel on the
ministry of Jesus. Yet to them that received him he gave
the right to become the sons of God. True equality is the
communion of experience. It is not in the possession of the
same sums of money, or the enjoyment of the same luxuries.
It is not in the appreciation of the same objects of art, and
it is not association in the same circles of society. It is the
fellowship of a common lot. It is the touch of common
humanity which our artificial life so often hides as far from
human gaze as it can. Here was one of the places at which
Jesus struck the basal note of human life. His own humble
birth, and the pathetic circumstances attending it, have been
to the masses of mankind in the earth the truest symbol of
the democracy of the religious communion, which must and
does precede social and intellectual democracy. Here was
an equality of birth. Here was a world Saviour, who sprang
from the simplest and most natural surroundings. Here was
a real child of the earth, and one that knew the lot of common men.

How powerfully that idea has stalked through the world!
Civilization's advance has been coeval with acceptance of this
idea. Equality among men is the last stage of the world's
development. Into that last stage we are coming. False distinctions still linger in the world, and unjust men and measures
are still in authority in many places. But the essential principle of equality has been accepted almost everywhere. There
is not an absolutism in the earth that does not feel in some
measure the force of this manifestation of the equality of man
and respect in some degree, at least, the rights of the humblest.
The human cause at least has been crowned by all men of
light and leading in every country and in every clime. Whatever there is in this world to-day of mutual respect among men,

and love and honor of man for man's sake, is the direct and immediate result of the gospel of Jesus Christ, whose central idea for social life was illustrated in the circumstance of his birth.   Christmas is the natal day of all movements toward social equality and mutual recognition of rights among men. Blood, possession and attainments go down on Christmas day before the child that was wrapped, not in purple and fine linen, nor heralded by the pomp and splendor that attend the earth princelings of what, by an archaic nomenclature, we still call "royal" houses, but the humble scion of the house of David enfolded in the crude garmenture of a workingman's home and laid in the manger of a stable.   But he was the Prince of Humanity.   He was the Messiah of all spiritual souls.   He was the mighty God incarnate.   He was the Lamb of God that must be slain for the sins of the world.

But equality thus introduced by Christ was not a concession to the human desire for equal life and fellowship in the intellect and the enjoyment of earthly privileges.   Equality was thus revealed that it might suggest another equality, the recognition of which is even more necessary than the other.   It was an equality of moral standing before God.   It was a comprehensive announcement that the one tie by which men can be bound together, and the reign of peace come in the earth, is the tie of a common love to a Saviour from sin.   This, too, was a novel idea.   How novel it was may be gleaned from the Saviour's parable of the Pharisee and the publican.   The moral life had become subdivided not less than the earth and the fruits thereof. Spiritual privileges were matters of heritage and caste as well as the more material things.   To some there appears to be some such notion still prevailing.   There is nothing men give up so reluctantly as the idea that they are better than other men.   Morally, almost every man is by nature an aristocrat of the worst type.   He may think that there are others better than himself, but he knows that there are many worse than he.   Upon the latter he rests his gaze, and while he does not give it the bald articulation that the Pharisee did, when he thanked God that he was not as other men, he feels it without saying so, and is hurt when the implication of moral democracy is broached.

Yet there it is, unmistakably bound up in the very name of Jesus Christ. There you have the symbol of his relation to every man. A Saviour must be for sinners. A Lord must be for subjects. A King must have a throne. A Redeemer must be for captives and slaves. And in the assumption of this mission, Christ announces us all as in the equality of sinfulness before God, not less than in the equality of his redeeming grace. So repugnant has this idea been to mankind that the dominant theology of Protestantism for centuries held to a doctrine of election, which was in effect nothing more than a spiritual aristocracy, which held that God had chosen from the foundation of the world some men for favor and some men for reprobation. Yes, even the Church could not wholly free herself from this itching for caste distinction. She is not wholly free from it now. But Christ is free from it, and the New Testament lies squarely across the path of any man who tries to bring it into the fold and life of the Church which Jesus established in the world.

But through the coming of Jesus Christ in this humble way, all races have not only been made equal, but they have been made one. The unity of mankind received here a new birth and a new interpretation. The idea of brotherhood, that strange, disturbing aspiration which has been the living rebuke to all efforts of men to separate themselves from their brethren, here blossomed into fruition and power. Men of different castes and education now looked at each other with the singular new feeling that both had common interests, and that the only interpretative word for them both was brother. Formerly it had been master and slave, or some other relation indicating the exalting of the one and the demeaning of the other. But now they looked at each other in the light of common sins and common salvation. The family idea broke national and tribal limitations, and became inclusive enough for all humanity. The chosen nation was every nation. Every child was a child of promise. The Jew was not the Jew of blood, but the son of the Most High, and the contrast between national religion and tribal salvation was swallowed up in the thought that, as of one blood God had made all the races of the earth, so by one Saviour they became a family of redeemed souls, Jesus Christ being the Elder Brother of them all. That made them more than equals. It made them one in hope and faith, and enforced the doctrine that life must be service, and that he loves best who serves best his fellow creatures in the earth, of whatever race or wherever found.

That was another channel through which these humble surroundings served to bring the minds of men into a common union of impulse and spiritual feeling. No royal pageant could have done it. No splendid demonstration in court or palace could have found the heart of humanity. But the manger could do it. The story of the crowded inn and the bed of straw could do it. The anxious shepherds peering into the face of the Christ-Child at midnight could do it. It was a song that ushered Christ into the world. It has set mankind singing ever since. It was a heavenly host that sent the good news to the watching men on the hillside. It is a heavenly host that sends it speeding to all lands of the earth to-day. And millions of souls to-day are catching fragments of that angel chorus and singing them to the music of ministering love and good will to the ends of the world. And through all these ages a little Child has been leading them. Each year reenacts the lovely scene. Each year renews the joyful sounds. Redemption's idyl is the one perennial theme which rejoices the human heart.

Christmas is, therefore, a festival of the union of humanity. It is the starting-point for real brotherhood and real fellowship under the leadership and by the redemptive grace of Jesus Christ. If it is true that our sins have separated us from God, it is not less true that our sins have separated us from each other. If we need union to God, it is equally true that we need union with men. If we need the forgiveness of the one, we need not less the forgiveness of the other. And is it not true that the true union of humanity would bring to our sorrowful earth relief from all its woes? Is it not that we battle for artificial life and artificial power and distinction, when we should be struggling for real power and real life ? When we are nearest to the hearts of our fellow men we are certainly nearest to the heart of God. Christmas is the annual renewal day of humanity's vows to itself. It is the one day when we strip off the winding-sheets of death into which our civilization and conventional intercourse so frequently wrap our humanity, and stand forth in the strength and brotherhood of our divine calling in Jesus Christ. This is the day of spiritual freedom and fraternal ministry. This is the independence day of the soul. This day's bells are the melodious harbingers of the regenerated humanity which is to come.

Ring out, then, the era of hatred and oppression and ring in the day of concord and helpfulness. Sing in with the angelic chorus the hopes of mankind and the glory of God on high. Sing in redemption through the love of God. Sing in the rule of love and peace. Sing in the farewell of castes and creeds and barriers that have separated men for ages past. Sing out the hard enmities of nations and men. Sing out the engines of war and destruction. Sing in the blessings of peace and faith in the Eternal God who is over all. Sing out the broken fragments of homes desolate and families divided. Sing in the reunion of common interests and charity for all. Sing in forgiveness. Sing in true love to God. Sing out the wrath and strife of business and law and competition in life. Sing in the sweet new vision of domestic joy and fraternal peace among men. Let prince and pauper, learned and unlearned, let rich and poor, let high and low, unite again as they did long ago around the cradle of the Christ-Child and give God the glory for him and for each other.

THE SPIRITUAL LIFE

THE SPHERE OF INFLUENCE

JOHN vii. 48.

THERE are many men still young who can remember the time when what represented the continent of Africa in the school geographies was little else than a large black spot. The coast line and a few hundred miles inland from the coast were known, but the vast interior was an unknown country. Through the enterprise of civilization, the zeal of missionaries and the energy of explorers that great dark spot has been almost completely effaced. The most enlightened races of the earth have now access to the whole of the Dark Continent. Nor have they failed to make use of · their opportunities. Block after block of the territory, belonging of course to the tribes inhabiting it, has been seized and converted into the domain of some European power. But the method of this seizure has been quite unique. They did not simply take the land and occupy it and subjugate or enslave the natives. That would have been too bald an exhibition of theft even for this day of brazen invasion of the rights of the helpless nations of the earth. No, they did not nominally claim the lands they seized at all, but veiled their occupation and control by a polite term which has since come to have vast significance in that continent. They called the territory subject to them their "spheres of influence." To be sure, the "sphere of influence" of Germany, for example, is as really German soil as any part of the national domain in Europe. But enlightened Christian sentiment would not permit so clearly expressed a robbery as simple seizure, so as a result German soil in Africa is called the "German sphere of influence."

This is equally true of the other great powers. France and England have their "sphere of influence." To all intents they are real parts of the empires of those nations. Aggression upon them would be construed by either as an act of war. They despoil these parts of Africa of their native wealth, they assign exclusive privileges to their own national trading corporations, and otherwise act as though they were the real and exclusive owners of the property. But they do not state that this is the case. Neither by cession, actual conquest avowed as such, or by purchase have they acquired any rights in these lands. Conquest is the civilized name for robbery. Exploitation is the diplomatic word for the same thing, and China is now the place where the thing is being illustrated. But no nation is willing to avow such a thing before the world. Hence this real though shadowy possession of the largest part of the Dark Continent is absorbed merely in "spheres of influence."

The interesting thing about all this is that though forced into it by the moral sentiment of this century and by the growing repugnance to the practice of unwarranted spoliation of the weak nations by the strong, the nations that have thus acquired "spheres of influence" in Africa have alighted upon a term which is truly descriptive of the thing itself. Influence *is* possession. Influence *is* authority. And while it may not require a standing army or a mighty navy, to have influence is to have all that these instruments of physical power can possibly accomplish. A sphere of influence properly considered is as much an empire as the best policed territory that can be selected in the earth. A man who will do under the influence of another what some other man will do under threats and blows is just as really a subject, though the means of his subjugation are less noisy and violent. Nations and men alike have their real spheres of influence. They are real and tangible possessions. Perhaps, like these insufficiently explored parts of the continent of Africa, their boundaries are rather indefinite and hazy, but there is a certain area which is nevertheless pretty well demarcated from the rest and can always be identified. Every man has his sphere of influence in which he is the ruling authority and the lawmaking power.

There is something in this identification of influence with power and authority which is a very proper theme for the

opening of a new year. As the years pass over a man's life
and he sees the opportunities for service narrowing and the
limits of his life becoming more and more fixed, and finds that
it is so much more simple than it used to be to predicate certain things of him, he begins to realize that he has for the
growing and further expansion of his life but one possible
field. That field is in the enlargement of his interest in other
men and other lives and the enlisting of their interest in him.
That mutual interest raised to a degree where it has a real
effect upon the lives of both is influence. There is nothing
about which a man ought to be so jealous as about what
influence is exerted upon him or what influence he exerts himself. There is nothing that has so vital an effect upon the
nature of his own life and thought, or that has so far-reaching
a result in his character, as this varying thing which men call
influence. It is more valuable than his real estate and is a
truer index to his wealth. It is a matter of deeper solicitude
to his friends than his ability to meet promptly his creditors.
It is somehow the world's judgment of his life and character as
a whole, a sort of spherical grasp of all that he stands for in
this world toward the life and well-being of our race.

In the text this morning you have an interesting illustration of this fact. The doctrines of Jesus made such a decided
impression in Jerusalem that the leaders of the people sent
trusted messengers to find out all that they could about the
new teacher. They were instructed to study his words, his
manner and the effect of his teaching upon the masses.
We know this from the report which they brought. "Never
man so spake," said these officers who had been sent to take
him. So moved were they by the words of Jesus and gave
such evident manifestations that they were impressed, that
the wrathful priests and Pharisees broke out at once with
the scornful reproach, "Are ye also deceived?" But the
very next moment their worldly caution and prudence came
to the surface again, and to measure the full effect of the
teaching which Jesus was spreading through the city, which
was causing so much division among the people and provok-
ing so much inquiry, note what they ask: "Hath any ruler

believed on him, or of the Pharisees?" That was the query of true men of the world. It was the knowledge that Jesus' teaching was beginning to interest the leaders of society that made Jesus comparatively safe so long. Right on the spot there was a Pharisee who had become mildly inoculated with the gospel, for Nicodemus, for it was he, ventured to temper their fierce judgment of Christ, and they turned at once upon him also with the rebuking question, "Art thou also of Galilee?"

These men of the world were not far wrong in this affair. If Jesus was making an impression upon the leading men of Jerusalem, then it was a matter that needed immediate attention. If the leaders of the social and religious life of the Jews were being carried away by such a message as Jesus taught, then it behooved the hierarchy of the temple to beware, for who could predict what would happen if the people of all classes were suddenly to seek to give practical expression to the doctrines which Jesus was preaching? It was a very vital and practical matter to them. They were right from their standpoint in being anxious about it. They showed themselves thorough students of human nature. They knew the value of influence, and especially the influence of certain classes of men. They estimated their own security by the influence which Jesus acquired with those upon whose support they must rely for their own safety. Their judgment in this respect was worthy of emulation. They were astute leaders and had at least in so far adopted the spiritual standards of their religion that they gauged the prophet's influence, not by the numbers, but by the character of his adherents. That was a wise method of measuring influence.

Let us see just how much that question meant and in what respects it showed a true knowledge of the situation, and in what respects it was faulty. The accession to the ranks of Christ's followers of any conspicuous ruler of the Jews would mean not merely that one man had accepted the gospel; it would probably mean that with that man went his sphere of influence too. Being a ruler would probably carry with it certain presumptions of education, carefulness in thought and a wise regard for all the interests of the nation. If such a man thinks well of the new Messiah, men would argue, there must be something true and attractive about him. It was not a meaningless question, therefore, to ask whether any rulers were believing in Christ. It had a very great interest to the men who believed, as these priests did, in the doctrines of which they were the official exponents. It has been so in all times. The conversion of a prominent man in a community has often been the means of bringing about a general revival. In a similar way the skepticism or opposition of a prominent man to the gospel has often been the direct cause of unbelief among those who looked to him for example and leading.

In a similar way this was true of the Pharisees. That name has become very odious to us from the manner in which they treated Christ and Christ's followers, but there is something to be said even for a Pharisee. He was at least a man who felt that he had a religious function and fulfilled it. That he was often a hypocrite does not invalidate the fact that he was exact and formal in his religious devotions. He was in his place. He observed certain forms and ceremonies. He was doubtless a great bulwark in the social order and religious faith of the Jews. Let us be just to him. Many a coward is just as much of a hypocrite as the Pharisees were, though he lacks their courage and zeal. Many men felt no concern about the religious interests of the nation. The Pharisees did. They were genuinely concerned about Israel. If they made long prayers for pretense, and if they despoiled the widows' homes, they were not different from a great many other kinds of hypocrites. They at least identified themselves with something tangible and clearly open to interrogation and judgment. Christ's strongest denunciations were directed against them. But has it ever occurred to you that Christ could direct his messages of scorn at no one else? It was their very virtue of definite profession that made them the target of Christ's wrath. And then let us not forget there were honest Pharisees, too, and noble-hearted ones, like Nicodemus, as well as the other kind.

Now if such a man, especially one of the good kind, became a disciple of Christ it meant much. It meant not that an ignorant mob was being carried off its feet, away from its reason, by some expert religious demagogue, but that a man of character and judgment had found that the cause was worthy of respect, and declared his belief in it by publicly avowing it. It is not essentially different with us to-day. We almost always ask of any cause who its sponsors are. We ask who believes in it, and our judgment is more or less influenced by the character of those who stand as its representatives. And it ought to be. We sometimes hear it said that Christ is not to be judged by his followers. But there was never a more foolish plea than this. Christ must be judged, to a certain extent, by his followers. If the Church of Christ were composed, as a rule, and led by ignorant, lawless and immoral men and women, it would soon destroy the influence of Christ in the earth. It is just because the followers of Christ, as a rule, are honorable, truthful and godly men and women that the Church is the power in the earth that it is. The influence of a good man means much to any cause which he espouses. The opposition of a bad man or a hypocrite is equally significant. The opposition of some men is a crown of praise to him who is fortunate enough to secure it.

Personal influence being then so valuable and important a trust, its guardianship should be a subject of the deepest reflection by every man who cares to have his life identified with the cause of Christ and the things for which Christ stands to men. The judgment of these priests was faulty in one respect, and that was in supposing that any cause is determined merely by the question of the rank of those who make up its followers. Right as they were on the question of the character of Christ's support, they were wrong in judging the rectitude of the cause by this means. Temporal power may be determined by this means, but righteousness never. Righteousness is not dependent upon official authority and power. It does not wait for the sanction of examining boards. It simply expresses itself with that sublime disregard of consequences which lies at the root of its deathless nature. But the question we have before us to-day is not merely the righteousness of Christ's service in itself considered, but the gain to its power in the world if men of influence — and all men are in their degree men of influence — were to make their personalities tell practically for the gospel. The opening year is an appropriate time for a man to ask himself whither the bulk of his influence in the world is being cast. It is a pertinent question for any man to ask himself, whether the sum of what he represents to his fellow men is what in his best moments he would wish it to be.

There are certain great laws of life which are worth remembering when the matter of influence is being considered, and may be useful as suggestions toward the desire to make the life helpful in its outlook and reach for God. One of these is the ease with which genuine Christian character is identified. It is only of the lowest forms of life of which it can be said that one does not know whether they belong to the animal or the vegetable kingdom. The higher we mount in the scale of life the greater the ease with which the nature and species of the animal are discovered. The same law holds good in the moral realm. Moral vertebrates are easily identified. The lower you descend in the moral and spiritual sphere the more difficult does it become to identify the species. Christian character is of such a nature that it may be fairly likened to the spinal column in the human frame. Take that away and you have the form of a man, but not the erect being who thinks and acts in accordance with his thought. If a man has the ideals of Jesus Christ in his heart he will act and think like Jesus Christ, and there will be little difficulty in identifying him with the species of moral beings known as Christians. Such identification should be easy, and is easy where the heart is set on God, and where the life shows forth the true elements of the Christ life. It is not easy in the shifting moral mollusks who are never one thing or another.

The nature of strong Christian character is in its lights and shadows. It brings out the deep, broad lines of contrast between selfishness and unselfishness. It shows in bold relief the difference between sincerity and insincerity. It may almost be said that the great characters of Christian history have been great just in proportion as they have been easily classified. Not that such character clearness means that the opinions are right, but that it shows the tendency and temper of the heart and soul. For this reason the Church has always loved and honored its strong characters, even when it did not assent to all their opinions. It will always love such men. It is in human nature to love such men. It is the nature of man to glorify such men. It is because Christ was such a man that it glorifies him. With what unerring distinctness does the thought again and again flash through the minds of the men and women with whom Christ talked, " Is not this the Christ ? " The Christ of their thought and hope and the Jesus of Nazareth corresponded so exactly and unmistakably that at once the Man of Galilee was known to be the Christ of God. The recognition was quick, decisive and accurate.

There is something titanic in the struggle for character that makes the combatants heroic, even though they are unconscious of the fact. One feels in Christ the heroic element of soul almost from the very first words that he utters. The solemn announcement of his mission in the words of an old prophet, and the stern, earnest way in which he set out to accomplish the things to which he was appointed in the providence of God, gave Christ a heroic cast before his deeds warranted the expectation of great things. The life that is influential has this same quality. There is a certain isolation about influential men and women which reveals power in itself. There is an atmosphere of discernment, of energy and of application of thought to action, which gives to all men instinctive knowledge that there is a hero present. The history of Christianity in the world is the history of the multiplication of just such men. Bribes and seductions fall away from them as the night-owls shrink from the sunlight of day. They are the moral Titans of humanity. They undertake the battles which seem to the unthinking observer to involve certain defeat, and wrest victory out of adverse conditions with an abandon that makes it seem like a miracle. But there is nothing miraculous about it. It is the joyous love of conflict that moves every righteous soul in the hope of making a new earth, wherein shall dwell righteousness. It is the unfaltering spirit of Christ that makes a man persist in labor and pain till he shall see the salvation of God.

Christianity is itself one grand defiance of all the natural habits of the unregenerate man. Notwithstanding our change of ideas with reference to many of the old theories of the moral nature and real growth in grace and manhood, it is still true that Christianity has a certain austerity about it which puts it at variance with what is commonly called the world. It enjoins a certain rigor of life and personal scrutiny of motive and action which make the Christian a separatist from the world in the best sense of that term. It need not make him a monk of the cloister. It need not drive him to a monastery. But it does take him out of many associations, for conscience' sake, which in themselves might be pleasurable and even to a degree uplifting. The crucifixion of the flesh and the lusts thereof is a defiance of the ruling theory of the world, which is, that we shall eat and drink, for to-morrow we die. Christ, on the other hand, bids us be sober and thoughtful, for to-morrow we *live*. Well may an unheroic and careless world, willing to leave a legacy of debt, trouble and confusion to its successors, say, To-morrow we die. It could with more truthfulness say, To-day we are dying. But the Christian separatist and hero can take no such stand. For him to-morrow means life, not death. To-morrow means to him a grander human race and a greater kingdom of God. To him it means a larger glory to God and a mightier sphere of influence for righteousness and truth. It is this underlying fact in the Christian gospel that makes the Christian life consciously and unconsciously heroic and grand when it is truly at the base of a man's life and purposes.

The Christian's sphere of influence will be great or small as he embodies these principles in his own relations to the world. Character marked by clearness, heroism and austerity is the influential character in the world. But these must not be confounded with their mock representations. A blustering hypocrisy is often just as clear as a consecrated sincerity. Falstaff is absolutely clear to us, though he is a craven, a coward and a liar. Many seem to think the Falstaffian ideal can persist in the Christian work of the world. But it is not so. The Christian clearness of character, easy to be understood, is that which is itself a law for righteousness. It was said of a certain statesman in our own day that his name was a platform in itself. This is what should be true of the Christian. His religion should itself be a declaration of principles that should make a creed and much profession unnecessary. Every Christian man has, by the very nature of the Christian life, the right to make his life his platform.

In the same way the mock heroics of Christianity deceive no one. Is any one misled as to the real purposes of Germany in China, at this moment, by the theatrical way in which the German Emperor announces his purpose to defend the Christian religion while he sends his fleet to China and seizes a large slice of territory and a valuable harbor and exacts over a million dollars for the murder of two missionaries? It was right and just to demand indemnity for the outrage to German subjects. But is any one deceived as to the real purpose of that expedition by this mock heroic talk about the defense of the Christian religion? What about the Christian religion in Armenia, when this same defender of the faith was exchanging presents with the assassin Abdul, who was slaughtering Christians by the thousand? Real Christians can feel nothing but disgust at this exhibition. But the same feeling follows the mock devotion to Christ's cause by men in everyday life who give us the pyrotechnics of gospel heroism without enduring any of the sacrifice. The world has become too practical and too full of common sense not to know the real hero from his counterfeit. It may be deceived for a while, but it is only for a while, and then it visits vengeance on him who tries to make it his dupe.

Real gospel heroism requires patience and hard work. Real strength of character under the standard of Christ does not shrink from the severe tasks of service and of suffering. Even heroism is under the operation of the divine law of growth and continual trial. Real heroism is heroism under law.

And equally true is it that the austerity demanded by Christ is one grounded in reason and principle, not in incident and indulgence. No man can be said to be austere merely because he does not do this or that *thing*. Virtue does not lie in doing or in not doing things. It lies in the principle which governs both doing and not doing. The Pharisee thought he was a beautiful religionist because he did certain things ; namely, gave tithes, fasted and all the rest. Many people are equally mistaken. Some think themselves Christian and self-sacrificing because they will *not* do certain things. They think that is the Christian austerity which is able to say, I do not *do* this or that. But this is not the austerity of Christian principle. The Christian may be required to-morrow to do what he would not do to-day. He may, on the other hand, be required to abstain to-morrow from what seems perfectly right to-day. It is the principle that makes the austerity. It is the ability and the readiness to change and alter the rule of life and the habit of conduct that mark the real austerity of the gospel life. This is the sacrifice which most people are not willing to make. They would rather float along with the prevailing tide and shrink from the unhappy prominence which adherence to principle often gives. But this is a harder task than to go into a monastery. The austere womanhood of principle is more of a sacrifice than going into a convent. In fact, the monastery and the convent are not symbols of austerity at all. They represent in the healthy Christian life and imagination rather a weak sentimentality on the one hand, or a cowardly flight from duty on the other.

Thus we see the gateways to a genuine and lasting Christian influence. They are not self-working appliances which open at the approach. They must be stormed to be entered.

But let no one be ashamed to earn his influence in an honest way. Let him not desire to have what is not his by the right of character and attainment in Christian power and devotion. Christ himself has told us that to be a son of God becomes not merely a privilege through his name, but a right. Mark that. To them that received him he gave the *right* to become the sons of God. It is this consciousness of right that gives influence and power in the world. One can have the gospel right only by having the gospel righteousness, too. The respect of mankind is not a thing that men can give or withhold at pleasure. Influence is what a man has by right, and no man can take it from him. The petty trumpery of outward show can be denied, as men of power in the councils of the nation cannot often be elected to office because they will not submit to party intrigues and discipline. But their power is not lost and their influence is not exterminated. Men of God still, they are like the flaming swords at the gates of truth and power, and only the chosen souls may enter. They are the real messengers of Christ to the world.

THE FAMILY FAITH

1 SAMUEL xx. 6.

THIS little passage in the history of David's experience at the court of King Saul is interesting, not only for the fact which it records, but even more for the incidental information which it gives as to the ideas of family life and religion which were prevailing in David's time. David, in suggesting to Jonathan a suitable excuse to make to the king for his absence, was likely to choose the one that would make the greatest impression on the king's mind for propriety and force. If the king is his enemy, it must be an excuse which will accord with the king's ideas of a youth's duty to himself, the nation and God. It must be one, too, against which the king can have the least to say. In view of all this, it is interesting to note what the excuse was that David selected as meeting all these requirements. He simply urged that he must go to a sacrifice at Bethlehem, to which all the family are bidden. In other words, he must go to the annual religious festival of the family. The statement that it was a family affair was evidently expected to answer any objection which Saul might make for David's absence, and, at the same time, prove David a loyal subject of the king, being a loyal son of his own family and household.

Just what the limits of the family were among the Israelites, no one can probably state with certainty. It meant all that we mean, and often a great deal more. Often it meant remote kinsmen, and not infrequently the servants and attendants of the household. Sometimes it had a wider limit even than this. But the essential thing about it is that the religion of Israel was organized on the family basis; that is, there was one faith for the whole household or establishment,

as the case might be. Hebrew society was essentially a con-
federation of homogeneous families. The faith of Israel was
not first national and then adopted by the families. It was
a family faith first of all, and from that, as the starting-point,
developed successively into tribal and then national. At the
base of all Hebrew institutions lies the family as the unit
intact. And it is an interesting feature of Jewish history
that national disruption almost always springs from a family
disruption. When the family faith is corrupted or divided,
the nation itself is soon rent in twain. There is no hint
throughout the whole of Hebrew literature that the family
was ever thought of except as a religious unit. A social unit
it is by its very constitution. Among the Jews it was also
the religious unit. By far the larger part of the institutions
of the Jews, their sacred festivals and their religious rites
are of a family origin. The most sacred of them all — the
Passover — is primarily a home rite, a family observance.

This idea is not different when we come to other pre-Christian religions. Not insisted upon with the same strenuousness
as among the Jews, it is nevertheless true that the religion of
the pre-Christian times did not contemplate the extreme individualism which is the distinctive type of religious development in our day. The older religions are all on essentially
the family basis, and this in part accounts for their solidarity
to this very day. Among the first and most constant questions that our missionaries in foreign lands have to meet and
deal with, is the question of the fate of ancestors. A heaven
where one's kinsmen are barred out is not a pleasant place
to contemplate. A salvation which has as one of its conditions that all those whom we have loved, and who have gone
before us, are lost, is not calculated to make us very happy
in its possession. Even the peoples whom we still, by a
curious misuse of language, call " heathen," feel the wrong
of such a moral ordering of the universe. It must never be
forgotten that the strongest ties in this world, in spite of the
scientists who have so confidently begotten us from the lower
animals, are still ties of kinship and of blood. It will be so
forever.

In the early history of the Church we find a similar practice and spirit. The early conversions of the gospel history are not merely of individuals, but oftener of houses, that is, of families. We hear of men being baptized with all their houses. We even hear of a church that was in the house of a certain Christian. And so throughout the New Testament the Old Testament idea seems to be continued; namely, that the family is a religious unit; that the titular head of the household gives to it, not merely its family life and family law, but not less so its family religion and faith. And down to our own day many of the historic churches still assume that children, born in a family whose head is in the church, are *ipso facto* members of that church. The Roman Catholic Church thus steadily counts its numbers. Children of Roman Catholic parents are assumed to be Roman Catholics till they prove themselves something else. This is the continuation of the family idea of faith and religion. In its essence it is a thoroughly Christian idea. It is grounded in the practice and habit of the Old Testament and New Testament times. It is sound as to social development, wise as to practical form and method and reasonable as to religious discipline and order.

Now it cannot be denied that among the Protestant population of this country the idea of a family faith has almost utterly disappeared. To a considerable degree it has also disappeared among the Roman Catholic populations. Let us acknowledge the fact, try to analyze the causes of it and examine the resultant effects. Perhaps that will suggest some practical duties in the premises. The Protestant teaching of the Christian life, which is also the New Testament teaching, is one of personal initiative and freedom, absolute liberty. That has been settled by the last four hundred years of Protestantism, and is presumably settled forever. We do not believe that any human being should be coerced in the matter of religion, even by the members of his family. We hold that faith in Christ is an individual act. No man can have it for any one but himself. But is this the whole of the Christian life, or is it a complete statement of individual faith even? Where does a man get his first ideas of religion ordinarily?

To whom is he indebted for the first exercises of worship in his life? Where is the first place that worship is brought to his notice? The answers to these questions show at once that the religion of parents, the teaching of a home and the parental place of worship are inseparably allied to a man's faith, no matter what it becomes ultimately. That is, in the first instance, all that a man knows about religion he knows from the life and practice of the home where he happens to be born. From this there is no escape. The enemies of the established social order and the enemies of the Church have always recognized this fact. They have always lamented that the Church laid her hand upon the young and reared them in the ideas of the gospel, so that unbelief has always had to be a work of disruption and tearing down. No man ever became an infidel naturally. No man ever became a church hater naturally. Something had to be torn away, as a rule, before these developments took place. It is for this reason that a leading antagonist of the ruling social ideas of the world said not long since: "If I had the power to banish the greatest afflictions of this world, plagues, wars, famines, I would renounce it if instead I could suppress the family." From this standpoint the Italian socialist Rossi was right. The family has always been and probably will always be the great bulwark against a destructive and irreligious socialism.

What has made the family that bulwark? The fact that it is still grounded in religion. There is still the semblance among us of a family faith. While we have the grotesque exhibitions of husbands in one church and wives in another, and the children variously divided among several, for the most part there is still at least the attempt at unity which for social purposes is preserved. The disruptive process has not become so securely engrafted that it has meant disunion in the family itself, though this is not unknown among us. The implied basis of the family is still religious unity. The habitual practice still assumes essential unity, though it often presents a most amazing variety. The assumption of unity is still potent enough to bridge us over many chasms which at first would seem to threaten destruction at once. But the main

fact to be remembered is that the sound understructure of a
true family life lies in its real religious unity, and in the
assumption that in its faith and practice it is at one, and
presents an unbroken front to the world. And in so far as
this idea has become impaired among us there has been a
falling away in religious life and faith, and social trouble and
disturbance of one kind and another. Without in the least
degree insisting on a rigorous uniformity that shall exclude
personal initiative and freedom, yet we may and do insist on
the truth that the family that is not one is nothing.

Perhaps this condition of things in America is the reaction
from the State Church life of the older countries. We have
for better or worse determined that we shall never in America
have a State Church into which we must all come. I do not
know a patriot churchman of any denomination who would
be willing to make his faith the State faith except by persua-
sion and voluntary adoption. Even then the more intelligent would regard the State's adoption of a given faith as a
calamity to that faith. I certainly should so regard it. We
have been emphasizing the doctrine of personal freedom a
great deal, and this is one of the results. Lack of church
control over men has produced the feeling of independence
to a degree that makes men feel that the Church has no
necessary place in their lives. This is especially true of the
ignorant classes, by which I do not mean merely the poorer
classes. I mean the classes who have no social knowledge
or social consciousness, who are simply so many of the population, mere human animals, who do not affect the life of the
community to any considerable extent one way or another.
A family without a church home, or connection of some
kind, is usually one of this character. The intelligent people
of the land are allied to the churches of the land. The
responsible classes are in the churches of the country.
These feel the need because they have the character that
creates the need of the recognition of the Divine wisdom and
guidance. A moral anarchist cannot of course have any conception of worship and the character of God.

Recognizing, then, all the qualifications of personal freedom enforced and taught by the New Testament, let me this morning bring to your mind the cause of a family faith as this is related to personal life, to the welfare of the nation and the government and to the moral life of the world. If the family is the great bulwark against all forms of disorder and social destructiveness, its unity is of paramount importance. Whatever affects that unity is of capital interest to every man, viewed from whatever standpoint he pleases. It certainly ought to arrest attention when a great socialist is willing to forego in the interest of socialism the privilege of abolishing war, famine and plague, choosing rather to destroy the family. And we may inquire whether these ideas are not making headway among us, too. Is there the same idea of the home that there used to be, the same loyalty, love and respect? Do we find the solidarity of the household kept in mind by all its members, and cherished as a possession which is of the highest value? Is the founding or the conserving of a family name and interests nowadays a matter of great interest to our people? Or is it true that whoever thinks about his family and its interests is at once sneered at as disloyal to our democratic traditions, and thought to be yearning for an old-world aristocracy? Must we all keep dirty just to show that we do not feel above the digger in the ditch? Must we send our children to incompetent teachers just to show that we believe in the public schools? Must we let our children grow up savages just to show that we are free in religion? Must we let them associate with all kinds of human vermin just to show that we are not proud? Is there no such thing as Christian selection and Christian exclusiveness? And is not the Christian family the place to begin it?

I think I am not mistaken when I say that the affirmative answer to these questions is the prevailing philosophy among us. A member of our school committee was reproached during the past week because he had not attended the public schools, and therefore it was assumed that he could not have a genuine interest in them. If a man keeps scrupulously clean, we have a whole vocabulary of jeers which are applied to him for it. If a man has a rule of religion in his family, and insists on its enforcement, there is a whole horde of sympathetic savages ready to pity his children because they are oppressed. This is called among us being thoroughly loyal to the democratic idea. Loyal as any man to the idea of a genuine democracy, I must nevertheless affirm my unwillingness to belong to one whose condition is dirt. I am likewise ready to be branded as an aristocrat who is not willing to give the training of his children over into the hands of amateurs and bunglers. If the choice of the companionship of the wise and the good, and unwillingness to delight in the company of the indecent, the profane and the obscene, make me a social aristocrat, then I am free to acknowledge myself one. Democracy is not dirt. Democracy is not loss of discrimination. Democracy is not a debauched morality and a miscegenation of social forces. Least of all do I believe that family democracy involves religious anarchy and confusion, with an altar to Jehovah on one floor, and incense to Baal on another. One form of religious life is ordinarily enough for one household. When there is necessity for more, the case is one for pity, not for envy. We have made the expression of Christianity various enough to secure emphasis upon almost every fundamental and upon many non-fundamental doctrines and modes of worship. I do not deplore it. I do not regard it as the unmixed evil that many do. But to carry that principle into the home is not only the greatest folly, but carries with it the loss of the profoundest elements of social and family unity. If in the worship and service of Almighty God concessions needful to unity cannot be made, what shall we say of the rest? Pity is the only emotion for such a situation.

The Christian religion rests for its continuance upon the unity and integrity of the human family. And this unity is not merely spiritual unity, but during a certain period a practical and disciplinary unity. A child who is reared in a home where the father never goes to church is another object of compassion. Likewise a child where a mother does not go. In some respects I regard the situation more hopeful for a child where the habit of the family in this respect is a unit, and neither goes, than in the other. The contrast at least is then a clear one when it is presented. A child who comes to the Christian faith in this way is far more likely to be influenced for right and good than one who has seen a halting faith on the one hand, and no faith on the other. For this reason it is usually wise that persons marrying shall settle the question of the religion in advance. With absolutely no prejudices whatever I should say, without any hesitation, that an agreement as to church relationships was one of the paramount conditions of happiness in married life. There are exceptions, of course. But these exceptions usually prove that one or the other or both the contracting parties are not good church people, in any case. It cannot well be otherwise. The whole ordering of life is bound up in this matter. The expansion and development of the home are included in it. The training and rearing of children become a kind of chaos without it. It leaves undecided and in the background the main issue of life and happiness. The only possible result can be moral and religious confusion. Among the various Protestant sects there ought to be few or no barriers to such union of worship as will present a family faith free and yet unified. Where the case is otherwise I have no hesitation in saying that the experiment is at least hazardous. God pity the man who regards the faith of his wife as a superstition. God help the woman who regards her husband's religion as a delusion. Thoroughgoing respect cannot live in such an atmosphere.

Now examine the personal effects of a family life religiously discordant and divided. If there is a factor in life where there is need for clearness of vision, and companionship in thought and action, it is in religion. But suppose that a man must throughout his life walk without the companionship of his wife in his religious life! Or, what is more frequently the case, what kind of satisfaction can there be to a wife walking one way while her husband seeks some other path, or does not take any interest in religion at all? Can there be any happiness in such an experience, and, unless a

man is prepared to abandon the idea of religion entirely, can
he see without regret, and something of shame, such a condition of affairs? What must be the personal effect of such a
condition? Without doubt it is one of regret, which sooner
or later becomes neglect, and finally lapses into utter irreli-
giousness and practical atheism. The moral companionship
and the religious fellowship which have been denied in this
way have resulted in just what may be expected in the physical life if you take away one of the great staples of human
food. The very need which draws people together to the
home is the one which should keep them together. The
same solemnity which makes the affection of the home, the
tie of blood, the sacredest thing in this world, is what demands for its nurture and sustenance the constant reproduction of the ideas and practices out of which it originally
sprang. Moral desolation comes first in such case, and after
desolation moral inertness, and then moral death. The religious life dies under such conditions, or, if preserved, is
like the hardy plants that survive the storms on the cliffs,
gnarled and knotted things, which show the hardships which
they have endured. The milder and kindlier elements have
withdrawn, and only the hardy surviving part of the fabric
remains. It is heroic. But there is a pathos in that heroism
which saddens while it inspires, and makes the tears that it
causes the weeping of regret, not of exultation. No man
who has not experienced it can know the enormous personal
loss which he sustains at the loss of a congenial religious fellowship in his home.

As a pastor I have often seen the perplexity of young boys
and girls moved with religious desire and feeling, yet per-
plexed and grieved because a decisive choice for God seemed
to reflect upon an irreligious father or a godless mother. I
have seen such feeling and desire pass away before the strong
passion of blood loyalty, and never return again. What that
must mean in mature life and in the continuing generations
only the Lord can know, but the thought of what is likely is
not encouraging or hopeful. The disparities of education
and culture in a home are infinitely less significant in this

respect than those of religion. Lack of education is a matter that kindness and fellowship and patience may overcome. Lack of social training, and even lack of mental fellowship, may be neutralized with time and earnest effort. But religious alienation and discord is a fatal and deadly wound to a rich and happy personal development, life being regarded as an opportunity for full growth in all that makes for moral power and happiness in the service of God. There is no room for much discussion on this matter. There can be but a single opinion, as there is but a single result usually where the condition I have described prevails. President Eliot thinks mental companionship the first requisite to a happy marriage. My own judgment is that moral companionship and religious fellowship are first, and are first because they are first in the human frame, and first in the kingdom of God. Jesus had little to say about the mental characteristics of the kingdom of God. He had much to say about its spiritual and moral nature. If the family is a miniature of the kingdom, then its first concerns are spiritual and moral. Moral unity and spiritual fellowship are first. Without them I believe marriage to be merely a contract slightly above a commercial agreement, and the home a hotel on the one hand and a shop on the other. It is possible that such an establishment can preserve the peace and keep out of the divorce courts, but think of the personal loss and the personal barrenness of it all!

That the State has a large interest in the home life of its constituent inhabitants is proved by the immense number of statutes which regulate it in all its details. The State has already made marriage and birth and death civil functions. It has determined the form and organization of the family, described its limitations and prescribed a certain measure of State control over it. Unhappily, the one thing that makes a successful family life, namely, religion, the State under our form of government cannot touch. The best laws in creation cannot secure happiness. And the best government that the sun ever shone upon cannot survive where the masses of the people are constantly unhappy. What is needful, therefore, for the stability of the State and the permanence of the government,

the government cannot give nor produce by enactment of any
kind. This again is because ultimately the State rests upon
religion just as the family does, and the religion which makes
the State strong is that which is most securely engrafted in the
homes of the people. The New Testament ideal of the Christian is also the ideal of the citizen for the strong and permanent State. Every man in that State is a king, but every man
is also a priest. The kingly life and the priestly life go hand
in hand. The State cannot survive merely because it has a
constituency of kings. Something depends upon the nature
and habits of those kings. If they be also priests, men of
sacrifice, and men in whose life the fellowship of brotherhood
in a common obedience to Almighty God rules as a purpose of
heart and will, then the State is secure. Otherwise it is a
battle of kings for the survival of the strongest. And kings
in battle grow to look very much like the common horde of
mercenaries who fight for plunder or for glory. Religious
union in the home is a patriotic duty as well as a religious one.
It is here that we build the foundations of a commonwealth
which shall through all the growing pains of a new civilization
endure and live to the glory of God and the happiness of unborn races of men. Only a citizenship which is in heaven
is a sure guarantee for a valuable and upright citizenship on
earth.

Looking out upon the moral life of the whole earth, there
is no one force which can do it so much good, give it such an
impulse, and lift it so surely out of degradation and misery
into peace and comfort and joy as a properly constituted
home. And the religious organization of the home is in this
way allied also to the larger development of the world in all
that makes for the kingdom of God here below. The home
character of the religion of the Jews has made that people not
merely a nation, but a religion. When you say "Jew" to-day
you mean not only a race but also a faith. It was the religious
faith, the family union in the worship of Jehovah, that produced this phenomenon, which twenty centuries have not been
able to alter or efface. May we not hope that when we have
put forth the proper effort we shall make " American " mean

" Christian " in precisely the same way ? When we say " Pilgrim " now, do we not mean a faith as well as a particular class of men ? Do not some names mean at once a personality and a prophecy ? And may not all the families of the earth be blest in our families as it was with righteous Abraham ? The foundation of personal, social and civic redemption is in the home. The corner stone of that home is also the corner stone of Christianity, Jesus Christ as Lord and Redeemer of all.

SPIRITUAL EXILE

LUKE XV. 18.

IT is one of the strange paradoxes of human nature that it often places the highest valuation upon those things from which it is the farthest removed. Distance seems to add an enchantment that overcomes both probability and judgment. The home life, the home blessings and the home virtues are somehow made, while this aberration lasts, to seem insignificant and unworthy, while the distant life and activity have about them a glamour which lures to their ardent and constant pursuit. And it seems to be utterly useless, while this passion for things foreign is raging, to appeal to reason, experience or recorded knowledge. Few men are ever swerved from their determination when once this flame of passion for the distant thing has been lighted. The experience of the world appears to be to-day what it has been for ages, that only sad and bitter disappointment can restore the sway of reason and truth.

Now there are many places in the world and many inviting scenes which can give pleasure and light to man. And the instinct to know, planted by God in the human heart, has made certain races especially capable for the business of foreign travel and colonization. Indeed, at different times different nations seem to have had the largest measure of this capability. In the matter of discovery and sea power, for example, sometimes Spain has been supreme, then Italy, then the Netherlands, and now England. God's way of discovering the world to the human race has been by implanting in the breast of man the desire to seek and see new things and foreign climes. Without this passion for search the expansion of the world might have been indefinitely

283

retarded. With it man has crept into the most remote corners of the earth, and is even now engaged in honoring the man who has made the most successful effort to find the long-hidden North Pole.

But the divinely implanted passion to search is a legitimately organized desire. It is a desire which in the main springs from thoroughly admirable and lofty motives. A Columbus seeking to find a way to the Indies by sailing through the Western Sea, though partly moved, no doubt, by the avaricious dreams of his age, is still engaged in the divine work of verifying a conclusion at which his mind has arrived by patient contemplation of the facts of God's world. Livingstone and Stanley, whatever may have been the subsidiary aims, were in the main moved by desires quite creditable to the God-impelling motive to uncover a hidden continent. A Darwin, though forgetful of the supreme privileges of religious sentiment and becoming a spiritual skeleton in the devotion to scientific pursuits, was nevertheless doing a work which was in accordance with a legitimate need and use of the human mind. Darwin's own lament in his later years shows how painfully he himself came to realize this fact.

But, as with every other divinely organized desire, man has perverted it to his own uses, which are nothing else than misuses of them as planned by God. This history of the prodigal son in the parable is an illustration. This young man, like other young men, did not say, Father, give me the necessary capital that I may organize industry in my own way, or develop my capacities for the larger results for which I am evidently designed by God, and for which I feel a special calling. What he said was, Give me the portion of goods that falleth to me. And the sequel in the story shows that he was thinking of selfish indulgences and riotous throwing off of the restraints of the home life and home duties. The distant country, with its freedom from close scrutiny and the absolutely unchecked indulgence in whatever passion happened to be uppermost, looked very inviting and brilliant. The parental counsel and wisdom immediately became trans-

formed in the filial mind into an odious tyranny; the maternal interest and solicitude, a mother's "apron string." The
normal duties of the home became the chains of a slavery,
and straightway all the benefits, the care, the parental responsibility and nurture of years are utterly obliterated in
the longing for the distant scene that now looks so brilliant
and so enchanting.

How thoroughly this spirit prevails in the world may be
judged from the fact that a Boston newspaper recently made
sport of the Princeton University faculty for their action in
forbidding young men to have or dispense intoxicating liquors
by giving the impression that the Princeton men were by that
fact reduced to the condition of children in the nursery.
Evidently the newspaper idea of a college man is a drunken
lout who has unlimited right to be drunk and to make others
drunk. But this is simply one more evidence of the fact that
the restraints which make for power, sobriety and thoroughness in habits of mind and life are generally reckoned in the
terms in which the young prodigal reckoned them. It is the
working out of the passion for the unlawful, the unusual and
the foreign. It is the desire to escape the scrutiny, the control and the regular demand of duty which the normal life
needs and has made upon it.

There is a difference in the result, however, which soon
brings an awakening. When a man goes of his own accord
to a foreign land with the knowledge that he can return when
he pleases, we call that traveling. But when he goes under
the penalty of not returning, or if, while he is away, conditions arise which prevent his return, then what was a pleasure
tour becomes a bondage. Absence becomes exile. And exile
is very different from temporary journeying from the place
called home. You all recall the story of the "Man without
a Country." This was precisely the experience of the prodigal son, and is the experience of every prodigal, whether he
leaves his home, his moral life, his spiritual nature or his
respect for law. Expatriation in the flesh is, in these days
of the speedy and increasing intercourse, becoming next to
impossible. If a man is in the earth at all, as our civilization

is developing, he may be in touch with his fellow men and cannot be totally separated from those whom he loves as regards the possibility of communication. Commerce and transportation facilities and the resources of invention follow him everywhere.

But spiritual exile is still and will always be possible. And in spiritual exile there are wandering multitudes of men who do not seem to know just what the trouble is. Many are feeding on the husks which even swine sometimes reject, not knowing that there is a Father's house where there is bread enough and to spare. Many are hearkening to the confused voices of the world, unable in the din to hear the voice of Jesus Christ calling them back to themselves, their manhood and to God. Others are in the helpless servitude of a false morality, like that to which I have alluded, which mistakes the restraints of the gospel life and the sanctions of the morality and religion of Jesus Christ for evidences of slavery and adolescence. A great many more are like this prodigal boy, without knowledge of themselves, having not yet "come to" themselves. But whether it is ignorance of self or self-indulgence or faint-heartedness, whether it is moral and mental confusion, or whether it is sheer obstinate rejection of the vital truths of Jesus Christ's teaching, the one specially depressing fact is that spiritual exile is one of the commonest of experiences and one of the saddest sights upon which the eyes of man can look.

Take first of all the exile involved in lack of respect for law. I do not mean merely the statute law, but for law in general, moral, mental and spiritual, as well as statute. The one thing that marks manhood from the absence of it is precisely this quality of respect for law. When a man has no such respect we cannot regard him as other than a savage. He is in fact a savage, and only lacks the necessary occasion to prove that the essential inspiration of his life is a savage one. He recklessly invades the rights of other men. He forgets the cardinal qualities of a beautiful and a sane life, which are courtesy, kindliness and tolerance. The fact that some one thinks otherwise is to him a signal for onslaught openly, or treachery secretly. Such a man is an exile from the simplest tie of humanity. He does not realize that he is breaking up the foundations upon which rational human life rests. He is a destroyer of industry because he robs men of the power of enjoying what they have created. He is the enemy of invention because he lessens the motives to mental effort. He is the abetter of vice because he obliterates the distinctions between a right life and a wrong one.

Think of the example of Jesus Christ in this quality of respect for law. Bringing a gospel which meant the utmost freedom for every man, he took no liberties with the religious ceremonials of his ancestors and his nation. Hating, as a Jewish nationalist he must have hated, the Roman rule, he still counsels to render to Cæsar the things that are Cæsar's. Chafing under the brutalities of a religious organization that made timid, shrinking natures go to the wall before the brazen assumptions of the bold and the pretentious, he nevertheless advises obedience to spiritual authorities and exactness in religious observances. The conservatism of Christ is not less real in his life than his radicalism. What is called the radical character of Christ was not violation of law nor the inculcation of disrespect for organized authority. Yet a great many people think of Jesus Christ as a reckless religious revolutionist, who has no respect for the things that had been handed down from the generations preceding. He had. No man had a better appreciation of the fact that in the past lie the foundations of both the present and the future. His radicalism was his denunciation of sin and wrong. In that service no man can be too radical. It is the truth alone that can make us free.

"Does Mr. Wibird preach against oppression and other cardinal vices of the time?" wrote John Adams to his wife from Philadelphia, soon after the Bunker Hill battle. "Tell him the clergy here of every denomination, not excepting the Episcopalian, thunder and lighten every Sabbath. They pray for Boston and Massachusetts. They thank God most explicitly and fervently for our remarkable successes. They pray for the American army." It is not wonderful, as Professor Tyler adds, that the "literary history of the pulpit of the American Revolution is virtually a history of the pulpit champions of that movement." "Oppression and the cardinal vices of the time" sounds very much like a slogan framed for our own day. Lack of regard for law is oppression, and oppression in its worst form. Such men are not merely men without a country; they are men without any humanity. Their success is the destruction of us all. Their persistence is the bane of the brotherly life of the world.

But this lawlessness of spiritual exile, if sad to contemplate merely as impatience under restraint, becomes positively painful to witness when it results in the utter loss of moral virility. We know what it is to lose our fine feelings of manhood and honor when we have done things against which our consciences still raised their protest. Self-respect is then still present, and there is hope for a man in whom the feeling of self-respect lingers. But when the moral nature becomes so stunted in its sensibility that we can violate good faith, truth and honor, and feel no pangs, then comes the painful beginning of the end. Self-respect vanishes, and the deeds, at first secretly regretted and perhaps apologized for, become the moral habit and take the place of the moral ideal. Sins that were exceptional, and the result of sudden passion or unlooked-for temptation, are indulged in as habitual necessities and cease to give twinges of reproach. The conscience, too, has been driven into exile, and the moral nature is following hard after it. What was at first a mere skirmish, where the man was defeated by the suddenness of the attack, becomes a rout where there is general devastation and ruin. The ordinary language of hope, and spiritual truth, too, ceases to have meaning. Conscience is merely a name for a thing that once existed, but which has no power to enforce its decree. He has lost that fine responsiveness which gave meaning to the line of Emerson when he wrote : —

When Duty whispers low, *Thou must*; the youth replies, *I can*.

When a man finds that he cannot give an affirmative reply to the dictates of conscience, he may rest assured that he is an exile from the dearest associations of mankind, those which make for spiritual purity and righteousness. In these straits there is but a single thing to do — back to the Father's house whence he came, even though the return be one of humiliation and pain! Back to the first pangs of remorse for wrong done and evil indulged! In the Father's house alone will he find again the symbols of truth from which he has become separated and find in the law of God his consolation and his safety.

An indication of spiritual exile which is not less destructive to the hope of the world and the growth of the individual in personal character and holiness is the absence of moral sentiment in the normal work of life. This is proof that the moral nature is in exile. Christ's example in respect to his labor was instructive and illuminating on this point. Work and service were to him things that could not be divided one from the other. "My Father worketh even until now, and I work." These were his words. But men seem to have the impression that there is a possible separation of work and service; that what is the work need not have in it the moral feeling, the fine sentiment and the noble aspirations that go into what we. call Christian service. But it is this alienation of the moral nature from the task of the daily labor that has played such havoc with the spiritual interests of the people when these have come into collision with their material affairs. *This* belongs to the sphere of Christian service. *This* is business. It is absolutely fatal to a high moral development to permit such an antithesis to exist in the mind. All labor is service. The moral nature cannot be banished at will. Sent into exile in this way often, it soon remains in exile and will not return when the possessor wants it. Indeed, he ceases to remain the possessor of it in any real way.

Here, again, the only restoration is return to the Father's house. And that return is not merely a longing, wistful glance toward the righteousness and the law of God, it is *return* to it. It involves confession. It calls for a recognition of sin. "I have sinned against heaven and in thy sight." Those words are the key to moral restoration, whatever the offense. Righteousness recognized as opposed to sin is the only righteousness that has sway in the heart and that makes for rectitude in the life. We sometimes hear a good deal about the higher life. But a higher implies a lower life. Elementary righteousness in honesty, sobriety, self-respect and other homely virtues may be a lower life to some idealists to whom only things metaphysical are real, but to the vast body of the world such virtues are still very ideal. There is not a single syllable of spiritual dreaming in the Word of God. Righteousness is its great theme. The kingdom of God is not like those early aberrationists whom the Apostle Paul rebuked,—a company of beings who speak words which nobody can understand. It speaks with the understanding. It talks to the heart and it takes hold on the conscience. It is the language of familiarity and simple intercourse. It is the tongue of a fatherhood and sonship, not the prattle of metaphysical courtiers of an Ideal Essence.

It sometimes takes such exile to reveal to us just what the conditions are from which we have wandered. Certain it is that the whole race has thus wandered away from the elements of God's loving fellowship and of simple intercourse with God. It sometimes seems as if even the Church were some huge machine erected by the ingenuity of man to obscure the face of the Father and fill us with vanity and self-love. We know that it is not. We know that Christ instituted the Church. We know that he loved it and loves it still. But we often need to be robbed of its privileges and denied its consolations to feel the sense of its home ties as binding us to our Father. That is because we are often exiles from ourselves, as well as exiles from God and his laws and his work. But almost every man is willing to be an exile from a part of his nature, the part which is hateful and degrading and that is forever entangling him in its passions and indulgences. St. Paul could not entirely escape this feeling. He saw the war between the law of the mind and the law of the flesh. The struggle sometimes grew bitter enough. He calls himself frankly enough a wretched man. But he found Jesus Christ, who giveth the victory, too.

The early life of the poet Virgil was spent in the rural districts of Northern Italy, but there is no evidence that during the period of his life there that he enjoyed the rural habits and the surroundings of the pastoral life. He was simply a gentleman farmer while others did the work. But when he became immersed in the cares and luxuries of the city, he thought with joy and delight of those scenes of his youth, and the Eclogues which he wrote are the mental transformations of them after years had separated him from them. Is not that characteristic of man? So also the life of sin and of selfishness looks free and ideal, too, till we get to it. Then its sordidness and its shame come to our view. Then we wake, as did the young man in the parable, and find out that the companionship of sin is not a loyal companionship; that the fellowship of pleasure-loving and immoral men is not a fellowship that makes for mutual helpfulness and burden bearing. When grim Want reared her head, the crowd that sang over the flowing bowl and that danced around the flower-strewn gardens of sensuality disappeared. Children of the night, they had flown when daylight came.

And so it seems to be continually. At home, we wish to be abroad. Abroad, we long for home. But what we long for is the love that makes home and kinship, and that makes forgiveness and peace. This is the real significance of the Father's house. The young exile knew, as every man knows, that when he comes to that home, while he is yet a great way off the Father will have compassion upon him, and will run to him and kiss him with welcoming tears of joy. Yes, he knows more. He knows that there is joy in heaven among the angels when one such exile comes back to the Father's abode. Have you ever thought how the first real appreciation of true sonship comes with the acknowledgment of sin and the willingness to give up the proud title of son of a noble father? When he knew that he was not worthy to be called a son, then he knew how great a title it was. "Beloved," said the Apostle John in his old age, "now are we children of God, and it is not yet made manifest what we shall be. We know that, if he shall be manifested, we shall be like him ; for we shall see him even as he is."

Poor John Howard Payne, seeing afar off in foreign lands the glamour of courts and civilizations that could not be matched in our young country, yet, with the true feeling of an exile, touched the heart-strings of humanity in his undying song : —

> An exile from home, splendor dazzles in vain,
> Oh, give me my lowly thatched cottage again.
> The birds singing gayly that came at my call,
> Oh, give me them with the *peace of mind*, dearer than all.

That finds the soul as well as the heart of man. No brilliancy of earthly power or keenness of earthly enjoyment can give quiet to the saddened heart that longs for home. The heart wants the comforts of the Father's house more than it wants the enjoyments of the most entrancing human existence. It wants peace of mind, it wants release from sin and it wants the work of restoration and forgiveness.

And all is welcome with the heavenly Father. No man need, like a Prometheus or a Faust, battle his way through, to the knowledge of the Eternal. It is here open and free to all who desire to know and love him. It need not be an eternal strife, with the painful consciousness of defeat and humiliation. In the Father's house are life and immortality. There is no resignation of strength or of manhood in this return. On the contrary, it is the finding of power, and the building of the foundation of abiding character, that shall bless and be blest. It is the casting off of all that can defile, and purging the nature of its besetting sins. It is the receiving of a new inheritance of power, moral reserve and spiritual insight. It is the renewing of the mind. It is moral and spiritual fellowship and citizenship. It is the home-coming of the soul to the place of its birth and the habitation of its love.

Exiles from God we have all been, and probably will often be. But we need not remain in exile, and shall not if we can grasp the spirit of Christ and learn from him what true sonship is and what it involves. He, too, was an exile in his earthly pilgrimage from scenes of glory which he had with the Father before he came to the great work of saving man. On earth he was an exile, having not where to lay his head. In his arrest he was again an exile, for all forsook him and fled; and even on the cross he thought his exile had pursued him into the very heart of God when he cried, " My God, my God, why hast thou forsaken me ? " But that was the exile of God-likeness and self-sacrifice. It was the wreaking of earth's bitterest vengeance upon the revealer of its sins. But he was not alone. Legions of angels stood ready to move at his call. That was the voluntary bondage of the Saviour of mankind. His earthly exile was man's spiritual home-coming. Well may we be exiles from the flesh, from passion, from selfishness! Well may we be outcasts from the ribald companionships of the world! But this is acceptance with God. This is the fellowship of the spirit. This is staying at home with the Father. It is the solemn compact-keeping sonship which is the glory of moral and spiritual existence.

Let other men taste if they will the bitter cup of sin and woe. Let other men if they must challenge the law of the Almighty in its operations on mind, conscience and moral nature. Let others strip themselves naked spiritually and find the fearful looking-for of judgment that pursues the unholy life and the defiance of piety and truth. But let your soul be at home with the Father. Let it endure without shame the reproach of childlikeness. A mother's "apron strings" are better than a jailbird's stripes. A father's counsel is better than the sentence of a police magistrate. A college faculty's mandate is better than a drunken debauch. A character is better than a good time falsely so called. A Father in heaven honored and a sonship with fellow men remembered in service, truth and fidelity are worth the restraint and self-mastery which they cost. Home is better than exile.

THE IMPERATIVES OF FAITH

I Samuel xvii. 46, 47.

A DISTINGUISHED college president of this country has written an interesting and impressive essay with the title "Some Reasons why the American Republic may endure."[1] He points out with great clearness and in a faultless style that the history of republican institutions is a most varied one and that the record of republican forms of government gives us little assurance for supposing that republicanism in itself is any guarantee for perpetuity. He then points out some of the reasons why the American Republic may survive the dangers which threaten it and continue indefinitely in the expanding civilization of the world. It is an interesting survey. It is discriminating and judicial. It bears the impress of a scholarly and cultivated mind.

But the most interesting feature of that essay was one which the author probably did not contemplate in such a light at all. There is evidence that the title was carefully chosen. And the subjunctive form of it is doubtless the result of deliberate choice. But a man less cumbered with the academic sense will at once wonder whether the subjunctive form of national feeling is the one that is calculated to assist in securing the perpetuity of the American Republic; whether a judicial estimate of the reasons why we *may* solve our numerous pressing problems or a scholarly setting forth of some hopes that we *may* keep the national honor unstained and the national integrity unspotted, is what the sixty-five millions of people would regard as the kind of discussion from which they could go forth determined to make the republic outride its storms and come into the fulness of

---

[1] "American Contributions to Civilization." C. W. Eliot, Century Co.

national expansion and moral excellence. The essay nowhere
asserts the author's positive belief that the republic will
endure. Throughout, his problem is to discover reasons why
it *may* endure.

That is undoubtedly the scholastic method of investigating
any problem while nothing serious is impending and important
decisions can be made to wait for further light and intelligence
is commendably rational and sane. But is it the attitude of
the vast majority of the people who are living on this earth
and to whom life is a mad struggle for simple necessities in
the desire to save themselves from being swallowed up nameless and unclassified in the mob? Does any man begin his
business with the subjunctive form of hope? Does any student go into college with the subjunctive expectation of a degree? Does any candidate for office undertake his canvass
with the subjunctive method of campaigning? To mention
these things is to state how absurd they are. Nobody makes
any venture in life without the firm hope and the confident
expectation that he is going to succeed. Without it he never
would undertake it at all. Young men do not take four years
of preparatory study to fit themselves for college with the
idea that they *may* pass the examinations. Men do not
marry with the thought that they *may* be happy and prosperous in life with their chosen companions. In all these
modes of human action the note is one of confidence and
faith. It is one which rouses to action and commands sacrifices which without the faith never could be made. Imagine
Wendell Phillips in Music Hall presenting some reasons why
we *may* hope to abolish slavery. Or General Grant sending
a message to General Lee stating some reasons why he *may*
take Richmond. This subjunctive way of looking at the
national life or indeed any kind of life may be academic and
scholarly, but it is not life.

Indeed, it may be questioned with propriety whether it is
in any proper sense academic even. For we must not suppose that the academic habit robs a man of that distinctive
thing which allies a man's ability to do with his ability to
think. When Emerson wrote, " 'Tis man's perdition to be

safe when for the truth he ought to die," he gave birth to a majestic philosophic truth, a product of the academic spirit and habit. And the boys of Harvard College who believed it in 1861 proved that the academic life is not necessarily linked to physical and moral inertness. Culture and action are not yet hopelessly divorced.

But this example of subjunctive patriotism is but the symbol of a larger subjunctive which is to a great degree prevailing in many forms of modern life. Especially is this true in the sphere of religion where men are apparently discussing things on the basis of whether they *may* be true or not, rather than on the sure basis of that they *are* true or not. Whatever middle state of thought a man may be in, on what constitutes devotion to country, the matter of religion admits of no such state of mind. In his religion a man believes or he does not believe. His belief may be soundly or unsoundly grounded in evidence. It may even to others than himself be foolish and absurd. But he himself, if it is religion to him sufficiently to make it the rule of his life, believes in it not with the idea that it *may* be true, but with the idea that it *is* true. And for him it is true. Faith is never a conjectural possession. A man has it or he has not. He possesses it and it possesses him. Without this reciprocal mastery by the man of his idea and by the idea of the man whatever else there may be, there is nothing that can be called in any real sense faith.

From this it will be observed that faith is something positive and imperative. That instead of being intellectual surrender, it is really intellectual independence. This 'is the explanation of the fact that the most severe persecution that can be visited upon a man for his belief is the surest way of making him hold to it most persistently. He links, in his mind, his personal freedom and liberty of thought with the faith that he professes. Abuse him for it, and you make him a martyr to it. Instead of taking kindly any attempt to lead him away from his belief, he closes his mind to any further light, and is hopelessly confirmed in it. This is a universal experience. It is as true of political opinions as of religious opinions. Direct attack upon them only intrenches men in them. Belief and liberty are thus twins in human thought. Faith in this aspect has in it all the heroic qualities that can be imagined as belonging to man. Weakness and surrender are as foreign to it as anything possibly can be.

Perhaps belief and faith are not philosophically interchangeable terms, but practically they involve the same faculties, and mean the same thing. A man's belief is his faith. And his faith is the totality of all that makes him what he is. Experience and judgment, expectation and desire, reason and feeling, all unite in the making of this quality of a man's faith. I do not mean by a man's faith a man's creed. Because things may be in his creed that are not in his faith, and there are always things in a man's faith which are not in his creed. A creed is usually only a kind of an index reference. It shows about where a man's religious life is found. But it is not a photograph of it, and is not intended to be. A great deal of the cant about creeds utterly fails to take cognizance of this fact.

The episode of David and Goliath, meeting in the wars of the Philistines and Israelites, furnishes a most signal illustration of the imperative character of the faith which gives power and victory in life. There is a sort of heroic cast about this battle of the shepherd with the giant which has always endeared it to men capable of feeling the impelling force of a high religious and national ideal. David the youth feels what the battle-scarred veterans of Israel are not able to feel. The young man trained in the freedom of the forest and the plain, who does not quail at the sight of the beasts of the forests, is surely not the man to tremble at the words of a braggart enemy of his people, his country and his religion. To challenge Israel's army in this defiant manner was to the youth, unspoiled by the subjunctive life of the court and the palace, something akin to blasphemy and was in fact to him defiance of the Lord the God of Israel. No wonder the young hero looked about him astounded that no man came forth to enter the lists against such an enemy.

The young life of to-day feels the same sort of surprise when it finds itself face to face for the first time with the subjunctive religious life of older men. It comes forth from the school with the mind charged with the sense of achievement and power. Its anxiety is only lest it shall not meet the Goliaths of business, politics, law and religion. But when it arrives at the battlefield, instead of seeing a host ready for conquest, it finds a terror-stricken mob trembling at the words of the Philistine. Experience rebukes it, as David's elder brothers rebuked him. Determined to fight the giant still, it tries to cumber him with antiquated methods and maxims of warfare, as Saul tries to cumber David with his own armor. But unlike Israel's young champion of long ago, much of our young life by this time catches the trick of falling into line, and loses itself in the subjunctive life of the host. A few, still remembering the power of a free arm and the steady aim of an unspoiled eye, find the smooth stones in the brook and slay the Goliaths and mount the kingly throne. Courage is restored for the time, and the note of possibility becomes the note of certainty. Victory, then, is not a thing that *may* happen. It is a thing that *must* happen. And then the times change, and the hosts return to subjunctive listlessness.

The faith that secures a victory like David's, or indeed any life victory, whether it be over evil habits, laziness or natural difficulty, is a faith that speaks in the imperative mode. It is a supreme authority, or it is no authority at all. It arrests the whole nature of man and fills it with new capacities and new desires. It gives new adaptabilities to old capabilities. It takes old experiences and applies them to new situations. It rises in a series of steady moral and spiritual gradations from lower thought and lower achievement to higher thought and higher achievement, until it looks with satisfaction only on the highest thought and the highest achievement. It does not permit the subject of it to doubt or retreat. It simply impels him like the gale on the seas, on and on, in a mighty and resistless course. His aroused nature is the outstretched sail, filled to its last nook and crevice with the powerful wind. Desire crystallizes into will, and will in turn becomes realization. It was faith's imperative that cut loose from the moorings and set sail on this boundless sea.

To the anxious existence which lives in the atmosphere of mere conjecture, this free, imperative life of genuine faith has always seemed mysterious and incomprehensible. The world looks on men of faith with a feeling in which wonder and pity are about equally mixed. Until the times of consummation, men feel by turns angered and amused with the reforming function which the man of faith sustains to the social body. But in the meantime the man of faith is driven by what he cannot resist. Like Paul he does not feel merely that he would like to preach the gospel. On the contrary, it is woe to him if he does not preach. One thinks of the pitiful wanderings of Columbus, type and symbol of all discoverers. One thinks again of Galileo, while he is recanting under pressure his famous doctrine that the earth moves, muttering under his breath, "Nevertheless it moves." It is the faith that thus holds men in its grip of iron. And the faith that moves men is greater than the faith that moves mountains. These living firebrands set the whole world ablaze. But faith makes them do it. It is the imperative within that creates the realized facts of history and life.

Inquiring now as to the reasons for the dominion which thus springs from the living faith which is in a man who believes, we note faith's recognition of the fact that life is not for material but for spiritual ends. The subjunctive life is practically on the same platform with Goliath: it believes that the Lord saves with the sword and spear. In other words, it subscribes to the infamous doctrine that the Lord is always on the side of the heaviest battalions. The reason why the Israelitish army became a set of cravens, who dared not go forth to meet Goliath of Gath, was because they saw only the great sword and the huge man. But the weapons of God's warfare are not carnal, but spiritual, and when the young shepherd comes, he thinks of the Lord God of Israel, rather than of the sword and the spear. On the sword and spear platform both the religious and the non-religious man are on the same ground. That makes the issue conjectural.

Victory is then a matter which can be determined only by brute force. The size of Goliath's sword and the strength of his arm are then capital considerations. But when the contest takes on a spiritual aspect, the whole affair changes. A smooth stone is as good as a long sword. And a stout sling and a free, active arm are better than armor and spear. And what is more, the faith of the shepherd is mightier than them all. Wise old law-giver Moses was, when he ordered that a timid man should not be permitted to go into battle; nor a man whose heart was elsewhere than in the service of the God of Israel. With such soldiers defeat was certain. But fighting the battle of the Lord was a different matter. A war of conquest might make men brave and daring. A war of defense might make them courageous and enduring. But a war for religion and faith makes them uncompromising and sacrificing beyond the power of conquest or defense. The battle was won with David long before he slew the giant. The Lord Almighty could not suffer defeat. It was the Lord Almighty's cause which was at stake. The real giant in that duel of champions was the Spirit of the Lord in the young shepherd's heart.

The men who have fought and are fighting the cause of industrial and social liberty in this and other lands are sometimes wont to make much of the carnal weapons. But their trust must be placed in higher things before the victory is won. The battle against monopolies and combinations, a chapter as pitiful as anything in the history of this country, embracing a hardship and suffering, danger to life, reputation, property and almost every other evil, an unparalleled recital of monopolistic crime and avarice, will not be won through courts and Congresses, strong allies as they may be of truth and justice. It will be won in the appeal to men's hearts and the renewal in them of the faith in God, that attempts things seemingly impossible and, though martyrs to them, believes them still. Christ dying the victim of treachery and intrenched ecclesiastical power was the victor, though he was crucified. But let the appeal be the imperative one of faith. Men must be free. Manhood must be restored.

The world must be redeemed. Let us have no more of what
may be or what can be achieved " perhaps." Let us only be
told where the rampart is that we must mount, and then send
the standard-bearer forward. We can dare anything if it be
for right and for God. We can suffer many things if they
are needful for the kingdom of Christ in the earth. Call on
us to believe! Bid us be confident! Tell us that we *must*
succeed, and under God we *shall* succeed.

There never has been a human advance that was not the
result of a spiritual aspiration. Somebody prayed it first, and
then it began to be realized. Somebody sacrificed for it, and
then it began to win souls. Somebody died for it, and then
it began to find that in the blood of the martyr was the resurrection of a triumphant cause. The struggle of life must be
taken as a spiritual task, not a carnal one. Business and religion are both spiritual matters. Law, politics and medicine
are mockery if they are not in deep alliance with the higher
spiritual interests to which they are only steps. Justice on
the earth should be but the reflection of the eternal justice of
God. Political and governmental strivings after equality and
economic well-being should be but efforts toward the brotherhood of man, which the gospel enjoins as obligatory on
all men. The practice of the healing art should have as its
final motive that the soul may have a healthier and holier
abode. St. Paul's view that the body is the temple of the
Holy Ghost should be the true impulse of medical science.
Luke was an apostle no less than Paul. And the life of
such a pioneer as the late Dr. Benjamin Ward Richardson
illustrates the power of the spiritual motive in the most
fleshly labors.

Again faith does not stop with the imperative requirement
that all life should be spiritualized. It goes farther and demands that the spiritualized life shall expand and develop
according to the new laws into which it has come. It does
not cease its imperative simply because the spiritual view
has become dominant. It requires expansion and extension
in the spiritual life. This is undoubtedly what the writer to
the Hebrews had in mind when he said, " Wherefore let us

cease to speak of the first principles of Christ, and press on
unto full growth," realizing, naturally enough, that a beginning
in the spiritual life is good, but it is only a beginning.   Full
growth is the final ideal.   And this is reiterated again and
again in the writings of St. Paul.   Beginnings are only beginnings even in Christian living.   Life grows larger as the
unvision extends.   And the faith that moved forward out
of the bondage of the material into the realm of the spiritual,
now moves on to a higher life in the spiritual realm.   Faith's
pressure is not lessened, and faith's note of authority is not
weakened.   It still says "must."   The stunned giant must
be slain.   The dazed armies of the Lord must be organized
for pursuit.   The spiritualized mind and the spiritualized
faculties must be set to work with increased zeal to hasten
the coming of the kingdom and the final triumph of Christ
in the earth.   Growth in the spiritual life is as imperative as
the assuming of the life itself.   Faith enjoins and enforces
this truth in most uncompromising terms.

The necessity of a constantly maturing life is as well established in the spiritual as in the bodily existence.   As a feature
of intellectual or social development it is so well recognized
that we are always ready for the changes which it will bring
out.   But the maturing of the spiritual faculties has not
always been seen to be so clearly commanded by faith as it
really is.   But the reasons are precisely those which apply
to the body.   When a man's body ceases to develop it begins
to decay.   There may be a period which can be described as
the high tide of bodily development at which there is a brief
interval which is neither increase nor decline.   But it is a
very brief period.   But there is no such thing in the spiritual
life because the will of God revealed by faith is an ever
widening vision of service and sacrifice.   Faith is therefore
constantly saying to man, Believe *more* and know *more*.   The
same vigorous voice which said to the carnally minded man,
Be spiritual, now says, Be more spiritual.   The shepherd
slayer of the physical Goliath must now become the King
of Israel.   The youth whose faith slew the lion and bear
must become the organizer of Israel's standing army, and

complete the organization of the kingdom. Likewise must the spiritual youth become the spiritual king. He must organize the kingdom for the larger use of all his own and others' resources in the service of God. The Christian who is not maturer at forty in the spiritual life than he was at thirty, is not less to be pitied than the man who does not know more at forty than he did at thirty in any other part of his being. His reason should be clearer, his appetites more restrained, his faculties more under control and his soul and spirit ampler in their receptiveness and interpretative power. Faith led him to this new life. Faith urges him to explore it. Grow, it is perpetually commanding. And as the growth of the spiritual powers increases, new energies are created and new tasks reveal themselves challenging performance and fulfilment.

To this outlook of unlimited power and growth there is no end. And it is here that faith has its most imperative note to offer. It is that there shall be no end. An endless life must mean to the man of faith an endless succession of new manifestations of God's greatness, goodness and love. On this point faith with mighty emphasis bids man never to waver and never to doubt. This is the reason why there is so much in the New Testament about believing. Not because any particular, intellectual view of the gospel or of the historic facts of the New Testament is in itself worth anything. But because the belief of a man's heart is the underpinning of his whole career. He must have authority there. He must be able to hear the voice of eternal and unchallenged right. He must hear God with his whole nature, the heart, the reason and the spirit. This makes his faith an imperative thing. And so long as he has it or it has him, then its command is one that cannot be trifled with or lightly disobeyed.

Philosophers and others have had a great deal to say in derision of the idea that a man's salvation is a matter of his belief. What a man is, they say, is of infinite more importance than what he believes. This criticism is true if by belief is meant merely the intellectual elements of faith. But the simple truth is that a man's faith *is* his life. His life is the outworking of the things in which he believes, not in any statement about them intellectually, but in the actual power which they exercise over his life and purposes. A ship might fly at the masthead the fairest flag of the world and still be a pirate. Not a few men in this world do substantially that thing. But it would be stupid in the extreme to suppose any flag useless because a pirate used it unlawfully.

Because faith is thus imperative and continuous in its note of authority, it must have an adequate object and illustration throughout the whole line of its appeal to men. That object and illustration of the life of faith is Jesus Christ. Any temptation to the subjunctive habit may at any time be utterly dispelled by simply inquiring, What did Christ do under similar conditions? When a man thinks he *may* possibly become self-sacrificing, let him look at Jesus Christ and he *will* become self-sacrificing. When one thinks he *may* learn to be meek and lowly in heart, let him give his mind the opportunity to dwell on the incomparable life of the Lion of Judah's tribe who became the Lamb of God. Let him reflect upon the majesty of the promise of the Saviour, "Because I live, ye *shall* live also." Life shall be enriched and the moral spinal column stiffened into strength and persistence in the divine life of service and belief. Christ never appealed to the world with such a splendid vindication in discipleship and service as in the Christianity of to-day, imperfect as it is in many respects. But while we are seeing new heavens with the great telescopes that bring the skies down to us, and while we are bringing out of the earth things that have been hidden for ages past, and while through air and ice we still search and expect to find the Northern Pole, let us remember that we nevertheless walk by faith, not by sight. We walk in God's knowledge and understanding, not our own. We live in the expectation of his glory, not our own. And we march on in the campaigns of service to the commands of a God-inspired and God-maintained faith. That faith is for us objectified in the life of our Lord. And it deals not with probability or possibility, but with certainty. Our victory is an assured one. Threats cannot move us, and perils cannot affright us.

Cheerful we tread the desert through,
While faith inspires the heavenly ray;
Though lions roar and tempests blow,
And rocks and dangers fill the way.

THE CONFLICT OF DUTIES

LUKE ix. 61.

THERE are people in this world to whom the next thing to be done is always perfectly clear. They seem to know from circumstances, from intuition or some other source, just what is required of them, and are never in doubt as to the precise task at which they should be engaged. The state of mind thus described may very properly be called beatific. For blessedness can have as one of its best compensations nothing better than just this.

But these are not the majority. They are not numerous enough even to make us feel that we are very greatly wronged in their having what most of us have not. Then, again, their blessed state does not seem to give them peculiar efficiency in life, or peculiar power in impressing their ideas upon us. They are undoubtedly without any doubts on this subject whatever. But they do not seem to have so enormous an advantage as to make us very envious. For such the message this morning is not intended. It is rather for that vast majority of people who are almost daily finding themselves face to face with what seems a veritable conflict of duties, out of which they must choose something, and are not always sure that they have chosen the right thing when the choice is made.

Take the illustration in our text. The Lord calls a man who after examining the matter, and hearing the Master's call, decides that he will become a disciple of Christ. I will follow thee, Lord, is his ready and unforced response to the appeal of Christ. But a moment's reflection makes him think that those in his house are also to be considered in

306

any decision he may make. And naturally enough he adds, But first let me bid farewell to them at my house.

Taken by itself in almost any ordinary occurrence in life, one would say this was a most reasonable request. One does not make decisions for one's self alone. The household must be considered. Even if only to say farewell, the breaking off of past relations at least should be done decently and in order. It seems a reasonable and a just thing to ask, and we rather honor the thoughtfulness which proposed it.

But here again we are brought face to face with the words of Christ, that a man must not look backward, and that looking back renders him unfit for the kingdom of God. That seems like a drastic requirement. It is not merely causing an amputation, it is making it with the coarsest instrument possible. And yet there are the plain words of the Master with their inevitable inference.

There is a qualification suggested here in the words, "having put his hand to the plough." It may be argued that the man had not yet taken up Christ's service, and therefore was not really looking back. That the real force of the message is, that duty once begun must be persisted in, and that here we are to find the true interpretation of the verse. But that seems so obvious a matter that we can hardly imagine Christ speaking to that simple duty at such a juncture.

No, he was addressing himself to a very real and practical experience of the human mind and will. That experience is the conflict of duties which is everywhere and never was more perplexing than it is at this time. But no more so in the matter of religion and morals than in any other department of life. The conflict is there as everywhere else. The choice of a profession, the determination of great life interests of one kind and another, are full of the same questioning that surrounds the matter of duty.

How do we discover duty at all? Just as we discover anything. A need arises which appeals to us. A sacrifice is demanded which we are capable of making. Christ passes our way and asks us to become his disciples. Christ appealing is a call to service. It suggests the duty of following.

Once in the presence of duty there is little ambiguity as to what it requires. In so far our problem is a very simple one.

But what when we stand in the presence of many duties at once and all are appealing and our own judgment is almost obscured in the endeavor to hear all the voices that are calling for assistance and support? That is a very different question to solve. It savors very much of the youth just on the brink of life asking himself, What shall I do with my life? And there are numberless answers to his question.

Now duty itself is born out of conflict. Righteousness was never a jovial affair. That is the reason why the blessedness of the easy-going people, who always know just what they ought to do, has so little attraction for us. Righteousness is no jollification meeting. It is not a sort of self-congratulatory gathering, where only pleasant things are spoken, and for the moment we forget that there is evil in the world. Righteousness is born out of strife. The conflict with evil gives the character of conflict to the choice of duties, as well as to duty itself. Right-doing is the product of strenuous effort.

It is fair to assume that every right-thinking man or woman wants to do what is best for him or her to do. That, at least, is a proposition which cannot be questioned. But because of the multiplicity of duties which seem to call for immediate action, it is very certain that a mass of people evidently do nothing, and the reason partly is that there are so many conflicting claims presented.

A man, for example, who has only a limited sum of money at his disposal, is and ought to be careful as to what he does with it. He may divide it into trivial driblets and touch philanthropy and charity at a great many points, or he may give his entire gift to a single aim. But in any case he cannot get away from the inevitable appeals of those causes. He may give only to one. But he must hear them all. What shall he do and how shall he quiet his soul with the burdens that are thus brought to him?

The same thing comes when he faces life itself. He must take up his cross and follow Christ. He is willing enough to do that. But how shall he follow? A multitude of denomi-

nations appeal to him as being the only custodians of truth.
Any number of enterprises ask him at once in Christ's name
to become sponsors for them. He cannot do everything.
He cannot take on his mind and heart every appeal which
comes along. What shall he do with the abundant sympathies which are called into being by the knowledge which is
so freely bestowed upon him?

This is a very practical question and becoming more so.
In the Congregational denomination we have already seven
regular societies, all telling us that their work is absolutely
necessary. These organizations have seven different treasuries and seven sets of officers, and are in this way made the
agents for an enormous and frightful waste of Christian
money. All our work is either in this country or in foreign
lands. Two treasuries at the most should answer for them
all. Two sets of officers should amply provide for the
administrative necessities. Seven societies for one denomination are as clear a case of administrative lunacy as seven
heads to one family.

But let the practical troubles go this morning and let us
deal with only the spiritual and moral ones. What shall
I do? Which duty is the most pressing? Which interest
really has the largest claim on my mind and heart? To
which should I devote the greatest labor and the most faithful prayer? For I take it that all prayer and work should
center and terminate on something definite and concrete.
These are the questions I want to answer this morning.

Let me answer first of all that Jesus' words, in reply to
the man whose desire to bid farewell to those in his house
are my text, form less a reply to the man than an incitement to intensity of conviction. What Jesus seeks to impress
in that saying is, that the man should look with tremendous
energy and earnestness at the thing to which he is to give up
his life. That in a great spiritual crisis a man does not
think of the minor concerns of life but only of those great
fundamental things which are the all-absorbing matter of his
thought.

That suggests that the conflict of duties is greatest where

intensity is least. When a man is on fire with a mighty idea
or cause, he has little trouble with the conflict of duties. It
is there undoubtedly at times, because duty is the result of
reflection and judgment, not of mere impulse or excitement.
But intensity of thought and conviction greatly lessens the
difficulty. It does not abolish it. That would be a calamity,
in my judgment.

Intensity, not of emotion, but of rational inquiry and knowledge, is the greatest need of the religious life at this present
time. We need to know with a masterful passionateness
that will not be denied. We need to question the very
sources of life and being, with an earnestness that will not
let go until we have what finally and substantially holds us
as the truth. Something of the spirit should move us that
made Jacob wrestle with the angel all night, and not until he
blessed him did he let him go.

Blessing comes with such an earnest struggle as that.
Light comes with it. Let me search for my duty not merely
when I can without inconvenience find it, but let me find it
when I must push through the thicket of doubt and distrust.
Let me not lay aside a difficult question when I am face to
face with it, but stay with it until I find at least some working
theory answer to it. Intensity enough to see present duty
to its end is the great need.

But this intensity must not.become irrational, blind devotion. The intense devotion to a good cause which persists in
ignorant disregard of plain facts is, in the long run, one of
the most damaging things which can come to it. Peter did
little good when he smote off the ear of Malchus, the servant
of the high priest, on the night of Jesus' arrest. John did no
good in calling down the fire from heaven on the Samaritans.
Both had to be rebuked by Christ.

And this, in connection with the example of Christ, proves
that intensity of purpose and aim is consistent with calmness
and repose. Not necessarily repose in manner, but mental
alertness and self-control. It is not needful to lose one's head
to be in earnest. On the contrary, real earnestness begins
with a perfectly balanced head. Christ was passionate and

often aroused to the deepest expressions of feeling, but there is no evidence that he ever lost sight of his mission, or the cost at which his aim was to be secured.

Now righteousness, because it is born of conflict, has just this quality. And the solution for the conflict of duties lies in the cultivation of a genuine zeal for righteousness. Then we shall be more likely to see duties in their logical succession rather than in a confused mass, of which we cannot make out which is first and which is last. The loudest call is not always the more pressing one. In fact, a man may well leave off saving the world until he has found his own soul and solved his own relations with God.

But some one says that there is no duty except present duty. I do not believe that. I believe there is a duty for to-day, and one for to-morrow. I do not think that the Creator, who by the orderly processes of evolution made the worlds, calls you and me to face duties of the gravest consequence, without the slightest intimations that they are coming. Rather do I believe that he helps us prepare for coming trials by the same laborious, patient training that made the earth habitable for man.

Then again, we must do in the conflicts of the spiritual life just what we do in the other relations of life. That is to say, we must be guided by what seem to be the exigencies of the time. Christ, it is observed, had nothing to say on the subject of slavery; very little that was suggestive of reform in the government; still less about a number of minor matters which have since grown to huge proportions. The gospel was not for an age, but for all time. Therefore by him the announcement must be made in universal terms.

This has led a great many people to suppose that obedience to Christ requires that we, too, must confine ourselves to terms of universal application. Denounce theft, but say nothing about the thief. Condemn crime if you will, but let alone the criminal. The minister may even denounce sectarianism, but woe betide him if he says aught against our particular denomination. This has been for years the irony of all movements toward church unity.

But it still remains that we must use our judgment in determining what is most pressing, and select out of the myriad of appeals what commends itself as the most meritorious and worthy of our service. The whole kingdom may hinge on some trifling matter, if that trifling affair is properly placed. The relation to the whole problem determines the importance of a thing. If an advancing army storming a fort finds a certain pass absolutely necessary to success, then it is good tactics to mass the troops at that point, and run minor risks at others.

But this again emphasizes the fact that duty is determined through judgment not through impulse. And herein lies the value of a life based on principle, as against one that requires the constant galvanizing of new motives and constant appeal. It is not far from the truth to say that fifty per cent of the energies of the Church are spent in keeping alive those who should live of their own spiritual strength and nurture, and thus free the Church for the larger problems before it.

There is also the best evidence for believing that the very perplexity which arises from the endeavor to determine what is the first thing to be done produces the attention which is necessary to the highest spiritual uses of the mind. The ministry of Christ was full of such moments of perplexity. It is often stated that his soul was troubled. He suffered the same anxieties which are a common experience with us. Even on the cross the human nature of the Saviour gives expression to this same questioning doubt.

But doubt fixes attention. The necessity for thinking produces thought. It is probable that the thought so centered on the moral difficulties of existence and action is the first step toward their proper solution. Nothing is ever clarified by avoiding it. But if we are compelled by conditions to make a path, if none has ever been made before, that is itself a notable work accomplished.

Life loses by too much discursiveness. Things of importance hasten to the form of issues and must be met as definite contests of strength. Saving the world is the problem of saving a man. All human problems can probably be found in some form in individual men. Indeed, the saving of a man is the great problem of redemption. It is therefore best understood and best dealt with when we take men singly as the subjects of labor and thought.

Yet while Jesus, whose example is here again suggestive, gave his thought to the man at hand, we must not forget that he sent out the seventy to preach and to heal. He sent them out two by two, also, giving by this act the recognition to the social fellowship which is the absolute requisite to the highest usefulness of the individual. In the presence of the multitude which needed the gospel, he did not forget that there were other sheep not of this fold. Remote duty was not neglected in the pressure of present activity.

After all, the main thing is to keep in motion. Give the mind a task of some kind and let that be the starting point to a natural growth of opportunity and privilege. It is wonderful what continued activity will bring forth even under the most unfavorable conditions. The recently published letters of Napoleon at Elba show that while Europe was thinking that it had settled the fate of the great usurper, his habits of activity were really preparing him for the famous Hundred Days which reawakened them to the power of the man.

The historian states that reduced as he was, to a small guard, he gave it the same attention that he did to the *Grande Armée*. He reorganized the administration, built bridges, started a navy, planned coast defenses, attended to sanitary improvements, all in miniature on the island of Elba, as he had done it in grand proportions at Paris. That was a true way of proceeding. Inaction would have seen Napoleon go out of the world insignificantly. As it was, Europe must needs bury him in the seas at St. Helena to be perfectly sure that his active nature would not disturb her again.

I take that to be a right spirit. Every man's own life should be to him what Napoleon made of the *Grande Armée*. Whether large or small in its resources make the most of it. Fidelity at Elba may mean a grand reentry into Paris. And to the standard of an active campaigner for a great cause a multitude are always ready to flock. Action in the field of moral conquest is not less admirable than action on the field of war. A moral nobility and a splendid moral dogmatism are as really objects of mental delight and as thrilling to the soul as any struggle at Thermopylæ or grim determination at Vicksburg.

And this leads me to say that, much as has been said about dogmatism in religion, what the world needs is not less of it, but more of it. The dogmatic assertion of things that cannot be proven is one thing. It may not be thoroughly commendable. But the unyielding, dogmatic assertion of determination to do what one conceives to be his duty, is altogether admirable. A genuine man cannot do less than that. Some men will call him obstinate. Others may call him a fool. But he knows that he is surrendering the citadel of his moral nature if he flinches from that position.

"In whatever situation fortune may place me," Napoleon once said to his treasurer, "I will never tolerate any *friponnerie*." That was the key to his almost miraculous successes as a military commander. That may well be the watchword of our young men at the opening of the moral campaigns which the new century will see forced upon us. In whatever may, in the providence of God, come to be our portion, let us never tolerate trickery with ourselves or the things around us. Let us keep things to the rule of right action and true ends.

And this trickery, this moral juggling, is at the source of much of our moral confusion. It is hard to find a moral evil in the world to-day which has not its organ, its coteries of apologists and its regular machinery for deceiving the public. Laziness will often be deceived into believing these smooth promises and these plausible falsehoods. But we must not tolerate it. The trick habit, once brought into the field of moral action, is like the sleight-of-hand performances of the sneak thief. It is hard to keep the hands off.

Rather let us have dogmatism at this point. Have it just as hard and fast as we can make it. "No," said General Burnside to General Longstreet's summons to surrender at Knoxville, "if you want my boots, come and get them."

That is how a man should feel about his moral integrity. If you defeat me, it must be in open battle. If care and patience and constant guarding can do it, I shall never be surprised into giving up what is the only thing I can possess that is worth having, a mind conscious of truth and rectitude. A dogmatism like that would mean much to the kingdom of God.

The conflict of duties tends to become less as we become identified with causes which are worthy of our best and most spiritual intentions. It is the lack of identification that brings about the hesitancy which leads to distress, and often to ruin. There is a great deal of cant about keeping the mind open to conviction. In certain respects this is true enough. In others it is a gross misconception of liberality. No man keeps his front door open to leprosy or scarlet fever! Why should he keep it open to attacks of moral disease?

Many a man has lost his own self-respect and that of his fellow men just because of this habit of lacking identification with the great interests of man and the kingdom of God. Church membership has for one of its uses just this thing. Not that it always succeeds. In some cases it lamentably fails. But for the most part, membership in Christ's Church identifies the man and simplifies for him, if he does not conceal the fact, many questions. The fact that he is enrolled there is itself a defense and a shield.

Politicians may, in this respect as in some others, teach us a lesson. They are careful to get a man to cast his first vote, knowing that it is a comparatively simple thing to hold him in the party after that. Having once cast his ballot for a party, he feels constrained to vindicate that first act, and so readily does it again until he is a full-fledged party man. It takes years to break the effect of a man's first vote.

Equally important is the fact of the first Christian decision which a man makes. The first time, for example, a man refuses to sign a license petition, is almost as momentous as signing a declaration of independence. But it goes easily the next time. He notes it. The rumseller notes it. The public note it. And public sentiment and his own manhood, if he has any, usually hold him to his standard. When it comes to the matter of openly confessing Christ as a Christian man, the importance of the act can hardly be exaggerated.

The advantage of standing out true and strong in the public estimation as an ally of right things and the cause of Christ in particular is the best advantage which the Christian life has to confer, in the effort of man to perfect himself. Hence it has always called men to come forth and be separate. That is, to keep clear to themselves and to all others that they stood upon the platform of Christ's theory of life and behavior. It is now among the greatest moral demands of the age.

While we are sorely tried and pressed by opposing powers of evil we do not want honeyed words, but help. We are willing to dispense for the time being with protestations of friendship and flower garlands of fine speeches. We want help. We do not want, as the Greek army was lately, to be supplied with scientific X-ray apparatus while common bandages have been forgotten. We will discuss occult things when we get to them. Life and work are anything but occult.

Christian living and Christian constancy at the very best are kept up to a high standard only by being reenforced daily from the Father on high. The world may be getting better, but is not getting better so fast as to abate one single effort in the work. This is no time for foolishness. Still less is it a time to get confusion to the mind because there is so much. The best disciplined army has its stragglers. The best Christian life has its moments of confusion and turmoil. Let not the conflict become a rout. Let us stand still long enough to find a point of beginning, and then, having found it, let the conflict of duties become lost in the conflict with the enemy of the soul.

And lest I seem to overrate mere working in the kingdom of God as the solvent of doubts as to what is most expedient, let me hasten to add that amid the greatest perplexity there is one thing never to be forgotten. It is the promise of God that if any man lack wisdom, if he will ask of God he will give liberally without upbraiding. Christ enjoined his disciples to have no fear on this point. They were to come before judges and magistrates and to be cast into prison for his name's sake. But they were to have no fear. A mouth and wisdom were promised, and the eloquent and convincing speeches of Stephen, of Peter, of Paul and of John are proof that the promise was fulfilled.

Pray in the assurance that a true seeker for light will not be upbraided for being helpless. But while we pray, let us still keep the armor on and stand girt about with the defenses of an unselfish purpose. Christ can honor that, however imperfectly expressed. God gives his gifts to the sincere workers in his kingdom. Light will break on the darkest spot if we keep close to the Light that lighteth every man that cometh into the world.

A SPIRITUAL LIFE

ACTS xix. 2.

THIS colloquy took place at Ephesus whither St. Paul had come on his third missionary journey. Before his coming Apollos, who had been taught in the rudiments of the gospel by Paul's friends Aquila and Priscilla, had gathered a few of the Jews together and had taught them all that he knew, and at this time was off on a journey to Corinth. Something evidently occurred in the earlier stages of Paul's conversation with these disciples which made him think that either they were very imperfectly trained in the gospel, or, if properly instructed, were not living up to their light, and with characteristic directness he comes at once to the point and asks them the question as we have it.

The reply is as frank as the question. They tell him that they know nothing about the matter at all. It cannot be supposed, as the Authorized Version would lead one to suppose, that these people had never heard of the existence of the Holy Spirit. Such a thing is utterly out of the question. Knowing John's baptism, they must have heard some things which would lead them to reflect about the Spirit of God. Besides, there was enough of general spiritual life and knowledge, such as it was, in Ephesus, together with philosophic teaching of one kind and another, to render it well-nigh impossible to believe that they had never heard of a Holy Spirit.

What they probably said is what the Revised Version indicates. They had seen no manifestations that led them to believe that the Holy Spirit was given or was being bestowed upon the disciples. They were living, it may fairly be supposed, in the light of the truth which is contained in the

elementary doctrines of repentance for sins and faith toward
God. Their faith in Christ was the acceptance of the hope
of salvation through him. They were endeavoring to live in
his obedience, and this formed the boundary of their conception of the Christian life.

It would be interesting to know what it was that arrested
Paul's attention and made him ask the abrupt and penetrat-
ing question that he did. But we can probably never know
to our satisfaction, only that we can infer something of the
spirit which prevailed in Ephesus from what happened to
Paul during the months of his sojourn at that place. It was
a spirit of materialism which put forth the thin veneer of the
worship of Diana as a medium for securing municipal greatness and personal profit. The ease with which Demetrius
the silversmith secured his mob and the cold brutality with
which he stated its motive are luminous as showing what the
general spirit of the city was.

But this much we can know. Paul was impressed that,
Christians though they were, there was something about them
which gave no evidence that they lived in the atmosphere
where the Holy Spirit is the constant witness and revealer
of Christ. They were everyday men of good intentions
and fairly excellent habits and making reasonably successful
efforts to live up to the light that was in them. But they
lacked what Paul evidently looked for first. They were obedient, they were faithful in the externals of their faith, they
had a reasonable hope in Christ, but they were not *spiritual*
men. That is, they were not men whose life showed the
power and the presence of the essential thing in successful
and effective Christian living.

They were good men. They were repentant men. They
were disciples of Christ and they were the servants of God.
But they were not *spiritual* men. That seems at the first
glance an impossibility. It looks like a very curious thing
to say that a man may be a Christian and a good man, and
yet be an unspiritual man. These qualities seem to be so
linked with the Holy Spirit's power and influence that we
seem unable to separate them. But it is nevertheless true

that there may be found many excellent people of whom we must affirm, if we speak truthfully, that their lives give no trace of spiritual power, and whose influence in the building of a spiritual life in the world is almost if not quite nothing.

It is the spiritual life, therefore, of which I wish to speak this morning. Not in the way in which the subject is often treated, which makes any allusion to a deeper spiritual experience seem but the gate to an odious pharisaism, but with a view to finding out just what a spiritual life is, and what the New Testament has to say concerning it, and what its bearing is on the whole subject of Christian living and habits. Obviously the Christian life must be a spiritual life at some stage of its development, or it is nothing.

That there are stages of Christian living is clear enough. A man who takes on the habits of Christian obedience and prayer late in life will not have the advantages of insight and penetration into spiritual things that we ought naturally to look for in one whose life has been reared under the spiritual conceptions which Jesus taught to his disciples. Just as no mature man can ever learn to speak a foreign language without frequently betraying the fact that it is an acquired tongue, so the later the acquisition of the mind of Christ the cruder the manifestations of its progress in practical life.

But the stages of the Christian life are in its ethical and practical manifestations only. There is nothing that need prevent a disciple of a month's standing from making the same spiritual impression as the disciple of a half century's experience. This is because the spiritual note is the same, wherever found. Truth and sincerity have their fixed characteristics. Its intellectual form may change. Its expressions are various. But the ring is the same, wherever found and by whomsoever uttered. If this were not so, how much the cause of Christ must have suffered amid all the grotesque ideas which have labeled themselves Christian! It is the spirit in man that is the candle of the Lord. And the spiritual note, once heard, is recognized forever afterward.

This is a necessity for another reason. It preserves the unity of life and thought in the Church of Christ. Our habits of speech and our modes of action are very diverse. Every four years we have in this country an election in which we divide into rival political camps, and fight each other's ideas of what is good and wise governmental policy with all the vigor and zeal of which we are capable. But nobody thinks of being anything else than an American all the time this struggle is going on. Sometimes we lose our heads, and seem to say that we believe that our political opponents are the enemies of our country. But we forget it after the election, or are ashamed of it if we remember it. In this same way there are diversities of operations, but the same Spirit. There are numberless ways of looking at the same thing. But the unity of the Church is not in its intellectual conceptions, and never has been. It is not in the social expressions of its life, though it can, and should, improve these very much. It lies in the same spirit throughout, which gives forth the note of regeneration and holiness in the soul.

It is, therefore, a reasonable expectation that every disciple of Christ shall give out the note of a spiritual life. Whatever else he may be, — ignorant or learned, rich or poor, of high degree or of low degree, — he should suggest something which we call spiritual. He should have, if I may so express it, something unearthly about him. Perhaps it would be better to say unworldly. But it is more than merely being unworldly. It is rising above the earth, and having the suggestion of the eternal and the infinite. It is literally unearthly. As Christ himself said, " My kingdom is not of this world," so the Christian who is a citizen of that kingdom is also, in a sense, not of this world at all.

Having said so much, let me appeal to your own experience if it is not true that there are multitudes of people of whom we are bound to believe that they are Christian people, but whose lives are wholly and almost absolutely without spiritual significance or power? Do you not know many such yourself? Are there not communities and churches which carry on all the external rites of religion and worship, but which seem as barren of spirituality and other-worldliness as anything possibly can be? What Christian has not himself watched with wonder and thought over with perplexity the strange absence of moving power in much of the paraphernalia of religion? It seemed religious enough. It seemed to say the right things. It was in good taste, and did not jar our intellectual conceptions of how religion should express itself. But it was utterly without the note of spiritual power.

I assume you all answer these things in the affirmative. Much of the religious machinery is the mere rattling of the lifeless instruments which have taken the place of the spirit which should be in and above them. Even the reading of the Scriptures sometimes takes on this lifeless aspect. Certainly prayers often do. Religious service becomes a seventh-day drudgery instead of a seventh-day delight. We exchange the clothes of business for the clothes of religion and Sunday observance. But it is all a matter of clothes. It is the merest seeming, and is hollow and without power over us in our lives. The Spirit that gives life is wanting and, lacking that, inspiration is gone.

There is enough religiousness in this world and to spare. In fact, the world seems to be overstocked with religiousness. But of the power that comes with the gift of the Holy Ghost there seems to be a lamentable lack. Few men seem to be making the large, deep impression on the race that made the prophets such notable figures in the history of Israel. The high-hearted courage of conviction, which is the Holy Spirit moving to the great battles of principle and righteousness, seems everywhere to lie prostrate before the manipulations of the machine. In politics the man is afraid to act independently because he dreads the vengeance of the party leaders. Teachers are becoming the mere exponents of the discipline of the schools where they were trained. No originality, no self-imposing personality, no uplifting inspiration, no breaking away from the beaten track of rule and precedent. Only the yardstick idea of instruction.

Religion is much of it of the same cast. It is formal and inert. It says, as a young man did in my study the other day, that it loves beautiful forms and gets great inspiration from them. But, like that same young man, it doesn't lift a hand for the cause of Christ anywhere or at any time. Machine-made and manufactured from week to week in the mechanical treadmill of religious routine, it is the form of godliness without the power thereof.

But you are saying, What, then, is the spiritual life, and what shall we do that we are not doing? If our lifeless inertia means that we have not something which we may have, how may we become otherwise? How shall we come into the fellowship of spiritual men and spiritual things, which shall bring us into contact with the Holy Spirit? What shall we do?

The answer to such an inquiry is not easy to give. The spiritual life is as much above rule as the formal religious life is under rule. We can make rules for the one, but not for the other. We can say what we shall do to be good church members or good citizens, which are matters of formal procedure. But with the spiritual life it is not thus. The spiritual life is over and above mere rule. It is not a thing that a man can *do*. It is a message that must possess us as the air we breathe, and must surround us as the sunlight from heaven. There are no rules for becoming spiritual which once followed give us the right to say that we are spiritual men. The discernment and the power which belong to spiritual natures are the fruit of imparted, not of self-extending, life.

Perhaps what the spiritual life is can best be shown in a contrast. Paul's own life affords us the fittest example of which I know. Look at Paul before his conversion. He was always an earnest man. He was a loyal churchman and a most rigid observer of religious forms and ceremony. Concerning the righteousness that was of the law, he has told us that he was blameless. He had the courage of his bigotry, too. When Stephen is stoned he is observing with evident satisfaction the martyr's death, and when there were Christians to persecute at Damascus, Paul volunteers to undertake the task. No man was ever better intrenched in the forms of godliness than was St. Paul before his conversion.

But observe him after he had seen the light on the way to Damascus. Writing of his former attitude toward the Christians he tells us that he was exceedingly "mad" against them. He says, indeed, that he did it "ignorantly in unbelief," but Paul nowhere impugns his sincerity as a persecutor of the Christians. Now if Paul's religion of that period had had the quality of spirituality, it is impossible to believe that so discerning and intelligent a man would have assisted at the stoning of Stephen. Paul everywhere shows that he was an appreciative man, especially as regards dialectic skill and argument. There is evidence in abundance that he was impressed with Stephen's great apology and exposition of the historical argument for Christ's coming. But incrusted in formalism, held in the grip of a lifeless religionism, cold and unspiritual, he prevented what would normally have made a great impression on his mind from having its legitimate effect. He could not exclude it wholly. He did prevent it from bringing the Holy Spirit to his heart.

See Paul growing in faith. See the maturing of his spiritual graces as he grows older. See how he acquires those most impressive words in the Christian vocabulary, adoption, sonship, heirs of God. All these things come to him with the wider knowledge of God's ways, and God himself. They are truths spiritually discerned. All the talk of all the theologies will never make a man know what adoption is. As well expect a child in a home where opulence and luxury are the rule, having known nothing else, to know what it is to be an "adopted" child. It never can possibly. But take some waif that has never had its little stomach filled with wholesome food, that has never known adequate clothing and shelter, that has been kicked and cuffed into orphanage and destitution, and let him be adopted by some loving couple to whom God has denied children of their own, and let him wake up some morning fed, clothed, sheltered and *loved*. He knows what adoption is.

But if spiritual life is not a matter of rules, there are nevertheless some landmarks which may guide us in the quest for it. St. James tells us that if any man lack wisdom, let him

ask of God who giveth liberally, and upbraideth not. That
suggests that prayer to God, constant and believing, is among
the primary agencies of the true spiritual life. It was the
long season of prayer that fitted the apostles for the Pentecostal outpouring of the Spirit. Christ was abundant and
constant in prayer. One of his choicest parables is in illustration of the doctrine that men ought always to pray and not
to faint. Prayer should be persistent and sincere. It should
not seek largesses of knowledge, but discernment in spirit.
Spiritual things are spiritually discerned. We need to see
what is actually about us ; to transfigure the daily contacts of
life ; to realize that under the thick coating of mammonism
and self-seeking there is still a hidden germ of immortality.
Pray through your hatreds to love. Pray through your impatience to a quiet heart. Pray through your anger to the
forgiveness of Christ. Pray through your selfishness to self-
sacrifice.

Prayer is genuine when it is supplemented by a prayerful
life. We cannot pray for the spirit of love, and then drive
roughshod over the rights of our neighbors. We cannot ask
for forgiveness of our debts, and then be hard and unyielding
creditors. If you must put the screws on anything, put it on
every false inclination and on every uncharitable thought.
Crucify the flesh and the lusts thereof. Brand the lies of life
as lies. Keep a road clear for the message of Christ, when it
calls to heroism and unselfish behavior.

The habit of regarding the things seen as the symbols of
things that are not seen will bring a spiritual atmosphere into
the most commonplace life. I go forth in the morning and
meet the men with whom I must do business that day.
There are two ways of regarding them. One is to regard
them as fellow warriors for a living and the gold that gives
it, who will either slay me or be slain by me. Another is to
regard every man of them a messenger of some truth of
eternal interest and significance. Every man, no matter what
his character, has such a significance about him to a spiritual-
minded man. The vicious become to him the incarnate
forces of evil and destruction. The kindly are ministering

angels of mercy. The domineering and the strong are the symbols of the vanity that frail man assumes to hide his weakness, and the patient and the gentle are the living symbols of the vicarious love of Christ. A man may find a whole theology written out for him in unmistakable signs at his own desk or bench every day that he cares to study it.

But this is not only true of men, it is true of things. I see a magnificent house. Beautifully built, of costly materials, I can at once take one of two ways of bringing that vision to my soul. I can compute its cost and envy the man who has it. I can bewail the social conditions which give that lovely building to him rather than to me. But then again I can think of the contrast between a house and a home, between houses and happiness, between a lovely home for the body and a lovely home for the soul, between the mansion on earth and the mansion in heaven, and before long, if I take this latter course, the envy flees if I had it, and the warmth of spiritual interest and illumination draws me near to God and to his kingdom. Transfigure what you see. Connect it with the holiest things in you and rejoice that they *are* rather than that they are yours.

There is a beautiful German story I used to hear in my childhood of a man of the peasant class who used to go about his work with such an air of repose and unaffected delight and used to see such beautiful things that he was known in the village where he lived as the "dreamer." By and by he married and it was observed that the same atmosphere reigned in the home. His wife and his children had the same cheerful contentment in their scanty fare and seemed full of the abounding joy of living. Asked finally what it might be that made him so, he said that he fancied himself a king and his wife the queen and his children the princes and princesses about him. Their frugal meal was a banquet board. Their occasional pleasures were the gayeties of their court. Their little plot of green was the royal gardens and everything about them was the trappings and habiliments of royalty.

No wonder they were content. If there ever was a being

who could rightfully apply to everything that is in the world the verbiage of royalty, it is the Christian and the spiritually minded man. All things may remind him of his royal estate and of his divine heritage. The Christian man is a king in truth, and his domain is all that the Father has made for his pleasure and enjoyment. Only that they may not be to him the corrupting treasures that moth and rust destroy, His love has surrounded them with the defenses of the spiritual vision, that only they who have eyes to see can see. But blessed are the eyes that are opened, for they behold in all things the wonderland of God !

But this is a vision which comes only to men who are conscious that they have been redeemed of God — men who have laid aside the common, earthly aims with their unyielding selfishness and the ignoble methods by which they achieved and have given themselves to higher tasks of the spirit. Such men see their own lives in the light of Christ's example and interpret themselves in the highest spiritual, not the highest earthly, terms. The difference is a fundamental one in the nature of the estimate. One looks to earth, the other looks to heaven. Between them is a great gulf fixed.

By far the most serious hindrance to the realization of a spiritual life is the consciousness of sins unforgiven. Men shrink from the attractiveness of a high spiritual ideal when they are conscious of a dark page of their own lives which has not been blotted out. It stands there as a sort of skeleton in the closet that may stalk forth any time to terrorize and destroy. No man can be spiritually minded while such a ghost is ever on his track. He must be freed from fear. He must be free from the sins that make the fear. He must be redeemed from himself and the thing that binds him.

This forms the specific work of the Holy Spirit. It is to reveal Christ as that very Deliverer from sins who can give spiritual freedom, and with it the vision of God. Until that Spirit has touched him he must continually be exclaiming, as Paul says in Romans, "O wretched man that I am ! who shall deliver me out of the body of this death ? " But, baptized with the Holy Ghost and with fire, one illuminating, the other purgative, he goes forth freed and spiritualized.

These two seem to be the functions of the Spirit of God as revealed in the New Testament. Illumination and Purgation! On the one hand there is ignorance to be dispelled, darkness to be driven out, and doubt to be banished, and in their places are to come knowledge, light and faith. On the other hand there is the sin to be burned out of its place in the carnal heart that is not subject to the law of God, and which neither indeed can be. There is the driving out of the consciousness and the memory of guilt. There is not merely chaining up the sin, but the forgiving of it. And in both the illumination and the purgation, Christ is revealed as the sacrificial offering of God for the sins of the world.

It is thus that we come into the companionship and fellowship of Christ. We walk with him now because we see with his vision. The world is not a malformed jumbling together of perfectly irreconcilable elements constantly at war, the material one and the spiritual another. Both men and things have their higher significance. The earth and the skies, the flowers of the field and the birds of the air, are bearers of a message to the spirit of man. And the Holy Spirit is the messenger of the revelation of Christ. He keeps Christ in remembrance; he cleanses from sin; he illuminates the mind, and he gives power. And the great awe-inspiring themes of righteousness, sin and judgment are unfolded in the daily working out of salvation here and now. And in the light of that unfolding we become the witnesses of the truth. "And ye shall be my witnesses both in Jerusalem, and in all Judæa and Samaria, and unto the uttermost part of the earth.' This, the final promise of the ascending Lord, is the highest fulfilment of a spiritual life, witnessing for the truth as it is in Jesus Christ.